MACHIAVELLIANISM

The world abounds with tricksters, swindlers, and impostors. Many of them may well be described with the term Machiavellian. Such individuals disrespect moral principles, deceive their fellow beings, and take advantage of others' frailty and gullibility. They have a penetrating, rational, and sober mind undisturbed by emotions. At times we cannot help but be enchanted by their talent even though we know they misuse it.

Recent studies have revealed that Machiavellians possess a complex set of abilities and motivations. This insightful book examines the complexities of the Machiavellian trait, in relation to attitude, behaviour, and personality. By integrating results and experiences from social, personality, cognitive, and evolutionary psychology, Tamás Bereczkei explores the characteristics of Machiavellianism (such as social intelligence, deception, manipulation, and lack of empathy), and the causes and motives guiding Machiavellian behaviour. The author also demonstrates how Machiavellianism is related to strategic thinking and flexible long-term decisions rather than to a short-term perspective, as previously thought, and explores Machiavellianism in relation to the construct of the Dark Triad.

The first comprehensive psychological book on Machiavellianism since Christie and Geis' pioneering work in 1970, *Machiavellianism* summarises the most important research findings over the last few decades. This book is fascinating reading for students and researchers of psychology and related courses, as well as professionals dealing with Machiavellians in their work and practice.

Tamás Bereczkei graduated as a Biologist, completed a PhD dissertation in Philosophy, and became a Doctor of Science in Psychology. He leads the Evolutionary Psychological Research group at the University of Pécs. Besides Machiavellianism, his main research areas include social intelligence, altruism and cooperation, and mate choice.

MACHIAVELLIANISM

The Psychology of Manipulation

Tamás Bereczkei

Routledge
Taylor & Francis Group

LONDON AND NEW YORK

First published 2018
by Routledge
2 Park Square, Milton Park, Abingdon, Oxon OX14 4RN

and by Routledge
711 Third Avenue, New York, NY 10017

Routledge is an imprint of the Taylor & Francis Group, an informa business

British Library Cataloguing-in-Publication Data
A catalogue record for this book is available from the British Library

Library of Congress Cataloging-in-Publication Data
A catalog record for this book has been requested

ISBN: 978-1-138-09328-7 (hbk)
ISBN: 978-1-138-09331-7 (pbk)
ISBN: 978-1-315-10692-2 (ebk)

Typeset in Bembo
by Apex CoVantage, LLC

CONTENTS

PREFACE

The world abounds with tricksters, swindlers and impostors. Many of them may well be described with the term Machiavellian. Such individuals disrespect moral principles, deceive their fellow beings, and take advantage of others' frailty and gullibility. They take advantage of others by using them to achieve their own goals while their victims are not in the least aware of being used. They have a penetrating, rational and sober mind undisturbed by emotions. At times we cannot help being enchanted by their talent even though we know they misuse it. We should also know, however, that they themselves often suffer from their ambitious and unattainable desires, which in many cases end in petty tragedies. History has witnessed several Machiavellian adventurers, so let us start by introducing one or two notorious figures.

Cesare Borgia: the unscrupulous

He was born in Rome in 1475 to a father who became subsequently known as Pope Alexander VI. The family included several well-known and notorious historical figures who were characterised by excellent abilities as well as by absolute moral nihilism. By his ninth year the boy had already been honoured with a dozen church offices, and he was inaugurated as the Bishop of Pamplona when he was 15. However, it soon became clear that Cesare was born to be a despot rather than a pontiff. Rome was rife with gossip about his increasingly violent acts after he embarked on an extermination campaign against noble families who were wielding excessive power. When his brother Giovanni also became a victim of murder, Cesare was suspected of the crime although the truth never came to light. The Borgias' notoriety is well reflected in the rumours circulating about the brothers fighting for the grace of their sister Lucrezia; many believe today that they lived in an incestuous relationship. It is more likely, however, that Cesare's jealousy concerned Giovanni's prospective bright military career.

Whatever the case, Giovanni's death opened up the way to Cesare's political and military career. When the Pope delegated his son to the French royal court to act in a diplomatic affair, Cesare won the hand of the younger sister of John III of Navarre. However, the couple only lived together for two and a half months, after which Cesare did not see either her wife or their subsequently born daughter (his wife died in a convent). Then his father sent him to Central Italy as a leader of Papal and French troops in order to establish a principality comprising cities nominally ruled by the Pope while in fact being independent. Cesare proved a talented and capable military commander and at the beginning of 1500 he returned home in triumph. He became a popular figure while people also dreaded him as several of his terrible acts came to light. He drowned the author of a pamphlet in the Tiber, shot unarmed thieves to death in cold blood, had a drunk man's tongue cut off for mocking him, and then he stabbed with his own hand the husband of his own sister Lucrezia, who had barely survived the attack of assassins set at him by Cesare previously.

Cesare Borgia became a firm-handed and cold-blooded ruler as the Duke of Romagna. Niccolò Machiavelli, who lived at the Duke's court for a while, took him as the exemplar of the successful prince, asserting his interests and will at any price (although later he regretted having idealised the fundamentally ill-natured prince). It is beyond question that Cesare did not hesitate to use any means to gain and keep power. Occasionally, he would graciously forgive his former adversaries, as was the case with the Orsini brothers whom he hosted at a grandiose feast, accompanied back to their accommodation and, after leaving them alone, had them murdered by his assassins. According to Machiavelli, Cesare was a good judge of people, and believed that anyone could be taken in by the right wile. When feeling that he could rely on the support of the masses, he did not hesitate to use any means he preferred, knowing that no one would pry into the case of a hated cardinal or mercenary commander drowned in the river. When, by contrast, he faced their former adherents turning against him, he strove to manipulate them by means of flattery and promises.

His career began to decline in 1503 when his father, Alexander VI, died (probably of poisoning). A sworn enemy of the Borgias, Julius II ascended the papal throne and ordered that Cesare, lacking political and financial support at the time, be arrested and resign his lands, titles and offices. Being deprived of wealth, lands and freedom, he might have found some satisfaction in the fact that rulers contested for him, none less than three princes wanting to engage him as a military commander. He could not escape until 1506 when he entered the service of his brother-in-law, the king of Navarre, since he could not return to Italy. Cesare Borgia died on 12 March 1507 during the siege of Viana. However, he could not rest in peace even after death: first he was buried in the local church but the indignant archbishop ordered that his tomb be torn apart and his bones, later placed at the main entrance of the church in 1945, be buried by the roadside.

Gregor MacGregor: the swindler

Born in Scotland in 1786, he was a supposed descendant of the famous folk hero Rob Roy. Since his father was a captain of the East India Company, he was also expected to pursue a naval career as a matter of course. He served the navy in the Caribbean Sea as early as at the age of 17 and then ascended as high as the rank of a colonel in the Venezuelan War of Independence. He sailed back to England in 1820 and in London he presented an account of an island named Poyais he had discovered near Central America, where he founded a governorship approved by the local tribal chief. Although the island did not actually exist, he provided exact figures describing its geographic position and demographic conditions. He reported that its area was 32,400 square kilometres and that the peaceful indigenous people inhabiting the island simply shared it with a few British settlers. He added that the island had ample mineral resources that had been unmined. He also reported that he himself as the governor had introduced laws, instituted the state apparatus and even recruited an army. He was only travelling to London to recruit more settlers and to collect money for further work. Since entering the South and Central American markets was almost impossible for the English nobility and merchants at the time, they were eager to seize the opportunity offered by an island where they could establish themselves and launch new conquests. England in the 1820s also offered an ideal field for MacGregor's large-scale endeavour in other respects. Napoleon had been defeated, peace ensued in Europe and the British economy saw unprecedented growth. Wages increased while costs of living decreased.

MacGregor also ingratiated himself with the upper class, not least by asserting he was a descendent of Rob Roy who was committed to serving the British Empire even at the cost of exposing his life to permanent risk. He had a bureau set up in London, the sole purpose of which was the foreign representation of Poyais, and he dealt out various assignments and titles to everyone whom he saw important to win over. Moreover, he also published a 350-page travel guide to the island under a pseudonym in which he reported, among other matters, that the island had enormous gold and silver mines. He even printed Poyais dollars in Scotland that he exchanged at a good price paid by the adventurers ready to set off. However, the business really began to flourish when he started to sell out each square metre of the imaginary island. What is more, he took out a loan of 200,000 pounds on behalf of the government of the island. (This is a considerable sum even today but it was an inconceivably large amount of money at the time.) Some were also granted leadership positions in the government and other high authorities of the island. A host of bankers, doctors and lawyers set off for the coast of Central America in order to take possession of their remuneration. The recruited settlers filled two ships which reached the Caribbean Sea at the beginning of 1823 with 250 would-be land and mine owners of Poyais who, of course, failed to find the promised land. A rebellion broke out, epidemics and famine decimated the settlers who desperately sought for King Frederic Augustus I and his people in the jungle. When eventually a British ship sailed by, took them on board and carried them to Belize, only 50 of the 250 travellers were still alive. Then the news quickly reached London and MacGregor's other five ships, being on the way, were returned by the British royal fleet from the middle of the Atlantic. The remaining "discoverers" only then realised that they had been victims of a swindle. Many of them chose to commit suicide as a way to escape the shame and the loss of all their wealth staked on the adventure.

Scandal reached the skies but MacGregor was sought for in vain: he was already far away with the money. He removed to France where he presented his tale once more while continuously releasing travel guides and articles. However, the French State became suspicious of a country which dozens of citizens applying for passport and visa wished to enter, yet the existence of which no official authority was aware. MacGregor had essentially been successfully deceiving people for eleven years when eventually, in 1839, facing the fact that things were getting too hot, he escaped to Venezuela where he was granted citizenship. He died in Caracas at the age of 58.

Ignaz Trebitsch: the chameleon

Trebitsch was born in Paks in 1879 to a wealthy merchant family. He received an excellent education, and spoke several languages. Moving to Budapest at the age of 18, he fell in love with an actress, and he himself also prepared to embark on an acting career. However, his father was against his plans and at once sent him abroad to see the world. From that time he started an adventurer's life which subsequently took many turns.

He frequently changed his name, identity and even personality; he had a genuine chameleon's character. Although born to a Jewish family, he became a member of the Presbyterian Church at the age of 19 and received the baptismal name of Timotheus. A few years later he left the Presbyterians following a dispute over financial matters and joined the Church of England for a salary paying 25 dollars more each month. He worked as a parish priest for a short while but finally he escaped from the "rat hole in Kent" – as he described the place. He "escaped" to London with his family and, aiming to pave the way for his prospective political career, he changed his named to Trebitsch, being easier to remember for the English, and added the surname Lincoln. He joined several political parties and movements and struggled his way up to a high position in each. His rhetorical skills and quick-wittedness were noticed by Winston Churchill among others, who more than once supported his political ambitions.

In 1907, Trebitsch moved to Belgium where he disguised himself in the role of a researcher employed by a "research bureau" studying the miserable conditions of the working class, while it appears that actually he was acting as an agent of the British Secret Intelligence Service for three years. Supported by influential friends, he started a highly profitable business enterprise that allowed him to live a luxurious life everywhere he turned up. He joined the intelligence service of the Austro-Hungarian Monarchy, something that became known to its British counterpart. From then on, Trebitsch acted as a double agent of the British and German intelligence services, and as such he lived in Galicia, Romania, the Netherlands and England again.

In order to make more money, he forged an old friend's signature in an indemnity bond of a usurious loan. The forging came to light but he was not reported due to the intervention of the Intelligence Service. Instead, he obtained a job at the office of censorship of the British ministry of defence. It was that office in which he devised the plan of ensnaring the German fleet. The plan was disapproved of on Churchill's advice and from then on, Trebitsch-Lincoln rather spied for the Germans. When things were getting too hot, he sailed to the USA where he primarily engaged in making money. He contracted an American publisher to write a book (which was subsequently published under the title "Revelations of an international spy"). At the request of the British government, he was arrested in New York and then served a three-year prison sentence in England. Thereafter he took benefit from the social chaos during the First World War in Germany, Czechoslovakia and Hungary and earned an excellent living through his political adventures.

At the beginning of the 1920s, he was already residing in China where he had apparently been sent by the American intelligence service. He offered his services to general Wu Peifu, who was the most important ally of the English. Trebitsch arrived in Venice with a Hungarian passport as the head of general Wu's delegation in order to negotiate and conclude agreements with German delegations. Trebitsch's fortune at Wu's side declined when the German-Austrian financial support failed to be delivered in accordance with the agreement he had concluded. Feeling the decline of his influence, he contacted the Japanese and British intelligence services and probably assisted the warlords supported by Japan and Great Britain to defeat Wu Peifu.

At the end of his life, he became a Buddhist monk under the name Chao Kung and had this name and personality when he died in Japan at the age of 64.

Kimberly Hricko: the cold-blooded

American Kimberly Hricko married a handsome fellow college student with whom they had a daughter named Anna. When Kimberly took up a job as a surgeon's assistant, her acquaintanceship altered at once: she was surrounded by wealthy doctors whom she envied their fortune and success. Her husband Steve, who worked as a superintendent of a golf course, was not fond of his wife's new friends. He complained that he had nothing in common with those arrogant doctors. This led to unceasing disputes. Kimberly wanted to escape from her marriage, while Steve devoted himself to keeping his family together. He even took his wife to a family therapist, convinced that their marriage would survive.

However, Kimberly was far from agreeing. She had been complaining about her husband to her colleagues for months. Moreover, she offered them 50,000 dollars several times to put her beloved man out of the way. Meanwhile, her husband was still trying to recover their relationship, surprising Kimberly on Valentine's Day with an exotic trip to a hotel which offered a mafia weekend combined with a murder mystery play. According to the plot of the play, the bridegroom's champagne was poisoned. Kimberly was inspired by the play and poisoned her husband's drink, which killed him. In order to cover up the traces, she set fire to the hotel room, running out and crying that her room was on fire. The police found the man's body before the scene of the crime burned down to the ground. When the wife was informed of the case, she burst into hysterical tears and became totally upset. She told the police that Steve had drunk too much that night and that they had had a row, so she had left the room. Initially, the police had no reason to doubt the account. In the next days, however, it turned out that only an insignificant level of alcohol was found in Steve's blood, nor was any trace of smoke inhalation found. When one of Kimberly's friends told the police that she had been considering ending the marriage for a while and that she even devising plans to get rid of her husband, the police arranged for her arrest. Soon it became clear that Kimberly had prepared for her husband's departure in other ways as well. Not long before, she had persuaded her husband to double the sum of his life insurance. It was also found out that she was having an affair with a man ten years younger than herself.

Other friends of the woman also testified against her, Kimberly reacting by harshly insulting them and making obscene gestures to them in court. The jury formed the impression that the woman had felt overly "burdened" by the divorce proceedings, and therefore she had chosen rather to get rid of her husband. The court sentenced Kimberly to penal servitude for thirty years.

1

WHAT MAKES A MACHIAVELLIAN?

The previously mentioned stories are the tips of the iceberg. We all know Machiavellians even if we do not recognise them. Some of us may be unaware that these people are generally willing to fish in troubled waters and that deceiving and manipulating others are essential features of their character. They do so in order to take advantage of others for their own sake. I therefore describe a Machiavellian as one who uses others as a means of achieving one's own goals.

The term "Machiavellianism" originates in the name of Renaissance writer Niccolò Machiavelli, who provided in his work titled *The Prince* a detailed discussion of the tactics a ruler should follow in order to gain and keep power (Box 1.1). Essentially, he described the ways of unemotional, sober governance. Machiavelli suggests that there are two alternative ways: one is peaceful and legitimate, while the other is based on force. If the first fails, one has to resort to the second. Therefore, the wise ruler should not adhere to his promise if it is against his interest. Of course, he would not be compelled to lie and deceive others if people were good. However, they are not. On the contrary, they are malevolent and traitorous, thus the ruler does not have to keep his word either. In any case, the prince always finds an opportunity to put his insincerity in a favourable light. "But it is necessary . . . to be a great pretender and dissembler; and men are so simple, and so subject to present necessities, that he who seeks to deceive will always find someone who will allow himself to be deceived."

Machiavelli always starts with a thorough observation of facts, that is, events of political and military history, when explaining what a ruler should do in order to successfully govern a state. He believes that governors should keep to generally accepted ethical principles if possible but they should not hesitate to employ cunning and lying if keeping their power so requires. Thus, for example, homicide should be avoided if possible simply because it results in uncontrollable emotional reactions, revenge campaigns and retaliation. Pretended kindness or flattery may yield more adherents. It is also true in general that a ruler should present himself

BOX 1.1 NICCOLÒ MACHIAVELLI

Machiavelli was born into a wealthy family of Florentine citizens. He followed in his father's footsteps by studying law and then working as an attorney. Meanwhile he read a lot and soon he became so educated that it made him an acknowledged and appreciated adviser in various affairs. When at the age of 29 he was assigned to be the secretary of the Council of Ten, he at once became one of the most influential citizens of Florence. During his fourteen years in office, he visited Italian princes' courts and saw the king of France several times, and he also made his appearance in front of the Holy Roman Emperor and the Pope. Meanwhile he wrote several books on the military establishment and on the eventualities and consequences of wars.

Florence faced ominous and ever-changing times. Italy was divided by the savage fight between King Louis XII and Pope Alexander VI; rivalry among the Medicis, Sforzas and Borgias became permanent. Machiavelli took part in these fights, not only as a leader of diplomatic negotiations but in taking an active part in the establishment of the Florentine army. It is no surprise that after the capture of the city he was imprisoned and subsequently accused of several political charges as well. In his mid-40s he chose to resign his office and withdrew to his nearby residence. However, he continued to be regularly invited by the rulers of Italy, who asked for his advice and ideas worthy of consideration in order to realise their dreams of power. Among others, he primarily provided useful advice for the Borgias and Cesare Borgia. The character of the illegitimate son of Pope Alexander VI veritably enchanted Machiavelli. Cesare was a cruel but brilliant military commander. His desire to unify Italy became the primary objective for Machiavelli.

Probably Cesare Borgia offered the model of Machiavelli's ideal ruler as described in his most notable work, *The Prince*. The work is about political leadership, gaining and keeping power, as well as about the relationship between the ruler and his subjects. Machiavelli suggests that actions carried out in the interest of the state are governed by practicability, utility and rationality, being in a sense independent of ethical reasoning. Such activity is unrelated to justice (which is the duty of the court), unrelated to goodness (which is the domain of religion) and unrelated to beauty (which is the subject of the arts).

Machiavelli was a truly Renaissance man: besides studies in politics, military science and diplomacy, he wrote historical works (on the Roman Empire and Florence) and he even tried poetry and prose, what is more, in the Italian language in an age when most authors wrote in Latin. He also wrote plays among which the most notable is the comedy *The Mandrake*. The play has stood the test of time since it is still performed worldwide. Already in his own time, Machiavelli was to become a well-known figure in contemporary Italian intellectual and political life, yet he died lonely at his residence at the age of 58.

as being good and *appear* to be gracious, loyal, humane, sincere and religious. He should, of course, act according to these five virtues on occasion but he should always be prepared to do the opposite if necessary. Machiavelli adds that "everyone sees what you appear to be, few really know what you are". "For that reason, let a prince have the credit of conquering and holding his state, the means will always be considered honest, and he will be praised by everybody because the vulgar are always taken by what a thing seems to be and by what comes of it . . ."

It is no accident that Machiavellianism was for a long time included in the vocabulary of political philosophy. The concept was used in relation to political leaders who ascended to high positions due to their despotic and authoritarian character.

American researchers Richard Christie and Florence Geis were the first to approach Machiavellianism from a psychological perspective, describing it as a personality trait, as an attitude to the world, and as a behaviour. They recognised that Machiavellianism, first, is not characteristic only of leaders; second, it is not equal to an authoritarian personality; third, it is not to be regarded as a mere psychopathological phenomenon. On the contrary, all ordinary people may exhibit a certain degree of Machiavellian thinking. Every individual, irrespective of their social environment and occupation, is more or less willing to dissemble and deceive others under certain circumstances. The above mentioned authors published a book (*Studies in Machiavellianism*) in 1970 in which they presented a large number of empirical studies and theoretical concepts. This volume is still seen as a crucially important work in the field, and it is used by contemporary researchers as a certain kind of starting point (Box 1.2).

Christie and Geis and their generation of psychologists delineated the personality profile termed Machiavellian. Essentially, it includes five major traits: manipulation, amorality, cynicism, emotional coldness and a lack of empathy. They deserve a more detailed discussion in which we will rely on more recent research findings as well.

BOX 1.2 THE MACH-IV TEST

The test consists of 20 items. Half of them are negative statements adopted from Machiavelli's original work while the other 10 items are positive statements added by the authors. Respondents find seven numbers under each statement. They are instructed to mark the number indicating the extent to which they agree with each statement. (1 = completely disagree . . . . . 7 = completely agree). Reverse score items: 3, 4, 6, 7, 9, 10, 11, 14, 16, 17.

1   Never tell anyone the real reason you did something unless it is useful to do so.
2   The best way to handle people is to tell them what they want to hear.
3   One should take action only when sure it is morally right.

4   Most people are basically good and kind.
5   It is safest to assume that all people have a vicious streak, and it will come out when they are given a chance.
6   Honesty is the best policy in all cases.
7   There is no excuse for lying to someone else.
8   Generally speaking, men don't work hard unless they're forced to do so.
9   All in all, it is better to be humble and honest than to be important and dishonest.
10 When you ask someone to do something for you, it is best to give the real reasons for wanting it done rather than giving reasons which carry more weight.
11 Most people who get ahead in the world lead clean, moral lives.
12 Anyone who completely trusts anyone else is asking for trouble.
13 The biggest difference between most criminals and other people is that the criminals are stupid enough to get caught.
14 Most men are brave.
15 It is wise to flatter important people.
16 It is possible to be good in all respects.
17 Barnum was wrong when he said that there's a sucker born every minute.
18 It is hard to get ahead without cutting corners here and there.
19 People suffering from incurable diseases should have the choice of being put painlessly to death.
20 Most men forget more easily the death of their father than the loss of their property.

1. Manipulation

Machiavellians are first and foremost manipulative: they use, deceive and shortchange others. They always take and even seek the opportunity to benefit from misleading others (Sutton & Keogh 2000). They are highly callous, selfish and malevolent in their relationships. It is not surprising that Machiavellian leaders were found to have detrimental effects on their employees' career success and well-being (Volmer, Koch, & Göritz 2016). At the same time, Machiavellians are careful: they only choose to fish in troubled waters when knowing there is little chance of being exposed. Mostly, they justify their actions by some rational reason, in many cases claiming that others would do exactly the same in their shoes. They employ a wide variety of means to deceive others: they may flatter, be intrusive or pretend cooperation and understanding as required by the situation.

At this point, however, Machiavellians should be distinguished from psychopaths, who embody an even darker side of human nature. Both are characterised by callousness towards others whereas psychopaths do not suffer from a guilty conscience. Machiavellians are not so hostile and aggressive but are more tactical in their relationships (Jones & Paulhus 2009). This is discussed in more detail in Chapter 4.

One secret of Machiavellians' success lies in the many diverse tactics they use to deceive others. In an early social psychological experiment, subjects completed a series of tasks (they had to find hidden figures in a picture) while the experimenter measured the time required for completion (Geis, Christie, & Nelson 1970). Subjects then temporarily took up the experimenter's role and presented the next subjects with the same test they had completed before. When a subject finished, the experimenter came and asked them to try to disturb another subject still working on the task by, for example, distracting their attention or confusing their mind, which would probably delay completion. However, it was up to the subjects by what means they would bring about disturbance. Practically, they were free to employ any tactic, trick or craft capable of producing the desired effect. The participants believed that the aim of the experiment was to study the effect of interpersonal power relations on reward and punishment. Subjects' behaviour was observed, video-recorded and noted down from behind a one-way mirror and then obtained data were statistically processed.

Results revealed that subjects with high Mach scores employed a larger number, more diverse and more effective influence techniques as compared to other subjects. They often lied, informing other subjects about false or distorted rules of task completion. Lies also included judging incorrect solutions to be correct and withholding important information as well as posing irrelevant or confusing questions and statements (e.g. "By the way, what camp did you attend last summer?"). Furthermore, they often employed various means of deception and distraction: whistled, hummed, kept sighing, tapped the pencil against the desk and constantly rearranged things on the desk. According to the authors, Machiavellians were distinguished not only by the intensity and frequency of influence but also by their using such techniques in extremely novel and innovative ways.

Obviously, it also matters under what circumstances they use such tactics. Christie and Geis (1970) suggest three types of situations where Machiavellians prove particularly effective and successful in overcoming others: 1) in a close personal relationship with the "victim"; 2) in a less structured and less regulated social environment or institution (e.g. workplace) which offers ample opportunity to find out unusual tactics; 3) with partners who are engrossed in, or occupied by, their emotions.

Manipulation has a multifaceted connection with lying. Machiavellians often lie and they lie convincingly and effectively (Box 1.3). A recent study aimed at assessing the participants' propensity to lie (Azizli et al. 2016). The extent to which individuals engaged in high-stakes deception was measured by different questionnaires. In one of them, participants were asked to respond to general items about their typical lying behaviours (e.g. "How often do you lie?"). The second questionnaire assessed how participants approve or disapprove narratives described in two scenarios. One of them depicted a hypothetical mating-relevant situation in which the participant goes out for coffee with an ex-partner behind a current partner's back. In the other scenario, the hypothetical situation was academic in nature and features the participant plagiarising a friend's assignment. Machiavellianism strongly correlated with all kind of deception. Yet, Machiavellians engaged in high-stakes deception to such a degree that even exceeded the psychopaths' propensity to lie.

BOX 1.3 LIES

In one study, high Machs reported they lied rather frequently especially when it promoted their wealth, social status and prestige (Baughman et al. 2014). Other studies accordingly found Machiavellians reported to be most willing to lie when it helped them to gain benefits (McLeod & Genereux 2008). Thus, for example, Machiavellians as compared to others found much more acceptable as well as personally applicable the behaviour of the actor in the following story:

> "Sean accidentally backs into a parked car. As he is driving away, the owner arrives and asks Sean if he saw who damaged his car. In order to avoid paying for the damage, Sean lies and says he has no idea who did it."

In an interactive experimental setting, subjects first completed the Mach-V test and then reported their emotional state in another test listing words and phrases related to emotions (Murphy 2012). Then they had to solve a quiz comprising ten questions, each of whose correct solutions was rewarded with a sum of money. Then came a twist in the setting: before the subjects were informed of the correct answer, the computer screen displayed the sum of the reward of which subjects had to verbally inform the experimenter (who could not see the screen). The study revealed that high Machs as opposed to low Machs were more willing to deceive the experimenter by reporting a false sum – increasing the amount, of course. Moreover, high Machs felt less guilty and remorseful. This was reflected by a second measure of their emotional state indicating insignificant change, that is, they did not become particularly tense or anxious.

However, it would be a mistake to think that Machiavellians are smooth liars, telling lies all the time. On the contrary, they do not consider lying a compulsory or inevitable tactic but view it as a necessary means to be used in a world where others are unreliable (Geis & Moon 1981). It is another matter that their judging others as unreliable results from their own malevolence in the first place. In any case, they choose to lie when they think the truth would not be effective. In sum, Machiavellians aim to appear sincere whereas non-Machiavellians hold sincerity important in its own right.

2. Amorality

Machiavellians are inclined to behave unethically; they can easily separate themselves from moral percepts. They always pursue their self-interest, and they are not particularly deterred by moral prohibitions. They become upset when facing unsuccess rather than injustice, that is, when they cannot influence others. They quite often provoke others, continuously testing where the red lines are in their relationships (Gunnthorsdottir et al. 2002). When they feel weakness or lenience in others, they launch an attack with no hesitation. They are particularly willing to break ethical norms when they expect material gain (Woodley & Allen 2014). Generally, they are uninterested in norms such as fairness, reciprocity and responsibility. They believe not to be bound by such norms, while they also believe themselves not to be different from others in this respect since others equally disrespect ethical principles, although they hypocritically claim the opposite. According to Christie and Geis (1970), one of Machiavellians' most important characteristics is resisting social expectations, not letting community rules and principles influence them – this is exactly what makes them successful manipulators.

A "classic" social psychological experiment demonstrates how unconcerned they actually are with conventional ethical standards and norms (Harrell & Hartnagel 1976). In the study, subjects first completed a couple of tests and then had to solve various tasks for money rewards. They solved the tasks in pairs: each pair consisted of an actual subject and a confederate of the experimenters (this latter is henceforward referred to as "partner"). The experimenter said that, unlike the confederate, the subject had two ways of making money: he could earn money for himself by pressing his button, or he could take money from the confederate by pressing another button. When this was done, the money being earned by the confederate would be diverted to the subject's counter. By contrast, subjects' partners had more limited opportunities: they could also access their own money by pressing a button but they had no chance to take away subjects' money. Then experimenters informed subjects that, since their partners suffered obvious disadvantage (being unable to access subjects' money), fairness required that they were given the opportunity to inspect the subject periodically to see whether or not to steal. This was followed by two alternative scenarios. In one case, partners publicly judged subjects to be fair by appearance and concluded that checking them was unnecessary (trust condition). In the alternative case, by contrast, partners declared that they did not trust subjects, who would most probably steal from them unless they kept an eye on them (suspicion condition).

Subjects with high Mach scores were more likely than low Machs to cause loss to their partners in the *trust condition*. Thus, they stole from those who had previously shown trust towards them. Obviously, they were unconcerned with conventional norms. This is also reflected in the finding that they never asked for their partners' approval in exchange for the chance to make more money and to enjoy a competitive advantage. Nor were they particularly concerned about how others would judge them. By contrast, low Machs did not steal at all in the trust condition. They chose to resign substantial material gain rather than violate the norms of fairness and responsibility. Apparently, they related these norms to the acceptance by others that is usually accompanied by increased self-esteem.

BOX 1.4 ARE MACHIAVELLIANS EVIL?

More recent studies confirm that Machiavellians have a rather lax attitude towards ethical principles, and they feel less bound by moral standards than "ordinary people". American university students were asked how important they held fundamental moral values (Jonason et al. 2014). Five such values were presented in the study: Harm (kindness, gentleness, nurturance); Fairness (justice, rights, autonomy); Ingroup (loyalty, patriotism, self-sacrifice); Authority (deference to legitimate authority and respect for tradition); and Purity (psychology of disgust and contamination). Beyond answering questions about these values, subjects had to specify the amount of money for which they would willing to engage in various deeds seen as immoral or placed under taboo. For example, they had to imagine a behaviour, such as "Kick a dog in the head, hard". Subjects rated their willingness on an eight-point scale. One extremity of the scale represented the answer "I'd do it for free". The other extremity was "Never for any amount". Response alternatives between the two extremities indicated specific sums, that is, 10, 100, 1,000 or even more money for which subjects would commit the wrongdoing in question. The authors found a negative relationship between subjects' Mach scores and the degree of importance they assigned to the values of Harm, Fairness, Ingroup and Authority. These results were very similar to those obtained for psychopathy but were highly different from those obtained for narcissism (that showed no significant relationship with any of the moral values mentioned).

Are Machiavellians evil? That would be an exaggeration. Usually they do not harm others for the sake of causing harm, and they do not find pleasure in others' suffering as opposed to psychopaths. Machiavellians act rationally: they use others to take advantage of them rather than to harm others for pleasure (although sometimes this may also be the case). The end justifies the means (benefits may be gained by deceiving others) whereas the means does not justify the end (benefits are not gained in order to deceive others).

Machiavellians are amoral rather than immoral. Amorality alone, however, also shows wide variation across Machiavellian individuals: some of them are not in the least concerned with ethical principles and norms. Others are clearly aware of the importance of moral standards yet do not see it necessary to be governed by them in everyday life. Finally, some feel guilty about harming others but do not see why they should choose not to come out the winner when others' ethical conduct also serves only as a hypocritical disguise to hide behind. We still know little about individual differences in Machiavellian thinking and behaviour but the findings of various studies – and also our everyday life experience – suggest wide diversity in the group of people commonly referred to as Machiavellians.

3. Cynicism

In the light of the previous statements, it is not surprising that Machiavellians are characterised by profound cynicism. They do not believe what others say and do not at all think of others in positive terms (Pilch 2008). On the contrary, they constantly attribute negative traits to people, assuming they are hypocrites, liars and malevolent beings. In an experiment, groups of subjects played a game in which they had to rank various things according to importance (Rauthmann 2011). Group members had the opportunity to make acquaintances during the game and finally they filled a questionnaire concerning their partners' personality and intelligence. Machiavellians usually rated others low on personality traits such as Nurturance (softhearted, kind, accommodating,), Gregariousness (cheerful, friendly, outgoing) and Openness (unconventional, abstract thinking, individualistic). Likewise, they rated fellow group members' intelligence low and judged that they showed poor performance and communication in the group.

One central feature of the Machiavellian worldview is distrust. Machiavellians maintain constant suspicion towards others whom they expect to be insincere (Geis & Christie 1970). They believe that others would do the same to them as they would do to others, that is, others would mislead them at the first opportunity given. In their own perspective, Machiavellians act in a preventive way: they deceive others before others can deceive them (McIllwain 2003). This is the perspective in which Machiavellians' callousness is best understood: "Why should I be considerate and generous if others are not?" What is more, they believe it is exactly others' false self-knowledge that makes them vulnerable since in reality they are not as sincere and benevolent as they suppose themselves to be. Discrepancy lies between people's attitudes and actions that makes them weak, and this weakness is worth taking advantage of. By contrast, Machiavellians are convinced they are honest with themselves, and they are aware of their willingness to do wrong to others. This may actually be the case; self-deceptive beliefs, such as thinking they are good people in reality, would decrease their chances of deceiving others.

McIllwain (2003) suggests that Machiavellians use their cynicism to create a certain kind of power imbalance between them and their potential victims. They do not regard others to be equal parties to negotiate with. They feel superior to others since they are convinced of having true knowledge of others' behaviour as opposed to others' own beliefs about themselves. They think that people are driven by external rather than internal forces. For this reason, ordinary people are unable to master their behaviour and to control their life. This is where the Machiavellian steps into action and, as another external force, controls others' thoughts and actions. Here the Machiavellian poses in the role of a naïve social scientist of everyday life who believes they know more about people than others. Moreover, they go beyond theoretical scope and turn their knowledge into practice to gain benefits. Later in this volume, we will return to the question of whether they actually have insight into people's thoughts and actions.

**BOX 1.5 SUSPICION TOWARDS CHARACTERS
OF THE STORY**

Machiavellians' cynicism was well reflected by an experiment (Szabo, Jones, & Bereczkei 2015) in which subjects were presented with stories about cases of deliberate deception (see Boxes 9.2 and 9.4 in Chapter 9). Such cases include denigrating someone whom one in a romantic relationship is jealous of, getting rid of an undesirable but devoted "friend", slandering a rival in a competition for being the best pupil in the class, and so on. After each story, subjects were presented with a set of paired statements from which they had to choose one according to their interpretation of the story. Their selections revealed how adequately they understood the stories. Some of the paired statements concerned how subjects held the characters in the stories responsible for wrongdoing, and whether they were willing to forgive the manipulator the deception. For example, one pair of statements related to the story presented in Box 1.2 reads as follows:

A) "Andrew's girlfriend lied to Andrew in order to show him his friend in an unfavourable light."
B) "Andrew's girlfriend did not mean to lie to Andrew, she just did not remember exactly what Andrew's friend said."

That is, one of these paired statements reflects a sincere attitude towards the protagonist (B) whereas the other statement represents a suspicious view (A), while either might be accepted as valid according to the presented story. Results caused no surprise: high Machs as opposed to low Machs more often chose statements expressing a suspicious view of characters. They were prone to recognise malevolence in characters' behaviour, rejecting the possibility of unintentional deception. Machiavellians rarely view others' behaviour as benevolent, even if the situation allows them to do so. On the contrary, they take a cynical position and mostly do not even consider the possibility that others have no negative intentions.

---

4. Cold-mindedness

Machiavellians are characterised by a reserved, cold-blooded and indifferent attitude. They detach themselves from the emotional aspects of situations, do not concern themselves with others' feelings and rather take a rational perspective on things and people. They are goal-oriented rather than person-oriented, focusing on their own interests and ignoring those of others (Christie & Geis 1970; Hawley 2006).

Their lack of emotional involvement is often accompanied by a certain kind of cognitive orientation: Machiavellians think rationally and consider possibilities in a cold-minded manner (Pilch 2008). Due to this approach, they are able to control the given situation; they focus on their goal first of all, analyse incoming information, purposefully sort out options and try to choose a strategy by which they can gain benefits. Meanwhile, they do not allow themselves to be distracted by the presence of others or their own emotions. Their lack of doubt as well as concentration on personal goals provide them with immense advantages over others in gaining material goods and favourable positions. In contrast, low Machs are much more concerned with their network of personal relationships and with moral norms that often make them vulnerable. Usually they are not willing to act according to the principle of "the end justifies the means", nor are they always aware of manipulators' intentions.

Machiavellians' emotional detachment and rational thinking are well reflected by the following experiment (Cooper & Peterson 1980). Subjects played the well-known game in which they had to combine letters into meaningful words according to specific rules. They were informed that each player should earn the most points possible. They were also informed that the average score in previous games was 26.5 points. Two alternative conditions were compared in the experiment. In one condition, subjects had no chance to cheat because the experimenter supervised the game and counted scores. In the other condition, however, subjects had the opportunity to cheat because the experimenter left the scene after instructing subjects to count their own scores. Subjects had several opportunities to cheat; these included exceeding the time limit, counting meaningless words or arbitrarily increasing scores.

The experimental setting was further varied in another respect. In one condition, subjects played the game alone in the room and tried to exceed scores achieved in previous games ("impersonal competition"). In the other condition, subjects played in pairs and they aimed to beat their partner ("personal competition"). Results revealed that low Machs rarely cheated in the impersonal competition, even when they had the opportunity. By contrast, this was the condition in which high Machs frequently cheated since they found it the least risky situation. In the personal competition condition, however, they did not break the rules since their partner's presence posed a high risk of exposure. Low Machs as opposed to high Machs were more likely to cheat in this condition, something which caused much surprise. The explanation is probably that personal competition aimed at winning against a partner elicits intense emotions. Such emotions, being related to beating the partner, reaching victory, the joy of victory and the accompanying anxiety, often make people forget about the importance of rational consideration. Some may even go as far as irregularly allocating extra points to themselves.

This is what Machiavellians do not do. They always keep their emotions under control and do not let either positive or negative feelings govern their actions. Previously we expressed this idea by noting that Machiavellians detach themselves from the emotional heat of situations and try to act in a cold-minded way. In the experiment described above, they considered which situation involved the lowest risk of being detected, choosing that in which they played alone *and* where the experimenter left the scene, and cheated only when the situation met these two conditions.

5. Lack of empathy

All of the previously discussed attributes are closely related to a lack of empathy. This is one of the most important Machiavellian characteristics, if not *the* most important one. It is very likely that they are unable to put themselves in others' shoes, that is, they cannot emotionally empathise with others. Numerous studies have demonstrated that in contrast with other people, Machiavellians show far poorer abilities to attune themselves to the joy, pain or disappointment of others around them. A strong negative relationship was found between Machiavellianism and empathy scores irrespective of the specific test used to measure this ability (Andrew, Cooke, & Muncer 2008; Wai & Tiliopoulos 2012; Al Ain et al. 2013; Jonason & Krause 2013).

BOX 1.6 A MEASURE OF EMPATHY: EXCERPTS FROM BARON-COHEN'S 60-ITEM SELF-REPORT QUESTIONNAIRE (BARON-COHEN, RICHLER, & BISARYA 2003)

Respondents rate each item according to how strongly they agree or disagree with it. Four response alternatives are offered:

A   Strongly agree
B   Slightly agree
C   Slightly disagree
D   Strongly disagree

- I can easily tell if someone else wants to enter a conversation.
- I often find it difficult to judge if something is rude or polite.
- I can pick up quickly if someone says one thing but means another.
- I find it easy to put myself in somebody else's shoes.
- I am quick to spot when someone in a group is feeling awkward or uncomfortable.
- I can't always see why someone should have felt offended by a remark.
- It upsets me to see an animal in pain.
- I can easily tell if someone else is interested or bored with what I am saying.
- Friends usually talk to me about their problems as they say that I am very understanding.
- I can sense if I am intruding, even if the other person doesn't tell me.
- Other people often say that I am insensitive, though I don't always see why.
- I can tell if someone is masking their true emotion.

It is not surprising that Machiavellians exhibit low levels both of helpfulness and selflessness (Paal & Bereczkei 2007; Bereczkei & Czibor 2014). Data obtained by the "Cooperativeness" scale of the TCI questionnaire (see Box 3.2 in Chapter 3) suggest that they show little willingness to cooperate with others ("It is usually foolish to promote the success of other people"; "I like to imagine my enemies suffering"; "I generally don't like people who have different ideas from mine"; "People involved with me have to learn how to do things my way"; "I don't think that religious or ethical principles about what is right and wrong should have much influence in business decisions").

Machiavellians' unwillingness to cooperate with and help others is probably not only due to their inability to empathise with others' pain and deprivation, thus preventing them from helping people in trouble. Another explanation may be at least as valid; namely, that their lack of empathy leads them to simply ignore the pain they cause or intend to cause to their victims. If one does not feel the negative emotions of others, one has no reason to be concerned that it was they who elicited those emotions. Therefore, poor emotional responsiveness to others may increase the efficiency and mercilessness of manipulation.

Machiavellians' lack of empathy pervades their entire life. A study surveyed career choices and professional interests of American employees aged 18 to 72 years (Jonason et al. 2014). Two types of occupations were found which Machiavellians preferred *not* to choose. They were less likely than non-Machiavellians to prefer jobs in the social service sector ("teaching children to read") and those requiring a caring attitude ("nursing diseased people"). Neither did they show either a positive or a negative attitude towards such other job types as practical, innovative or traditional occupations. Similar vocational interests of Machiavellians were reported in a Canadian study (Kowalski, Vernon, & Schermer 2017). However, irrespective of their working activities, employers are dissatisfied with the attitude and behaviour of Machiavellians. Maybe more importantly, neither are Machiavellians satisfied with the job and role they fulfil in everyday life (Ali & Chamorro-Premuzic 2010).

We have seen the most important five characteristics of Machiavellians: manipulation, amorality, cynicism, cold-mindedness and lack of empathy. There is no doubt that others with low scores on Mach scales may also show one or several characteristics from time to time. Machiavellians, however, pose danger to others because they embody all five characteristics simultaneously (Slaughter 2011). They desire to mislead others in a cold-minded and self-seeking manner while they are unconcerned with either moral standards or the emotions of others. They are unable to empathise with others' pain while placing their own views and ambitions above everyone else's. They are distrustful to others while they are convinced that others deserve to be deceived. We have seen Machiavellians' attitude to life and people, their views on morality and their social deficits. Now we can turn to their basic personality structure.

BOX 1.7 MACHIAVELLIANS AND SEXUALITY

Machiavellians' sexual behaviour provides an excellent field to illustrate their nature since it reflects all of their typical characteristics. Their romantic and intimate relationships provide a peculiar picture of their motives for taking advantage of others, as well as of their cynicism, amorality and lack of empathy. Christie, Geis and their colleagues as the pioneers of research on Machiavellianism paid relatively little attention to this subject. Decades later, John McHoskey (2001) was one of the first researchers to explore the habitual behavioural styles, emotions and motives characteristic to the sex life of Machiavellians. To that end, he developed a test embracing a wide spectrum: it measures the attitude to promiscuity, the level of sexual arousal, the level of guilt related to sexuality and a number of other motivational and emotional factors. In addition, he asked questions about specific behavioural instances, such as the time of the first sexual experience, the number of partners up to the current time or the frequency of masturbation.

He found that those scoring high on the Mach-IV test answered almost all questions differently than did low Machs. Especially great differences were found in sexual curiosity, arousal and promiscuity: Machiavellians positively seek new experience and diversity in their sexual life. At the same time, they are also characterised by a certain kind of malevolence in that they frequently intimidate and humiliate their partner when they judge such behaviour to be the most effective means to sexually conquer the partner. In the light of these characteristics, it is not surprising that they prefer "free sexuality" to obeying moral standards and laws regulating sexuality. Regarding specific life events, all Machiavellians reported more intensive sexual experiences compared to others. They started to engage in sex earlier, had had more sexual partners in past years, made their partners more frequently drunk in order to have sex and so on. Probably not surprisingly, however, it is also Machiavellians who are dissatisfied with their sex life, always seeking for something different, something new. Gender differences accurately reflected the distribution of the entire population: male Machiavellians reported more frequent promiscuity and sexual fantasies than female Machiavellians.

Subsequent studies clearly confirmed these observations. Machiavellians as opposed to others are much more likely to change partners frequently, to prefer short-term relationships, to engage in sexual coercion and to abuse those of the opposite gender (Jonason et al. 2009). They show low levels of closeness, intimacy and commitment towards their partners (Ali & Chamorro-Premuzic 2010).

BOX 1.7A THE SOCIOSEXUAL ORIENTATION INVENTORY (SOI)

The relationship between Machiavellianism and sexuality has often been assessed by the Sociosexual Orientation Inventory which measures the willingness to engage in casual relationships and uncommitted sexual encounters. One of the most recent versions of the inventory comprises nine items including questions and statements divided into three groups according to three facets of sociosexual orientation (Penke & Asendorf 2008). Respondents rate each statement on a 9-point scale, according to how strongly they agree with it.

1   The first group of items includes questions concerning specific behaviours, that is, the frequency of engaging in short-term sexual encounters.

   For example: "With how many different partners have you had sex within the past twelve months?"

2   The second group of items consists of three statements assessing respondents' sociosexual attitude, that is, their attitude to uncommitted sexuality.

   For example: "Sex without love is OK."

3   Three questions forming the third group assess sociosexual desire. (This is a certain kind of motivational state related to concepts such as the interest in sexuality, sexual fantasies and sexual arousal.)

   For example: "How often do you have fantasies about having sex with someone you are not in a committed romantic relationship with?"

The sum of the scores obtained for the three facets provides a measure of so-called global sociosexual orientation. Relatively high SOI scores indicate respondents' willingness to engage in short-term relationships (such respondents are described by the term unrestricted sociosexuality) while low SOI scores rather suggest a preference for long-term relationships (such respondents are characterised by restricted sociosexuality). Pertinent results show that Machiavellians are more willing to engage in emotionally uncommitted sexual relationships. Their preference for casual relationships equally manifests itself in their behaviour, desire and attitude, thus it is not surprising that their overall sociosexual orientation is typically unrestricted.

2

MOTIVES AND CONSEQUENCES

In Chapter 1, I enumerated Machiavellians' most important attributes and discussed their typical ways of thinking and action. The present chapter essentially expands this focus to the underlying motives driving Machiavellians' behaviour, as well as to the consequences of that behaviour. More specifically, I examine the motivational factors underlying manipulation strategies as well as the advantages and disadvantages of Machiavellianism in everyday life.

1. Reward-driven behaviour

Facing the question of what the most fundamental and direct motive driving Machiavellian behaviour, most of us would highlight one single word: reward. Machiavellians strive to be the winner of the situation and aim at gaining the largest profit possible. This is reflected in studies based on experimental games modelling everyday life situations. One type of study is based on the so-called trust game in which subjects alternately take on the role of the first and the second player (see Box 2.1). All existing results show that high Mach players, in contrast with low Machs, earn more at the end of the game (Gunnthorsdottir et al. 2002; Bereczkei et al. 2013). Distrusting their partners in the first place, they subsequently offered a relatively small amount when taking up the first player's role. Moreover, they did not feel bound by the norm of reciprocity (or by moral standards in general), and therefore they also returned small sums as second players. They made no exception of those who previously had made them fair or even favourable offers. This latter observation makes the profiteering tactics of Machiavellians particularly salient: although they are aware of their partner's cooperative intent, they do not concern themselves with it but solely pursue their own self-interest.

Machiavellians actively seek opportunities to gain profit while trying to avoid situations that might possibly deprive them of rewards. With Machiavellians, high

BOX 2.1 TRUST GAME, ULTIMATUM GAME

The experimental games presented below are typically played by subjects sitting in separate places but connected by a computer network. They can see sums offered by their partner on the screen and they can respond to the offer (usually specifying another sum) by using the keyboard. This means that players remain anonymous during the game: they have no information about their partner's physical appearance, age, gender, etc., rendering the experimental setting highly objective. The screen displays either real currencies or points that are subsequently converted to money. In both cases, players actually receive the sum of money they win in the game. This condition increases the "seriousness" of the game and the lifelike quality of the decisions made in the game.

Ultimatum game: Two players interact in order to distribute a given amount of money. Player 'A' makes a proposal regarding how to distribute the sum. That is, player 'A' may transfer a part of the money received from the experimenter to player 'B', who may either accept or reject the offered distribution. In cases of acceptance, both receive the sum according to the agreed distribution. In cases of rejection, neither of them gains anything. The game comprises one single round, that is, the response of player 'B' ends it. The game is primarily used to study the conditions under which player 'A' shows generosity to player 'B' as well as the limit under which player 'B' refuses the offered sum considered unfairly law, thereby essentially punishing player 'A'.

Trust game: The game involves two players who have equal funds at the start (say, 10 USD each). Player 'A' makes the first move: he has two alternatives. 'A' may choose not to trust their partner and thus not to transfer any money to player 'B'. However, 'A' may instead choose to trust 'B' and to transfer a part (or the whole sum) of their money (say, 4 USD). In the latter case, the experimenter doubles the transferred sum, so that player 'B' will have not 14 but 18 USD. Then comes the turn of player 'B', who also has two alternatives: they can either keep the whole sum, thereby inflicting a loss on player 'A', or return a part of their funds to 'A' (say, 6 USD). This is the end of a single-round game. To summarise the alternative outcomes of the exemplary transaction: if 'A' transfers nothing to 'B', both keep their initial funds (10 USD each). If 'A' transfers 4 USD whereas 'B' does not offer anything in return, then 'A' earns 6 and 'B' earns 18 USD. If, however, 'B' "shows gratitude" for their partner's trust by returning 6 USD, then eventually both gain a larger sum (12 USD each) compared to their initial funds. The game serves to study two decision-making situations and the corresponding psychological states: first, to what extent 'A' trusts their partner and second, to what extent 'B' is willing to reciprocate.

reward dependence is combined with high harm avoidance. In one experiment, subjects played the so-called ultimatum game (see Box 2.1). In this game, one player offers a sum and the other player decides whether or not to accept it. If the second player accepts the sum, both receive the money credited to them whereas in the case of a negative response, neither of them gains anything. From a rational point of view, people have an interest in accepting even the smallest sum since it is still more than nothing. In reality, however, people usually act otherwise: most of them refuse sums they consider unfairly low, even though they are depriving themselves in that way (Gintis et al. 2003; Heinrich et al. 2005).

High Machs behaved in this sense rationally: they were more likely to accept small offers than low Machs who refused offers they judged unfair (Meyer 1992). Likewise, when subjects were asked to specify a "resistance point", that is, the minimum amount they would accept, Machiavellians chose not to refuse even sums smaller than one third of the funds available to their partner. This behaviour suggests, on the one hand, that Machiavellians seek to gain rewards while not bothering overmuch with ethical issues such as injustice or unfairness. On the other hand, they try to avoid even the smallest loss by putting up with the smallest offers. Finally, they seem to be able to master negative emotions elicited by freeriders, that is, by those offering unfairly small sums. Inhibition of negative emotions and the underlying neural processes are discussed in Chapter 11.

Of course, Machiavellians' dependence upon reward goes beyond financial profit. It is generally true that their behaviour is strongly influenced by their striving for gains. Such gains include material benefits, overcoming others and reputation among group members. In a recent study, subjects completed a test assessing sensitivity to reward and punishment (SPSRQ; Birkás et al. 2015). Reward orientation was assessed by questions such as "Do you generally prefer activities which result in immediate gains?"; "Do you often pursue activities aimed at achieving your colleagues', friends' or family members' appreciation?"; "Are you often concerned with making a good impression on others?" The degree of Machiavellianism (as measured by the Mach-IV scale) showed a positive relationship with these indicators of sensitivity to reward: there is no doubt that Machiavellians resolutely seek to win and gain whether money, prestige or position is in question.

However, they not only seek to gain but often seek to gain *immediately*. In the above mentioned study, subjects played a well-known card game (the IOWA gambling task) which essentially is a form of gambling. Players drew cards from four decks one at a time. Each player had a certain sum of labour money at the start and all were informed that each player's goal was to win the largest sum possible after drawing 100 cards. Two of the card decks (A and B) mostly contained cards which earned a relatively large sum (reward) to the player turning them up but some of the cards imposed considerable losses (punishment). Cards in the other two decks (C and D) yielded smaller rewards while the sums of possible punishment were also smaller. Decks A and B proved unprofitable in the long term because they involved large sums of punishment not counterbalanced by the likewise large rewards. By contrast, decks C and D ensure a safe game involving low risk in which relatively small sums may be earned. A negative relationship was found between Mach scores and the amount of money the players eventually gained. Machiavellians as opposed to others were more willing to draw from the decks offering large rewards even though they should have realised over time that their losses would exceed their earnings. They had a preference for immediate rewards despite the potential negative consequences.

It has to be noted, however, that Machiavellians do not go for direct and immediate rewards at any price. The presented gambling game comprises a number of uncertain and unpredictable situations. Under such conditions, Machiavellians typically seeking to gain profit may judge that there is no reason in playing a safe game because outcomes are unpredictable. "Take what you can and forget about everything else." Low Mach players were not necessarily cleverer; they were simply driven less by the greed for gain and thus they made more considered decisions.

Nevertheless, Machiavellians are in many cases able to achieve success in the long term as well. Although they lose under the very special conditions of gambling, they often win in situations resembling everyday life. In the upcoming chapters, we present many studies which reveal that Machiavellians flexibly adapt to changing circumstances and that they develop efficient strategies ensuring success in the long term.

2. Conflicts in the brain

Reward-driven behaviour, and especially behaviour aimed at gaining immediate and direct rewards, includes seemingly simple, almost instinctive actions: persistent and confident efforts for the largest gain possible at others' cost. In fact, it is a complex decision-making process as confirmed by studies on the underlying neural processes. In an fMRI study (see Box 2.2), subjects who are placed in the machine played a trust game with a partner sitting outside. Subjects were enabled to play by having a screen inside on which they could see their partner's offers while they could set the size of their own offers with their free hands. Before making an offer, subjects had a few seconds to decide on the amount of money they offered. Changes in brain activity taking place in this phase were recorded, enabling the researchers to infer the cognitive processes underlying decision-making.

Increased activity was found in the anterior cingulate cortex (ACC) of high Machs fulfilling the role of the first player (Bereczkei et al. 2013). This brain area is one of those most studied in relation to social relationships, and a wide range of cognitive functions have been ascribed to it. It is involved in reward-based decision-making as well as in processing novel, non-automatic stimuli (Etkin, Egner, & Kalisch 2011; Weston 2011). It is well-known for monitoring and eliminating conflicts emerging between various brain areas (modules). It monitors conflicting responses emerging during information processing and signals if action performance requires further cognitive control (Rilling et al. 2002; Dulebohn et al. 2009). The ACC seems to be especially involved in the assessment of negative performance that it then uses as an avoidance signal during the selection of future action plans (Dreisbach & Fischer 2012).

In the light of these functions, increased activity in the ACC of high Machs suggests that Machiavellians experience intense conflict during decision-making

BOX 2.2 BRAIN IMAGING

A major advance in neuroscience was the development of brain imaging techniques. They enable the observation of brain areas responsible for specific functions or malfunctions. Such techniques meant a revolutionary innovation: images of changes in human brain activity enabled direct observation of neural events. Today, magnetic resonance imaging (MRI) is the most frequently applied brain imaging technique in neuroscience and medical diagnostic procedures. The technique is essentially based on measuring changes in cerebral blood flow, more precisely, changes in the amount of oxygen bound to hemoglobin in the blood. Such changes provide information of metabolic activity of the studied brain areas that in turn indicates the intensity of neural activity in those areas. The technique enables clarification of what functions various brain areas are involved in. Initially, the technique was primarily used to localise brain areas involved in various basic functions such as, for example, colour vision. Subsequently, sophisticated experimental procedures were developed to explore relationships between different types of stimuli and neural responses. For example, it has been determined what brain areas are activated by images presenting threatening stimuli (e.g. an angry face) compared to neutral images.

Probably the most common application of brain imaging techniques includes experiments comparing individuals or groups in order to reveal their differences at the level of neural events. Such experiments have provided, for example, a much better understanding of the particular brain functions, or the lack of such functions, underlying the poor mentalisation ability of people with autism, that is, their poor performance in understanding the mental states of others.

Functional MR studies have also been conducted with Machiavellians. These studies usually involved subjects scoring extremely high or low on the Mach scale, that is, those scoring at least one standard deviation away from the mean (usually 100) in either direction (approximately, scores above 115 and below 85). In general, the former are typical Machiavellians while the latter are typical altruists. In the experimental setting of the studies, subjects were lying in the fMRI machine while playing a social dilemma-type game with a partner.

The experimental procedure was rather complicated, comprising 40 to 50 rounds each including a decision-making phase of 6 to 8 seconds as well as a feedback phase of 10 to 15 seconds, while players' current account balances were displayed. Brain activity measures were recorded in the decision-making phase, that is, when players selected the sum to be transferred to their partner as the first step or as a response to their partner's previous step. The experimental procedure required a total of 40 to 60 minutes per subject.

in the trust game. Distrusting their partner, they transfer small sums whether they are the first or the second player. Nevertheless, they are probably aware of their violating the norm of reciprocity that may prove disadvantageous in long-term reciprocal relationships. This produces a conflict between their short-term goals (shortchanging others) and long-term interests (gaining more in a stable partnership) which probably causes the increased ACC activity in the moment of decision-making.

This explanation is apparently corroborated by the obtained reaction times. Positive correlation was found between Machiavellians' ACC activity and their reaction time (the lapse between perceiving the partner's offer and pressing the response button). This was precisely the expected result: assuming that high Machs as opposed to low Machs experienced a more intense conflict between their different motives, they would need more time to prepare the adequate decision and to process relevant information. Inferring backwards, prolonged reaction time may indicate that Machiavellians struggle with a dilemma that causes a delay in the optimal response.

BOX 2.3 ANTERIOR CINGULATE CORTEX

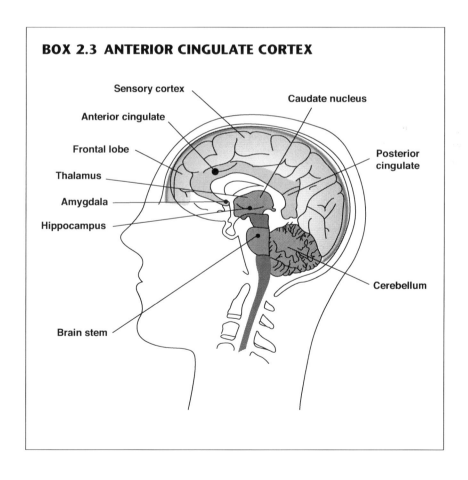

It is important to note that the employment of brain imaging techniques has not displaced "traditional" psychological experiments; in fact, they represent the same processes at different levels. Various questionnaire studies, social psychological experiments and other methods are used to measure behavioural processes, personality dimensions and motor responses. However, they cannot map the underlying neural processes that are explored by fMRI studies which, at the same time, do not concern the observable behavioural outcome. Only the integration of the two levels can provide a complex and comprehensive understanding of the phenomena in question. Research on Machiavellianism has just undergone such an integration process. First, Machiavellians' most important personality dimensions, behavioural patterns and decision-making processes were revealed and only since then, practically during the past five years, have investigations into the involved brain areas and processes taken place. Future research on Machiavellianism will still require all the various methodological procedures on different levels.

3. Extrinsic and intrinsic motivation

Reward-driven behaviour is closely related to the regulation of need fulfilment and goal-oriented behaviour, that is, to motivational factors. Research shows that Machiavellians' goal-oriented behaviour is mostly motivated by external factors (Fehr et al. 1992; Jones & Paulhus 2009). Extrinsic motivation is the term used in the literature to refer to the drives related to the achievement of tangible goals or rewards as well as to the drives serving to avoid harms and damages. By contrast, the term intrinsic motivation covers internal drives, that is, the pleasure of activity, interest and striving for development.

Studies suggest that Machiavellians are typically driven by extrinsic motivation; their actions are a means to obtain external gains (money, power, influence). John McHoskey (1999) used various tests to reveal the different motivational factors held important by people with different Mach scores. A four-item test focused on the importance of pursued goals: material success, communion, self-love and family ties. Subjects rated the subjective importance of these goals on 9-point scales. Machiavellianism was positively correlated with material success whereas negatively with all intrinsic motivational factors (communion, family ties, self-love). High Machs are firmly convinced that external circumstances have a stronger influence on their life than internal drives. This probably lies at the core of their strong feeling of alienation in their personal relationships as far as they believe that they live in isolation and their life is essentially meaningless.

Another motivational factor is related to pursuing individual versus community interests. A recent study (Jonason et al. 2014) found that Machiavellianism was positively correlated with an individualistic value orientation (emphasising autonomy, independence and competition) while negatively correlated with collectivistic values (underlining loyalty to the community). This finding corroborates the picture suggested by previous social psychological studies: Machiavellians are characterised by markedly low sociability; as compared to others, they are less able to go beyond self-interest and to show concern for others.

In this regard, the Machiavellian repertoire displays a certain duality. On the one hand, they believe themselves to be slaves to circumstances; they are characterised by a certain kind of fatalism insofar as they believe that the outcome of all their actions depends on chance, circumstances or the behaviour of others (see also Box 2.3). On the other hand, however, they are unconcerned with

---

BOX 2.3 TIME PERSPECTIVE AND FATALISM

In a recently published study, researchers investigated the time perspectives of Machiavellians (as well as of psychopaths and narcissists; Birkas & Csatho 2015). People's time perspectives are subjective points of view; the forms and ways they experience the events of their past, present and prospective future. Subjective time perception strongly influences the understanding of life events as well as the way of attributing meaning to them. In order to assess time perspectives, the researchers used a 56-item self-report measure developed by Boyd and Zimbardo. Subjects rated each item on a five-point scale according to how strongly they agreed (or disagreed) with it. The construct measured by the scale is based on the assumption that there are great differences in the ways people orient themselves towards the past, present or future when making decisions. These differences were sorted under five categories. *Present hedonistic* people strive for immediate satisfaction, take risks, seek for exciting stimuli and ignore future consequences ("I find myself getting swept up in the excitement of the moment"). *Present fatalistic* people believe in the fatefulness and predestination of life events ("My life path is controlled by forces I cannot influence"). *Past positive* people take a rather sentimental and nostalgic perspective on past events ("Happy memories of good times spring readily to mind"). By contrast, *Past negative* people rather focus on previous failures and misfortune ("I have taken my share of abuse and rejection in the past"). Finally, people oriented towards *Future* set goals and make plans that they strive to realise by persistent efforts ("I am able to resist temptation when I know that there is work to be done").

The researchers found that Machiavellianism was positively correlated with Present-fatalistic and Past-negative perspectives. (Similar results were obtained for psychopaths as well.) The Present-fatalistic orientation is understandable from the previously mentioned research findings: Machiavellians tend to think their life is governed by fate rather than by themselves. Their preference for a Past-negative perspective; that is, their tendency to recall bad rather than good memories from the past is probably related to their negative childhood experiences. As Chapter 10 will discuss in detail, a Machiavellian's childhood is characterised by a rather low degree of parental care. As adults, Machiavellians recall a lack of clear rules and stable family ties. Possibly this childhood environment causes their subsequent inability to be attached to others and their failure to learn the norms of cooperation. What is certain is that their time perspective is strongly influenced by the shadows and ghosts of the past.

others' views, and they keep themselves from being emotionally involved in close social relationships (McIllwain 2003). In fact, Machiavellians are characterised by a certain kind of internal drive leading them to deceive others and obtain gains. Fatalism, at the same time, suggests passivity and resignation: "we are toys in fate's hands having no chance to interfere". To resolve this contradiction, it is worth recalling Machiavellians' cynical attitude and distrust towards others. They believe it is inevitable to take advantage of others in order not to be taken advantage of by others. In this regard, Machiavellians' behaviour is motivated by the need to avoid being exploited rather than by their own independent goals. In sum, these people are simultaneously characterised by passivity and activity, resignation and goal-orientation. They strive to exploit all situations; at every moment, they seek the opportunity to deceive others. At the same time, they actually consider themselves the plaything of circumstances. They believe that their fortune is in the hands of others who scheme against them, therefore their only chance is to get ahead of others.

This duality is also true in another, similar respect. On the one hand, they are not particularly concerned with social norms, and they resist community expectations. This is suggested by studies demonstrating that Machiavellians deceive those who trust them and cause losses to those who offer cooperation (Exlinne et al. 1970; Bereczkei, Szabo, & Czibor 2015). On the other hand, they do concern themselves with the opinions of others, trying to make a good impression and win others' benevolence. This has been clearly demonstrated in an experiment revealing that while Machiavellians are unwilling to help people in trouble when fellow group members are not present, they are more likely to give charitable donations when they are aware that others are informed of their activity (Bereczkei, Birkas, & Kerekes 2010, see Chapter 10).

They not only try themselves to make a favourable impression: others also often judge them as being intelligent, while research has clearly demonstrated that the general intelligence of Machiavellians does not exceed the average (Wilson et al. 1996). Their most prominent characteristic through the eyes of others is that of being charismatic and effective leaders (Deluga 2001). Others possibly judge them as good leaders of a group because they may employ the same strategy against rival groups as that against fellow group members: they fully realise their interests; they are unconcerned with the innermost thoughts and feelings of others; and they seek opportunities to attain the largest gains possible. If they rise to power, their personal interests often become intertwined with collective interests of their group since in many cases they can realise the former through the latter. Therefore, it is in their interest to protect the group and to stand up against other groups. In such cases, people presumably tolerate Machiavellian behaviour from members of the group and even place them in high positions in the hope of sharing the benefits gained in intergroup competition. Thus, one may raise the question: who takes advantage of whom?

4. The strategy

Machiavellians do not always cheat, and altruists do not always give aid. It would be a mistake to think that certain personality traits and motivational factors consistently and constantly lead people to act in certain ways. No one will become another's exploiter once and for all simply because they have Machiavellian characteristics.

Exploitation also requires certain environmental conditions. The social context has primary importance, that is, whom one is associated with, what one knows or thinks about others, what the chances of successful cheating are, how great the risk of exposure is, and so on. It is the interaction between personality and situational factors that influences the intention and success of deception.

In accordance with this line of thought, Machiavellians are mostly ready and willing to cheat and deceive others when they personally benefit from doing so. This requires that the benefits of manipulation exceed its costs. In other words, Machiavellianism is context-dependent. It is beneficial when one (1) successfully avoids being detected; (2) will not be punished for cheating; and (3) conforms to community norms and expectations when the conditions of exploiting others are not given.

Reasoning backwards, Machiavellians only enter deception against others when the circumstances make cheating and manipulation profitable. A cornerstone of Machiavellian strategic decision-making is the continuous weighing-up of the situational conditions. In an early social psychological experiment, subjects completed tasks in pairs (Bogart et al. 1970). Each pair included an actual experimental subject who was informed that the study was aimed at revealing whether cooperation between people with similar or different personalities would make teamwork effective and successful. The other person in each pair was the experimenter's confederate, who had previously received detailed instructions on what to do. Subjects were informed about their partner at the very beginning. However, different information was given in two different conditions of the experiment. In one condition, subjects were informed that their partner was similar to them in several respects while at the same time being a rather unpopular person who had performed below average in psychological tests administered previously. In the other condition, subjects were informed that their partner was different from them in most respects while being a popular person in the eyes of others, having high prestige and favourable traits.

This was followed by the tasks in which subjects were asked to choose from alternative interpretations of puzzling stories. The tasks gave subjects plenty to think about. After finishing the first task, the experimenter had an "unexpected" phone call in the neighbouring room and left in a hurry. Then the confederate began to sigh and moan painfully and eventually suggested to their partner (the actual subject) that they have a look at the experimenter's notebook left open on the desk in front of them.

The experiment revealed that the high Mach response to this suggestion depended on the situation. They rejected the suggestion when previously receiving a negative evaluation of their partner, whereas they showed no such reluctance to cheat when they believed that their partner was a popular person enjoying high prestige and with an attractive personality. The authors' explanation was that Machiavellians had obtained a certain kind of justification for their wrongdoing in the latter case, since they could benefit from collaborating with a person acknowledged and supported by the community. That is, they did not base their decision on ethical considerations (since in that case, they would have agreed to cheat either in both conditions or in neither). They rather cheated or refused according to the descriptive labels given by the experimenters. By contrast, the decision by low Machs about cheating was unrelated to the partner's label. They were influenced by personal involvement with their partner, and by personal feelings for their partner which developed in the face-to-face interaction between them. These findings are in line with other results suggesting that Machiavellians use rational cognitive cues during problem-solving more often, while non-Machiavellians rather rely on their emotions (Christie & Geis 1970).

5. The disadvantages

So far, the reader may have formed the impression that Machiavellians skillfully manoeuvre in a wide range of situations, efficiently deceiving their fellow human beings and successfully making material and social gains. While this is frequently true, it is only one side of the coin, and Machiavellians are often condemned to paying the price.

This was the subject of a study in which young American men and women were asked to read a story and project themselves into it (Wilson, Near, & Miller 1998). The story presents three shipwrecked young people who drift ashore on a desert island (for the sake of simplicity, all three are either men or women). Prior to the shipwreck, they had only met on board and did not know each other. They manage to save food and drinking water sufficient for three days. Each subject was asked by the experimenter to write a first-person account of the events which they expected to take place on the island in the following days. Subjects were expected to primarily write about the development of their imaginary relationships with the other two survivors. They had 50 minutes to write this story, and then they completed the Mach-IV test.

Other subjects (as readers or judges) were asked to read two stories each, one written by a low Mach and the other by a high Mach, and then they had to indicate according to various criteria how willing they were to develop a relationship with the author of each story (see Box 2.4). It has to be noted that the judges did not know the authors' Mach scores. In addition, they had to describe the main characters (authors) of the stories by negative and positive attributes they selected from a list. Finally, they were also asked to complete the Mach-IV test but they had to rate the main characters instead of themselves. That is, they were asked to describe the main characters according to how selfish, manipulative and exploitative each was in their view.

BOX 2.4 EXCERPTS OF THE STUDY REPORTED BY WILSON, NEAR, & MILLER (1998)

I   In reality, how willing would you be to enter into the following social relationships or situations with the author (main character) of the story? Indicate your willingness on a scale ranging from -3 (absolutely unwilling) to +3 (absolutely willing).

1   Partner in a small business
2   Sharing an apartment
3   Confidante (someone with whom to share problems and secrets)
4   Member of your debating team
5   Employer (someone who directly supervises your work)
6   Someone to whom you would loan money

II   What advantageous or disadvantageous attributes does the main character of the story have?

a   Advantageous: realistic, effective, a good friend, self-confident, cooperative, optimistic, intelligent, caring, hard worker, helpful
b   Disadvantageous: selfish, uncaring, immoral, unintelligent, judges others, pessimistic, untrustworthy, aggressive, irritable, shy

III Examples of typical accounts of the shipwreck situation:

1   Low Mach male author: We are all together in this plight. We realise that we must all cooperate, and John, Peter and I decide to equally distribute the limited supplies.
2   Low Mach female author: Mary, Jane and I seem to be getting along pretty well . . . It's funny how we immediately began to trust each other.
3   High Mach male author: I didn't particularly care for John and Peter, and I suspected that there were going to be problems real soon. . . . They are two and I am one. . . . I hope that I can get rid of the human threat soon.
4   High Mach female author: Mary and Jane are cold bitches who constantly complain . . . when I got really hungry I wondered how I could cook them with the limited cooking equipment we had.

This rather complex study provided several interesting findings. First, close correspondence was found between the authors' self-reported Mach scores and the main characters' Mach scores estimated by readers. That is, the readers were able to infer the authors' degree of Machiavellianism solely from their stories while being unaware of their actual scores obtained on the Mach scale. Second, not surprisingly, readers attributed far more negative traits to the authors with high Mach scores, compared to those with low scores. The former were judged as selfish, untrustworthy and aggressive, who were unconcerned with others' troubles. Third and finally, readers preferred to enter into various types of social relationships with low Machs as main characters much more than they did with high Machs. They were more willing to accept the former as a partner in a small business, as a flatmate sharing an apartment or as an employer or teacher.

These findings clearly led to the conclusion that Machiavellianism has a serious price, namely, deprivation of social relationships in the long term (Wilson, Near, & Miller 1998). People coming to know their motives and intentions seek to avoid any closer relationship with them. The authors concluded that Machiavellians are rather successful in the short term; that is, in cases when there is no time or opportunity to detect them. They launch an immediate "first strike" and then move off seeking after new prey. However, research done in the past decade suggests that such dichotomy between the realisation of short-term and long-term interests is not as sharp as previously believed. It has been revealed that Machiavellians can also successfully deceive others by analysing the situational factors and others' behaviour throughout a longer period (see Chapter 10). That is, Machiavellians are characterised by a certain kind of strategic thinking which primarily pertains to their flexible adaptation to a changing social environment. Nevertheless, it is still true that Machiavellians often have to pay the price of manipulation, often becoming isolated, especially in a close-knit community such as a company of friends, a workplace community or a sports club.

6. Social success or unsuccess?

The above observations sharply raise the question of how successful Machiavellians are in various areas of social life. That is, the question concerns how efficiently they get along in everyday life rather than how they perform under laboratory conditions and how they rate items of questionnaires. They should be brought into focus not as experimental subjects but as real everyday people who lead a life, work and pursue their everyday businesses. In this regard, it is practical to study social variables which represent relatively reliable measurement and make more or less accurate comparisons possible, such as occupational status or income.

A meta-analysis embracing several previous studies included data from various countries and social groups on workplace performance of individuals with different scores on Mach tests (O'Boyle et al. 2013). Data was obtained from a total of more than 43,000 subjects included in 245 independent samples. The analysis found that Machiavellians as compared to others had a lower average income while they were more frequently engaged in "deviant" behaviour at the workplace. Thus, for example, they spent more days absent from work without permission and more complaints were filed against them. In fact, these findings are not surprising in the light of the previous studies. On the one hand, Machiavellians try to make a good impression on others at the workplace. They seek to earn the largest rewards possible (higher income, promotion, etc.) and to that end, they often try to develop close relationships with colleagues. On the other hand, they cannot deny their true selves, and their employers sooner or later notice that they generate tension around themselves due to their being secretive, lying and intriguing. They do so in the hope of advancement and gains but exposure in most cases upsets their plans. All things considered, they clearly appear to be relatively unsuccessful in workplace communities.

Other studies suggest, however, that in certain cases high Machs reach higher income, occupational statuses and positions than low Machs. This may in part be accounted for by their aspiration for success and influence that may guarantee material growth and control over others. But it may also be due to the tendency by others to attribute traits to them which are generally associated with a good leader, that is, charisma, charm and the ability that may be used in favour of the group (Jones & Paulhus 2009). In a Hungarian study, Mach scores of people working in different positions were compared (Sárkány & Bereczkei 2013). The authors found that top leaders had the highest scores of Machiavellianism while mid-level managers and team leaders scored in lower ranges of the Mach-IV scale. This relationship was more pronounced at companies with a past of only a few years compared to longer-established ones. This finding presumably reflects that longer-established multinational companies operate under well-organised and controlled conditions whereas younger Hungarian companies established during the past two decades following the collapse of socialism have not yet fully elaborated the rules of effective management and cooperation.

The pioneers of Machiavellian studies revealed that (Christie & Geis 1970). This explanation is supported by studies pointing out that Machiavellians positively prefer organisations where no strictly defined roles and regulations prevail and where events are not closely controlled (Gable, Hollon, & Dangello 1992). Under such conditions, they may feel that they have more freedom of choice and that they can pursue their business without any serious risk of punishment. Furthermore, they have more opportunities to improvise, that is, to employ individual strategies of deception. A German study has also revealed that at less strictly organised companies lacking top management instructions, high Mach employees earn twice as much as those with lower Mach scores and that this also applies to employees within the same age group (Shultz 1993). The old slogan may be true: some people like fishing in troubled waters.

3
PERSONALITY

Many experts consider Machiavellianism as a specific set of personality traits that are, in themselves, more or less characteristic to each individual's psychological condition (Paulhus & Williams 2002). Naturally, each individual has a complex psychological constitution characterised by interactions among various personality traits. Some psychologists have developed typologies which describe various personality traits as stable and real components of the psychological organisation. For example, each individual shows a certain degree of Extroversion that is related to sociability and impulsiveness (Eysenck 1970). Extroverts tend to enjoy human interactions and live very actively and intensely. They are dominant, dashing, optimistic and talkative as compared to others. By contrast, introverts are rather quiet and introspective; they avoid being in a larger company of people, and they are prone to anxiety. Naturally, these two "prototypes" are the extremes of a continuous dimension encompassing tremendous intermediate variations. It is generally true that personality traits are continuously distributed in the population, and people show wide variation in these traits.

In recent decades, the Big Five model has become dominant in psychology (Digman 1990). In this model the basic structure of personality comprises five superior traits (called principal factors or dimensions) that essentially determine each individual's psychological constitution. One of these factors is the above-mentioned Extroversion. Another factor is Agreeableness that encompasses various degrees of likeability, emotional support, care, altruism and their negative counterparts. The factor of Conscientiousness is related to responsibility, achievement motivation, persistence and goal-directed behaviour. The factor of Emotional Stability or Emotionality (or Neuroticism in an alternative terminology) refers to the way people emotionally react to environmental effects such as negative stimuli (e.g. a stressful situation) that make some people upset easily while eliciting a calm and balanced response in others. Finally, Openness to experience, or Intellectual

Openness, includes imaginativeness, creativity, interest and the quickness of uptake. The most important characteristics of the five factors, that is, the adjectives which best describe them, are shown in Box 3.1.

It should also be noted in this short introduction that each principal factor may be divided into several sub-factors describing the specific or concrete contents of personality. For example, one subfactor of Extroversion is sensation- or novelty-seeking, which refers to the willingness to actively seek novel, intense, varied and possibly

BOX 3.1 THE BIG FIVE MODEL

Bipolar and unipolar adjective scales characterise the five principal factors of personality (Carver & Scheier 1998). Unipolar scales describe the contents or "theme" of each factor while bipolar scales specify the extremes of the personality traits in each factor. Naturally, the scales defined by these extremes encompass many intermediate degrees; personality traits show wide inter-individual variation in a given population.

Factor	Bipolar scales	Unipolar scales
Extroversion	Bold – timid	Sociability
	Assertive – compliant	Outspoken
	Self-confident – irresolute	Energetic
	Talkative – silent	Happy
	Spontaneous – inhibited	Reserved
Agreeableness	Friendly – unfriendly	Jealous
	Warm – cold	Considerate
	Kind – unkind	Malevolent
	Polite – rude	Touchy
	Good-natured – quarrelsome	Complaining
Conscientiousness	Cautious – rash	Practical
	Serious – frivolous	Persistent
	Responsible – irresponsible	Prudent
	Thorough – careless	Careful
	Diligent – lazy	Extravagant
Emotionality	Nervous – stable	Worrying
	Anxious – calm	Nervous
	High-strung – imperturbable	Timid
	Relaxed – tense	Tense
Openness	Imaginative – unimaginative	Intelligent
	Intellectual – unintellectual	Sharp-witted
	Sophisticated – unsophisticated	Imaginative
	Uninquisitive – curious	Verbal
	Uncreative – creative	Original

unusual experiences. Some people find pleasure in situations offering new and exciting experiences whereas they positively avoid common everyday situations that they
find boring. By contrast, others are clearly made anxious by unusual, unexpected and
intense stimuli. Research has recently revealed that such reactions are closely related
to the reward areas of the brain. Moreover, genetic effects underlying sensation-
seeking and avoidance behaviour have also been revealed (Plomin et al. 2005).

1. The Machiavellians' personality

In accordance with the introduction, the question in focus is whether Machiavellians have characteristic personality traits and, if they do, how they differ from
others in those traits. The answer to the first question is a definite "Yes" according
to studies conducted in different countries, the results of which show a rather universal pattern. These studies found a negative relationship between Machiavellianism and Agreeableness. High Machs report compared to Low Machs (Jacobwitz &
Egan 2006; Paulhus & Williams 2002; Egan, Chan, & Shorter 2014). This is not
surprising given that Machiavellians typically use others as means to achieve their
goals, generally describing others in negative terms and often showing malevolence
towards others.

Other studies likewise revealed a negative relationship between Machiavellianism
and the principal factor of Conscientiousness (Jacobwitz & Egan 2006; Paulhus &
Williams 2002 etc.). Again, this is not a surprise since Machiavellians are notorious,
among other things, for lacking a sense of responsibility, being cynical and unconcerned
with the moral implications of their actions. At the same time, some studies found
a positive relationship between Neuroticism (emotional instability) and Machiavellianism (Jacobwitz & Egan 2006). This suggests that high Machs are characterised by
their seemingly cold and reserved behaviour. They often experience intense emotions
in their personal relationships, especially in stressful situations such as when obtaining
a desired reward or being exposed is at stake. However, they are unable or unwilling to
express their intense emotions; their behaviour and appearance reveal nothing of their
feelings. Since this is an essential characteristic of Machiavellianism, we will discuss the
subject in detail in a separate chapter (Chapter 7).

An unfriendly attitude, a poor sense of responsibility and high emotional instability: are these the characteristics which constitute Machiavellianism? Is it the
people who possess such personality traits whom we call Machiavellians? From
this perspective, one may verifiably argue that those individuals strive to deceive
and exploit others who happen to combine these traits in their personality. These
characteristics of one's mental constitution develop during childhood as a result of
the child's adaptation to certain, presumably negative, effects of the family environment (see Chapter 5).

However, I think Machiavellianism cannot be limited to a specific personality con-
struction. It is a wider psychological phenomenon that also includes characteristic
processes of thinking and cognition. As the subsequent chapters of this book reveal,
Machiavellians employ very specific mental operations in order to exploit others. They

make rational decisions, monitor and forecast others' behaviour and devise strategic plans. Moreover, there are specific neural networks underlying these processes whose activity patterns differ from those observed in the brains of non-Machiavellians. In this more comprehensive sense, Machiavellianism is a complex behavioural system comprising various components from cognitive and learning mechanisms and affective information processing to the particular personality structure.

2. Temperament and character

In any case, it is beyond question that personality traits shape the Machiavellian character. The close relationship between Machiavellianism and certain personality features was revealed not only by Big Five-type questionnaires. Claude Cloninger et al. (1994) developed the so-called Temperament and Character Inventory (TCI) that measures seven personality traits including what are called temperament factors and character factors. Temperament factors represent innate, that is, genetically prescribed patterns of environmental information processing. They determine the individual's basic patterns of automatic responses to effect-eliciting stimuli. The four temperament factors, namely, novelty seeking, harm avoidance, reward dependence and persistence, remain relatively stable throughout life irrespective of cultural and social environment. The other group of personality traits, that is, the character factors, including cooperativeness, self-transcendence and self-directedness describe individual differences which gradually develop as a result of the interaction between temperament, family environment and individual life experiences. The TCI questionnaire enables us to measure a relatively wide spectrum of personality due to its seven principal factors and twenty-four subfactors.

In a study, high negative correlation was found between Mach scores and the scores obtained for the cooperativeness factor of the TCI test (Bereczkei & Czibor 2014). Machiavellians, as we have seen, lack openness to others and show low levels of empathy, care and helpfulness towards others. They are likely to agree with such statements of the TCI test as "I have no patience with people who don't accept my views"; "Principles like fairness and honesty have little role in some aspects of my life"; "Members of a team rarely get their fair share"; "It gives me pleasure to see my enemies suffer"; "I enjoy getting revenge on people who hurt me"; "It is hard for me to tolerate people who are different from me".

It clearly seems that Machiavellians subjects in the mentioned study not only completed the TCI test but also made decisions in a social dilemma situation. Namely, they participated in the experimental Public Goods Game in which they had the opportunity to take financial benefit from others' benevolence and trust (see Box 10.3 in Chapter 10). In most cases, they monopolised the large part of the amounts of money transferred to the group's account and left the game with the highest profits (Czibor & Bereczkei 2012). Machiavellians' poor cooperativeness is, of course, not surprising, and it is in line with those previously mentioned studies which found them to display low empathic concern and a highly manipulative attitude.

BOX 3.2 A SHORT DESCRIPTION OF THE PRINCIPAL FACTORS OF THE TCI

I Temperament factors

1 Novelty seeking – behavioural activation, initiative, curiosity

High scorers: impulsive, willing to explore novel environments, irritable, irresolute, inconsistent, disorderly, uncontrollable, prone to get bored easily

Low scorers: not attracted to novelty, willing to be occupied with details, think long before making a decision, rigid, organised, persistent

2 Harm avoidance – behavioural inhibition, passive avoidance, aversion to negative stimuli

High scorers: cautious, timid, worrying, tense, inhibited, easily exhausted

Low scorers: carefree, uninhibited, self-confident, relaxed, optimistic, energetic, sociable

3 Reward dependence – dependence on others' approval, sensitivity, social attachment

High scorers: sensitive to social stimuli and acknowledgement

Low scorers: socially detached, practical

4 Persistence – achievement-orientation, diligence, ambition

High scorers: diligent, industrious, ambitious, perfectionist, steadfast

Low scorers: idle, negligent, easily give up goals

II Character factors

1 **Self-directedness** – The ability to follow rules and to adapt

High scorers: responsible, reliable, efficient, lead a purposeful life

Low scorers: lack responsibility, self-acceptance and goal-directedness

2 **Cooperativeness** – acceptance of others, empathy, conscientiousness

High scorers: helpful, merciful, tolerant, empathetic

Low scorers: socially uninvolved, self-seeking, unconscientious

3 **Self-transcendence** – identification with a cosmic force independent of the individual

High scorers: patient, creative, wise, spiritual

Low scorers: impatient, self-respecting, lack humility

Importantly, another interesting finding was also obtained in this study. At the end of the experiment, subjects had to describe and render a reason for their previous behaviour, that is, the strategy they used in the game. The resulting texts were content-analysed by means of a software developed for such purposes (Czibor, Vincze, & Bereczkei 2014). The analysis primarily focused on the occurrence of verbs describing cognitive states, emotions and intentionality. Results revealed that high Machs less frequently used first person plural verb forms (e.g. we thought/hoped/approved) compared to low Machs. Furthermore, they used fewer words indicating emotions (e.g. fear, excitement, joy). According to the authors, these results indicate that high Machs have a weaker sense of group orientation and belongingness as opposed to low Machs, who are much more prone to highly value such ties among group members.

Returning to the personality traits measured by the TCI, a lack or at least insignificant level of moral principle was indicated by low scores by Machiavellians on Self-directedness and Self-transcendence (Bereczkei & Czibor 2014). These results confirm that they are unable to go beyond their ego, which they hold the center of the universe. They do not feel obliged to accept social rules if this would go against their self-interest, nor do they feel particularly accountable for their harming others. Furthermore, their high scores on Persistence suggest that they try to permanently adhere to their decisions based on rational considerations. In the Public Goods Game, for example, they consistently transfer smaller sums to the group's account than others in each round and, as a result, they collect more money in their individual account. They are not deterred from such persistent manoeuvring, even given the possibility that they may lose their fellow group members' benevolence since their self-seeking behaviour sooner or later becomes obvious. This result is strictly related to the relatively low scores of Machiavellians on the Reward Dependence factor, which measures sensitivity to the approval and acknowledgement received from the community as a fundamental source of reward rather than the sensitivity to immediate material reward. For Machiavellians, the approval of others seemingly does not count.

3. Sensation seeking, impulsivity, risk taking

Machiavellians score high on the Novelty seeking factor of the above mentioned TCI test. This means, according to Cloninger's definition, that they are impulsive and willing to take the initiative and explore new environments on the one hand, while on the other they are irritable, uncontrollable and easily bored.

This description in itself reflects that novelty seeking is an immensely complex and heterogeneous psychological category. One may seek novelty in work, in extreme sports as well as in sex. Moreover, novelty seeking is closely related to such concepts as sensation seeking, impulsivity or risk taking. The contents of these categories in part overlap while each category has unique contents that distinguish them from the others.

Maybe sensation seeking is the concept most closely associated with novelty seeking. The term was coined by Marvin Zuckerman (1994) who used it to refer to the responsiveness to new and unusual stimuli as well as the willingness to seek exciting, challenging or adventurous experiences. Sensation seekers, that is, those scoring high on Zuckerman's Sensation Seeking Scale (SSS) are a type of hedonists who find pleasure in facing varied, novel and possibly risky circumstances. By contrast, low scorers prefer always to stay in their habitual environment and to avoid unexpected events. Sensation seekers appear to need a constantly high level of arousal that is related to increased brain activity. In other words, such people need more stimuli than others to feel comfortable and to optimally perform tasks. Such internal comfort may be reached by several means such as by sports, travelling or risky behaviour (e.g. bungee jumping), among others.

Machiavellians are also characterised by above-average levels of sensation seeking (Crysel, Crosier, & Webster 2013; Linton & Power 2013). This implies, on the one hand, that they find new stimuli, situations and rivals positively challenging. On the other hand, it suggests that novelty seeking may be related to risk taking. Zuckerman himself also considered risk taking an essential component of sensation seeking (novelty seeking). It is not by accident that the Sensation Seeking Scale he developed and, most of its revised versions, include many items specifically related to risk taking (see Box 3.3). Various studies found that those scoring high on this

---

BOX 3.3 A SHORTENED VERSION OF ONE OF ZUCKERMAN'S SENSATION SEEKING SCALES (SELECTED ITEMS)

Subjects are asked to choose one of two alternative statements that best describe her/him.

- A   I would like a job that requires a lot of travelling.
  B   I would prefer a job in one location.
- A   I get bored seeing the same old faces.
  B   I like the comfortable familiarity of everyday friends.
- A   I sometimes like to do things that are a little frightening.
  B   A sensible person avoids activities that are dangerous.
- A   I would like to try parachute jumping.
  B   I would never want to try jumping out of a plane, with or without a parachute.
- A   I enter cold water gradually, giving myself time to get used to it.
  B   I like to dive or jump right into the ocean or cold water.
- A   I prefer people who are emotionally expressive even if they are a bit unstable.
  B   I prefer people who are calm and even tempered.
- A   People who ride motorcycles must have some kind of unconscious need to hurt themselves.
  B   I would like to drive or ride a motorcycle.

scale generally like gambling, drive faster, prefer exciting sports involving risk, have an inclination to choose hazardous occupations, more frequently engage in casual sex and are more likely to take drugs or consume alcohol (Zuckerman 1994).

One might expect that Machiavellians are genuine risk takers. Of course, this is in part true. They are prone to getting immediate reward even if they risk future success by doing so. In the previous chapter we presented an experiment which revealed that Machiavellians in a gambling game mostly drew from the card deck which offered large rewards even though they realised over time that through that strategy they incurred a disproportionately high risk of losing everything. We also know that Machiavellians often violate norms that are closely related to risk taking. In the hope of gaining profit, they refuse to meet the norm of cooperation or reciprocity, by which they run the risk that their partners will refuse to trust them in the future or even abandon them (Wilson et al. 1998; Gunnthorsdottir et al. 2002).

Nevertheless, Machiavellians cannot be considered typical risk takers. No relationship was found between Mach scores and the levels of alcohol consumption, drug use and smoking (Jonason, Koenig, & Tost 2010). Several studies suggest that Machiavellians positively avoid deceiving others under circumstances involving a high risk of being exposed (Cooper & Peterson 1980; Bereczkei, Birkas, & Kerekes 2010). At other times, they act as prudent strategists who try to prevent themselves from losing previously gained profit. In an experiment, subjects played a gambling game in which the amount of reward was kept by the player who earned it whereas in the case of loss, the sum was deducted from the next player's (and not her/his own) funds. In turn, this latter player was allowed to punish the previous player who could thereby lose all their money. The study found that Machiavellians played rather cautiously and did not lose too much money under the threat of punishment imposed on them by their harmed partners (Jones 2014). They made a strategic decision: they did not take unnecessary risk which would have yielded unfavourable results regarding their closing balance. By contrast, non-clinical psychopaths displayed marked inflexibility during the game: they steadily continued gambling and lost their money.

Both sensation seeking and risk taking are related to impulsivity that may be described by such terms as quick decision, instant responsiveness, spontaneity, enthusiasm and adventurousness. The difference between impulsivity and the other two psychological categories lies in that it refers to an internal readiness to act without specifying its contents or object (as opposed to sensation seeking focusing on novel stimuli and risk taking focusing on hazardous situations). This research field also provides rather contradictory findings for Machiavellians. Some of the studies employing various questionnaires found positive correlation between Machiavellianism and impulsivity (McHoskey 2001; Crysel, Crosier, & Webster 2013). This is possibly because Machiavellians frequently (but by no means always) act in accordance with the principle of the "first strike": they immediately take advantage of their partner's vulnerability and pounce on the opportunity offering itself.

Other studies, however, did not find a significant relationship between the levels of Machiavellianism and impulsivity. Several analyses of the members of the Dark

Triad revealed that certain forms of impulsivity were related to narcissism and psychopathy but not to Machiavellianism (Jones & Paulhus 2011; Malesza & Ostaszewski 2016). Our knowledge on Machiavellianism offers a consistent explanation of this finding as well. Machiavellians are characterised by a certain kind of impulse control: they are able to make a cold-minded decision on the optimal manipulative strategy in the given situation. They rationally consider the most important situational factors while concealing their emotions (see Chapter 7). Such lack of impulsivity may be adaptive since it prevents hasty decisions and supports carefully considered action.

It is not a favourable omen in science when a phenomenon and its opposite could be equally well explained. Machiavellians prove to be impulsive in one study and not impulsive in another, while each finding is supported by empirical data. The dilemma may possibly be resolved by focusing on the multi-faceted and diverse nature of Machiavellianism itself. Machiavellians sometimes employ the tactic of the first strike while at other times their actions serve longer-term goals depending on the social environment they face. When deception is expected to lead to benefit, and when it does not involve any obvious risk, they primarily rely on their intuition and act immediately. In such cases, the readiness to act, spontaneity and quickness resulting from impulsivity may prove crucial. However, when the situation requires an analysis of its complex and changeable effects, it may be more expedient to step back and appraise possible alternative outcomes. Soberness and cold calculation enabled by reduced impulsivity may in the long term guarantee the success of such a rational and analytic form of manipulation.

4. Antisocial personality

Machiavellianism is not a disorder. It may not be considered a psychopathological phenomenon. However, it may be related to several personality traits which may be classified as mental disorders according to the most diverse diagnostic criteria. The above-mentioned impulsivity, risk taking and norm violation raise the question: to what extent may Machiavellians be considered antisocial characters? In the most general terms, an antisocial personality is characterised by absolute disregard to others and by violation of their fundamental rights. People with antisocial personality disorder ignore social obligations and norms, refuse to follow rules, despise authority and exhibit cold indifference towards others' feelings. Although they mostly know that their conduct goes against general social expectations and norms, they remain unconcerned. As the saying goes: the antisocial personality does not love, does not fear and does not learn. Of course, antisocial behaviour is not necessarily equal to violence and physical abuse, although this also occurs frequently. The repertoire includes harassing and threatening others, recurrent conflicts with the authorities (e.g. document forgery), ceaseless involvement in illegal practices (e.g. marriage swindle) and so forth. Box 3.4 shows the clinical classification criteria for antisocial personality disorder.

BOX 3.4 DIAGNOSTIC CRITERIA FOR ANTISOCIAL PERSONALITY DISORDER ACCORDING TO THE DSM-IV

A   There is a pervasive pattern of disregard for and violation of the rights of others occurring since age 15 years, as indicated by three (or more) of the following:

   (1) failure to conform to social norms with respect to lawful behaviours as indicated by repeatedly performing acts that are grounds for arrest
   (2) deceitfulness, as indicated by repeated lying, use of aliases, or duping others for personal profit or pleasure
   (3) impulsivity or failure to plan ahead
   (4) irritability and aggressiveness, as indicated by repeated physical fights or assaults
   (5) reckless disregard for safety of self or others
   (6) consistent irresponsibility, as indicated by repeated failure to sustain consistent work behaviour or honour financial obligations
   (7) lack of remorse, as indicated by being indifferent to or rationalising having hurt, mistreated, or stolen from another

B   The individual is at least age 18 years.
C   There is evidence of Conduct Disorder with onset before age 15 years.
D   The occurrence of antisocial behaviour is not exclusively during the course of Schizophrenia or a Manic Episode.

Considering the above listed features and criteria, it is no wonder that high Mach scores were found among people under psychiatric treatment for antisocial personality disorder (Rada, Taracena, & Rodriguez 2004). Obviously, the two groups have a set of common features: disregarding ethical norms, taking benefit from deceiving others, cynicism, cold-bloodedness. Machiavellians showed higher antisociality according to a 99-item self-report measure (PDQ-4) than those scoring lower on the Mach-IV test (McHoskey 2001). In a recent study conducted in England, randomly selected subjects were asked how many times they were involved in acts of violence as offenders during the past 12 months (Pailing, Boon, & Egan 2014). They received questions such as "Have you thrown something at anyone in order to cause injury?"; "Have you pushed, grabbed or shoved anyone during an argument?"; "Have you hit anyone with a fist or object?".

It is not surprising that those showing a high level of psychopathy proved the most violent according to the self-report measure. It is surprising, however, that they were immediately followed by Machiavellians (with a mean score of violence hardly below that of the former group). It is somewhat strange that while Machiavellians are known as smooth-spoken, cunning and intriguing people who prefer to deceive their victims by wit and words, they are not far from overt violence either. The fact that they are actually inclined to employ physical violence may possibly be due to their malevolence and prejudice, which form an integral part of their character. Usually they do not think of others as individuals with their own emotions and desires, but as impersonal objects of manipulation. Essentially, they see their potential victims as tokens of some faceless type, and that particular type determines the way they choose to manipulate and deceive the victim under the given circumstances.

I have the suspicion, although no related empirical experience has yet been provided, that Machiavellians resort to violence when their tactical moves fail. It may be their frustration caused by failure or being exposed that eventually leads to violence. It is also possible, however, that they are oriented to success and reward to such an extent that they choose to commit violence rather than give up their plans and resign from exploiting others. Another possible explanation is that their sensation seeking and impulsive nature leads them to commit acts of violence, in which case they fail to exercise self-control. This idea is supported by a study in which a close relationship was found between Mach scores and the willingness to employ physical and verbal aggression (McDonald, Donellan, & Navarrete 2012). Machiavellians agreed with statements such as "Once in a while I can't control the urge to strike another person" or "I cannot help getting into arguments when people disagree with me." Obviously, only future research may verify or falsify these alternative explanations for Machiavellian violent behaviour.

BOX 3.5 MACHIAVELLIANISM AND AGGRESSIVE HUMOUR

At first sight, humour is in no way related to antisocial behaviour and aggression. This is only apparent, however. Several disciplines from ethology and ethnography to social psychology have pointed out that jokes, funny remarks and laughter often convey aggressive content and meaning (Eibl-Eibesfeldt 1989). A recently developed self-report scale (Humour Styles Questionnaire) not only measures the understanding and use of humour but also provides a clear-cut category system (Martin et al. 2012). At the primary level, positive and negative humour are distinguished by the respective scales, after which both are divided to further dimensions. The authors define positive humour by the condition that all involved parties benefit from the use of humour and that no one is harmed (e.g. by being ridiculed). Within this category, the Affiliative Humour scale measures one's willingness to communicate humorous contents, telling jokes and teasing others wittily and spontaneously which are aimed at entertaining others (e.g. "I enjoy making people laugh"). The scale for Self-Enhancing Humour, that is likewise positive, measures one's attitude to humour. This includes a humorous outlook on life, the ability to find the humorous aspects of ambivalent everyday situations and using humour as a means of coping (e.g. "My humorous outlook on life keeps me from getting overly upset or depressed about things"). By contrast, Negative Humour always harms someone by reducing their self-esteem. This category includes Aggressive Humour that serves to criticise others (sarcasm, ridicule, mockery) or as a means of threat or offense as does racist and sexist humour, for example (e.g. "If someone makes a mistake, I will often tease her/him about it"). Finally, Self-Defeating Humour is also a type of negative humour manifested in self-criticism and self-disparagement aimed at entertaining others (e.g. "I often try to make people like or accept me more by saying something funny about my own weaknesses, blunders, or faults").

A Canadian research team used this questionnaire in a study which found that Machiavellianism was only correlated with negative humour, and the correlation was found to be positive (Veselka et al. 2010). This means that Machiavellians prefer to tell jokes and make funny remarks which harm, degrade or disparage others (e.g. "If stupidity made you grow, now you could lick the moon while sitting!"). This style of humour, which speaks of a lack of empathy, often becomes a means of exercising control over others and thereby may contribute to the achievement of personal goals.

Interestingly, Machiavellians also scored higher on the Self-Defeating Humour scale than average. This may possibly be explained by their intention to show a negative, pessimistic image of others by degrading themselves: "I am ridiculous but not in any way different from you." Machiavellians as opposed to psychopaths and narcissists do not necessarily set themselves above others. They rather think that everyone is a liar and hypocrite, including themselves. However, they also think that while they are aware of their true self, others cherish illusions about themselves and think they are better than they really are. This may enable Machiavellians to confidently and resolutely hold that deception is the best way to treat others.

Another study not only focused on those engaging in antisocial behaviour but also on their victims. Young Canadian employees were asked about the frequency of workplace bullying (Linton & Power 2013). Researchers in this case did not primarily focus on physical violence but on a wide behavioural spectrum including several antisocial acts ranging from intimidation and emotional abuse to brutal violence. The questionnaire used in the study accordingly included such diverse items as "Humiliated or ridiculed in connection with work" or "Ordered to do work below level of competence". Subjects were asked to indicate how often they had been involved in such acts during the past half-year, either as perpetrators or as targets. The study found that subjects scoring high on Machiavellianism (as well as those with high narcissism or psychopathy, that is, the Dark Triad members) more frequently committed violence against their colleagues than other subjects, while they were also more frequent targets of violent acts. Taking all three groups of the Dark Triad into account, 41.7% of the targets reported that they had bullied others at least once a week, and vice versa: 89.7% of the perpetrators frequently became targets of violence. It seems that both parties are prone to being involved in negative events. People with certain personality types often behave in a way provoking others who in turn respond with violence. For example, it has frequently been observed that superiors in a workplace environment often act aggressively towards those who violate a norm (e.g. by idling working hours away). Moreover, it seems that perpetrators and targets of such workplace violence possess similar personality traits. Machiavellian behaviour is characterised by angry reactions, hostility, verbal aggression and risk taking in both roles. All of these traits make them suitable to become either abuser or victim.

5. Borderline personality

John McHoskey suggests that Machiavellians exhibit a series of personality problems (1995). His findings revealed that while they show symptoms of several mental disorders (antisociality, paranoia, schizotypy), it is probably the borderline personality whose traits are most characteristic to them. This observation was subjected to a closer examination in a study reported by András Láng in which the author used a 53-item questionnaire (Borderline Personality Inventory; BPI) to assess symptoms of the personality disorder (Láng 2015). The borderline personality disorder is highly prevalent, affecting 2–3%of the population. Subjects with this condition behave in an unpredictable and chaotic manner; they often show intense emotions and make scenes, while at other times they withdraw and occasionally sink into complete passivity. They are almost continuously anxious and very frequently react with extreme emotion. Generally, they have difficulty controlling their emotions, often verging on the boundaries of ethical behaviour, and it is not uncommon that they come into conflict with the law. Their social relationships are also characterised by extreme and unpredictable events: they are equally able to love and hate to an extreme, and these feelings are often directed at the same person.

The study found strong correlation between Machiavellianism and borderline personality disorder in three different fields assessed by three subscales of the inventory. One of these subscales is "Identity diffusion" in which the individual perceives themselves as a formless entity without boundaries and unity ("I feel like I'm falling apart"). This state, of course, entails several negative consequences in the individual's life, from a feeling of inner emptiness and inferiority to drug abuse. It is possible, however, that Machiavellians, among whom this state is much more typical than among non-Machiavellians, are able to employ the indetermination and plasticity of their personality to serve their actions. Namely, one core of their success is behavioural flexibility, that is, their ability to quickly adapt to changing circumstances (see Chapter 8). The Machiavellian individual may also be described as a certain kind of social chameleon who assumes different faces in different relationships that they treat neglectfully and impersonally.

Another important field where the relationship between Machiavellianism and borderline personality disorder manifests itself is "Fear of fusion" – the fear of being closely attached to others emotionally ("If a relationship gets close, I feel trapped"). This leads, on the one hand, to loneliness and to the loss of social support while, on the other hand, it may help the Machiavellian to maintain emotional distance. They are able to distance themselves from the emotional atmosphere of the situation and cold-mindedly consider possible tactics. Such a cold reaction may serve manipulation and deception since the efficient exploitation of others is undisturbed by feelings of regret, guilt or generosity (in detail, see Chapter 5). Possibly the same function is fulfilled by the so-called Primitive Defense mechanisms that form the third field where borderline personality and Machiavellianism is interconnected. Their function is to prevent the individual from recognising and realising experiences which threaten their self-esteem and lead to anxiety and distress ("People appear to me to be hostile"). Several defence mechanisms are based on what is known as splitting, where the individual divides their social environment into two opposed groups including "good" and "bad" people. They trust the former while showing distrust, caution and often even contempt to the latter. It is possible that Machiavellians use their defence mechanisms as a means to develop an impersonal relationship with their victims as well as to prevent themselves from facing the emotional consequences of the situation.

Machiavellianism most probably shows the closest relationship with psychopathy among mental disorders, so much so that Machiavellianism is commonly referred to as the non-clinical form of psychopathy. This latter is discussed in the next chapter on the Dark Triad.

4

DARK TRIAD

In the 1990s, the idea was raised that Machiavellianism might be a part of the personality complex related to the negative side of the human psychological constitution. Some researchers traced back human malevolence and evil to the so-called Dark Triad personality that encompasses the traits of Machiavellianism, narcissism and psychopathy (Paulhus & Williams 2002; Furnham, Richards, & Paulhus 2013). These authors did not deny that each of these three personality types had a unique profile but they did argue that a more accurate approach would have been to integrate them into one single construct. They proposed that we could gain a deeper insight into human frailty if approaching and analysing it from the wider perspective of the Dark Triad as opposed to examining it in relation to single personality traits. Neither did the authors argue that the Dark Triad or any of its members necessarily described pathological personalities. As we have seen, Machiavellianism is not considered a mental disorder, something also reflected by the fact that Machiavellians in general are not treated as patients in clinical practice. By contrast, narcissism and psychopathy do have pathological forms since their extreme levels require psychological and psychiatric intervention as diagnosable mental disorders. However, the "less severe" types of narcissism and psychopathy remain within the range of non-clinical behaviour in the normal population. In other words, the Dark Triad includes Machiavellianism as well as non-clinical forms of narcissism and psychopathy. It is beyond question that these are malevolent expressions of human nature but they still form a part of everyday life. Those showing such behaviours are not mentally ill; their personality is not pathological, and even less abnormal. Mostly, they are everyday people even though they make a lot of trouble for others (and for themselves).

1. Narcissism and psychopathy

Narcissism is commonly associated with notions such as self-importance, vanity, conceit and selfishness. Essentially, it is defined as self-adoration, a feeling of grandiosity and a chronic need for affirmation. The narcissistic person is self-centred and self-adoring; they consider themselves unique and continuously suffer from a lack of due attention and respect. They are arrogant, complacent and possess a seemingly highly self-confidence that often serves, however, to conceal their dissatisfaction with themselves. They hold they have special privileges and they are immensely envious of the success of others. They are extremely selfish and convinced that everyone is there to serve their interest. They are unable to have regard for others' needs and feelings although they are in most cases capable of empathic concern and often exhibit guilt. Their relationships with others are shallow and they need them purely to serve, respect and acknowledge them. Over a short time, they are even able to behave persuasively in order to win others' acknowledgement. In accordance with the narcissistic persons' preference for being superior and a propensity to dominate others, a positive correlation was found between narcissism and the level of testosterone, the dominance-related hormone (Plattheicher 2016).

Narcissistic personality disorder as the pathological form of narcissism comprises all these symptoms at pathologically extreme levels. Such individuals are characterised by abnormal self-adoration, claiming superiority, megalomania, needing and expecting unconditional admiration from others and by hypersensitivity to criticism. These characteristics seriously endanger their relation to reality.

The extent to which one may be considered a narcissistic personality is assessed by various questionnaires and tests in the same way as it was presented in relation to Machiavellianism (Box 4.1).

Although both narcissistic and Machiavellian individuals make a lot of trouble for their fellow beings, it is most probably psychopaths who bring the greatest danger on their environment. People with a high level of psychopathy are primarily characterised by poor moral judgement, a lack of regard for the emotions of others and a lack of regret and guilt. Psychopaths are convinced that they are above others and have privileges, and so they disregard social norms. They are unable to love; they do not feel anxious before harming others and do not feel remorse afterwards. They are extremely impulsive, almost all of them showing some form of antisocial behaviour, and they are unable to control their desires. They often engage in criminal conduct, from marriage swindles to murder. In most cases, their actions seem to lack any reasonable intention, and they rarely see any use of their achievements. They are often quite intelligent and smooth-spoken individuals who may delude even experts with their charm. There is no consensus regarding where the "criterion level" of psychopathy should be set, above which the individual requires psychiatric treatment.

BOX 4.1 NARCISSISTIC PERSONALITY INVENTORY (NPI) (SELECTED ITEMS)

The test consists of forty pairs of statements. For each pair the participants are asked to select the one that they feel best reflects their personality.

1.a   I have a natural talent for influencing people.
1.b   I am not good at influencing people.
2.a   Modesty doesn't become me.
2.b   I am essentially a modest person.
3.a   I would do almost anything on a dare.
3.b   I tend to be a fairly cautious person.
4.a   When people compliment me, I sometimes get embarrassed.
4.b   I know that I am good because everybody keeps telling me so.
5.a   The thought of ruling the world frightens the hell out of me.
5.b   If I ruled the world, it would be a better place.
6.a   I can usually talk my way out of anything.
6.b   I try to accept the consequences of my behaviour.
7.a   I prefer to blend in with the crowd.
7.b   I like to be the center of attention.
8.a   I will be a success.
8.b   I am not too concerned about success.
9.a   I am no better or worse than most people.
9.b   I think I am a special person.
10.a   I am not sure if I would make a good leader.
10.b   I see myself as a good leader.
11.a   I am assertive.
11.b   I wish I were more assertive.
12.a   I like to have authority over other people.
12.b   I don't mind following orders.

Two basic types of psychopathy are distinguished:

- *Primary psychopathy*: the most callous, most brutal form of antisocial behaviour that is hardly responsive to interventions. It is largely based on genetic predispositions which are presumably involved in the regulation of the temperament and physiological arousal states. They are insensitive to social stimuli (e.g. unable to properly decode emotions from facial expressions) as well as to almost any form of punishment.
- *Secondary psychopathy*: Forms of behaviour included in this type are mainly influenced by environmental factors rather than genetic effects. Secondary

psychopaths typically grow up in an unfavourable social environment where they develop deficient models of social behaviour. As opposed to primary psychopaths, they have moral scruples and to a certain extent they are able to feel guilt and empathy.

BOX 4.2 LEVENSON SELF-REPORT PSYCHOPATHY SCALE

The test consists of 26 statements. The participants are asked to rate each on how much they agree with it on a scale of (1) strongly disagree, (2) disagree, (3) neither agree nor disagree, (4) agree, or (5) strongly agree.

1   Success is based on survival of the fittest; I am not concerned about the losers.
2   I find myself in the same kinds of trouble, time after time.
3   For me, what's right is whatever I can get away with.
4   I am often bored.
5   In today's world, I feel justified in doing anything I can get away with to succeed.
6   I find that I am able to pursue one goal for a long time.
7   My main purpose in life is getting as many goodies as I can.
8   I don't plan anything very far in advance.
9   Making a lot of money is my most important goal.
10   I quickly lose interest in tasks I start.
11   I let others worry about higher values; my main concern is with the bottom line.
12   Most of my problems are due to the fact that other people just don't understand me.
13   People who are stupid enough to get ripped off usually deserve it.
14   Before I do anything, I carefully consider the possible consequences.
15   Looking out for myself is my top priority.
16   I have been in a lot of shouting matches with other people.
17   I tell other people what they want to hear so that they will do what I want them to do.
18   When I get frustrated, I often "let off steam" by blowing my top.
19   I would be upset if my success came at someone else's expense.
20   Love is overrated.
21   I often admire a really clever scam.
22   I make a point of trying not to hurt others in pursuit of my goals.
23   I enjoy manipulating other people's feelings.
24   I feel bad if my words or actions cause someone else to feel emotional pain.
25   Even if I were trying very hard to sell something, I wouldn't lie about it.
26   Cheating is not justified because it is unfair to others.

2. Common features

Previous research has revealed that the three members of the Dark Triad have several features in common. Although the authors put emphasis on different shared elements, the strongest candidates are maliciousness, dishonesty, lack of empathy, and interpersonal antagonism (Jones & Paulhus 2011). Other authors place more emphasis on unfriendliness, insincerity and callousness as common features (Furnham, Richards, & Paulhus 2013). A study using factor analyses has revealed that manipulation and callousness are necessary and sufficient components of a malevolent personality (Jones & Figueredo 2013).

In recent decades, studies using a wide variety of questionnaires and tests have established a more or less close relationship between measures of Machiavellianism, narcissism and psychopathy. The closest relationship was found between Machiavellianism and psychopathy, which is not surprising since both are associated with a poor sense of responsibility and low moral commitment (Paulhus & Williams 2002; Wai & Tiliopoulos 2012). Moreover, this relationship is mediated by strong genetic influence; a twin study found a genetic overlap between Machiavellianism and psychopathy (Vernon et al. 2008). Machiavellianism shows a particularly strong correlation with primary psychopathy, the coefficient of which may even exceed 0.7 (Ali & Chamorro-Premuzic 2010) although in most cases it remains in the range between 0.5 and 0.6. Secondary psychopathy is less closely related to Machiavellianism, and narcissism is the most weakly associated with it (Paulhus & Williams 2002; Jacobwitz & Egan 2006). It is generally true that narcissism is more or less the "odd one out" in the Dark Triad since most studies found that it was rather loosely related to the other two components (Rauthmann & Kolar 2013; Vernon et al. 2008).

A common feature of all three members of the Dark Triad is a low level of Agreeableness. This is reflected in characteristics such as being cunning, authoritarian, selfish, arbitrary, rigid, stubborn, impatient, intolerant, unyielding, aggressive and quarrelsome. Not only Machiavellians but also narcissists and psychopaths show a low level of emotional empathy, that is, they have a relatively poor ability to attune themselves to the feelings and needs of others (Wai & Tiliopoulos 2012). They also overlap in their negative relationship with cognitive empathy (Wai & Tiliopoulos 2012; Jonason & Krause 2013), which refers to the understanding of others' emotional states and that is clearly related to mind-reading ability (see Chapters 8 and 9). All Dark Triad members are associated with a low level of self-control involved in several behaviours from antisocial tendencies to a preference for short-term partner relationships (Furnham, Richards, & Paulhus 2013). Narcissism and psychopathy are closely related to Extroversion, and all three Dark Triad members, including Machiavellianism, are characterised by high sensation seeking with a strong orientation towards novel and unusual stimuli (Crysel, Crosier, & Webster 2013). Finally, all Dark Triad members predominantly include men.

BOX 4.3 MACHIAVELLIANISM AND PRIMARY PSYCHOPATHY

It is somewhat surprising that Machiavellianism is most closely related to primary psychopathy. This is unexpected because psychopathy is considered the "darkest" side of the Dark Triad (Pailing, Boon, & Egan 2014) that is synonymous with evil in this context. Primary psychopaths are not only self-seeking and malevolent but positively cruel and merciless. They feel no remorse or regret. By contrast, Machiavellians are much more "humble" and peaceable, as has probably been made clear throughout previous chapters. They rarely bring themselves to employ violence, nor do they even prefer to humiliate others; rather, they are the masters of deception. Furthermore, they do not harm or hurt others for the sake of pleasure but in order to gain something.

Taking these essential differences into account, the close correlation found between measures of Machiavellianism and psychopathy calls for an explanation. This should most probably be embarked upon from psychopathy since psychopaths have several characteristics in common with Machiavellians: both manipulate others, think rationally and prevent themselves from being affected by their own emotions. One may say that Machiavellianism is the "basic level" of psychopathy, and that this is where their relationship originates. However, psychopaths develop further characteristics on this foundation which strongly differentiate them from Machiavellians as reflected in their behaviour. They are antisocial, violent and cruel people who enjoy harming others. These characteristics pertain to no, or only very few, Machiavellians. Future studies will have to clarify those developmental pathways and parental effects that canalise their adult behaviour on divergent routes.

---

3. Differences

How should these findings be interpreted? On the one hand, the three members of the Dark Triad actually have overlapping personality profiles as far as they have several traits in common. On the other hand, several fundamental differences also appear that question the overstrict or even exclusive use of Dark Triad as a unified framework in understanding the three components.

Essentially, the Big Five model (see Box 3.1 in Chapter 3) has only one dimension which shows a strong negative relationship with all three Dark Triad components, namely, Agreeableness (Paulhus & Williams 2002). Regarding the other four Big personality factors, the Dark Triad members do not show any consistency. Narcissism and Machiavellianism differ so much that there is no other personality trait besides Agreeableness to which both are related. One might expect Machiavellianism to be more closely related to psychopathy in personality construct, but many studies have revealed differences between them in Extraversion and Emotional stability (Paulhus & Williams 2002; Rauthmann 2011; Vernon et al. 2008). Furthermore, a likewise marked difference between Machiavellianism and psychopathy is that the latter are far more prone to anxiety (Al Ain et al. 2013). As has been previously discussed, Machiavellians usually do not show high impulsivity, although studies in this field have yielded rather contradictory results. By contrast, psychopaths are clearly very impulsive, with especial regard to the dysfunctional impulsivity that includes inattention and risk seeking (Jones & Paulhus 2011). Psychopaths, similarly to Machiavellians, are incurable liars whereas narcissists are not: no relationship was found between the level of narcissism and either the frequency of lying or the number of deceived people (Jonason et al. 2014). In general, compared to the Machiavellians and psychopaths, narcissist persons are considered as less malevolent, as they show a socially more positive character and a higher self-rated happiness (Egan, Chan, & Shorter 2014; Kowalski, Vernon, & Schermer 2017).

Similar differences were found regarding antisociality and risk taking. As was presented in the former chapter, Machiavellians are only willing to take moderate risk in order to gain immediate reward, due to their long-term strategic orientation. This is not the case with psychopaths; they strive after profits at any price even if it entails punishment. They do not moderate themselves in gambling, and as a result they lose much due to the punishment they incur (Jones 2014). Such insensitivity to punishment is only one manifestation of the inflexibility generally characterising psychopaths. The other related trait is aggression, also characteristic of psychopaths: they often assault others and are ready to take immediate revenge for any harm they suffer (Furnham, Richards, & Paulhus 2013; Jones & Paulhus 2010; Pailing, Boon, & Egan 2014). Although Machiavellians also commit antisocial acts, they remain far behind psychopaths in brutality and cruelty, which probably originate in a lack of control of aggressive impulses. If looking for the most prominent difference between the two groups; one will probably point out the almost absolute lack of remorse and guilt in psychopaths. Machiavellians are mostly unconcerned with others' feelings but they do not exhibit that kind of mercilessness which is characteristic of the way psychopaths relate to others. It is not by accident that psychopaths lag far behind the other two groups in such ethical values as fairness and altruism (Jonason et al. 2015). A further important difference is that while both psychopaths and narcissists claim their own greatness and superiority, Machiavellians are rather characterised by a certain kind of realism. They do not place themselves in a more favourable light; contrarily, they think they are just as selfish and hypocritical as others.

Essential differences were found by a recent study in the domain of coping strategies (Birkás, Gács, & Csathó 2016). In psychology, coping means to solve personal and interpersonal problems in order to minimise or tolerate stress and conflict. The reduction of the effect of stressors can be accomplished by various coping strategies. It turned out that the members of Dark Triad choose different strategies for mastering personal and interpersonal problems. Narcissism was the only Dark Triad member that was positively associated with coping strategies aimed at altering the stressful situations. In line with their self-controlled and friendly–dominant personality, narcissists performed well on tests that measured active problem solving approach to stressful situations, and a deliberate effort to change the effect of stressors. Machiavellians and psychopaths, in contrary, do not tend to face and alter stressors. Their essential feature is a neglect of social support: they do not seek informational, emotional or tangible support from the others for solving their personal problems: that may be due to their cynical, exploitative social attitude.

In the light of these evidence, several authors suggested that narcissism does not belong to the cluster of malevolent personality traits (Egan, Chan, & Shorter 2014; Kowalski, Vernon, & Schermer 2017). Instead of Dark Triad, they proposed to use Dark Dyad (Machiavellianism, psychopathy), and a related but separate narcissism. This concept is based on empirical finding showing that most of prosocial behaviours are strongly and negatively correlated with Machiavellianism and psychopathy, but not with narcissism, although the latest obviously has some negative connotations (e.g. low agreeableness).

Whereas an emphasis has been put on the strong association between Machiavellianism and psychopathy, and whereas narcissism is considered as a third personality character weakly linked to them, several studies depict another picture. A Polish study investigated the relationship between Dark Triad and materialism which is a tendency to place material possession very high within an individual hierarchy of values (Pilch & Górnik-Durose 2016). Higher narcissism and Machiavellianism were strongly connected with materialistic orientation but psychopathy did not. The authors concluded that possessing material assets cannot be, in itself, the motivational drive for psychopaths. On the other hand, as we seen above, profound differences were found between the members of Dark Dyad (Machiavellianism and psychopathy) in terms of anxiety, impulsivity and aggression. Additionally, a recent study has revealed that a difference exists in the emotional coping with psychological stress. Whereas Machiavellians are characterised by engaging behaviours such as ruminating or becoming emotional in response to stress; psychopaths show no sign of making emotional control in stressful situations. This result confirms the former evidence on the psychopaths' impulsivity, cruelty and antisocial attitudes (Birkás, Gács, & Csathó 2016).

4. Summary

What is the Dark Triad, then? Dan Jones is probably correct when explaining that the Dark Triad is a complex construct which is rooted in a basic structure of traits equally characteristic to all three components (Jones & Figueredo 2013, etc.). A detailed analysis of this basic structure shows that it comprises two major components. One is callousness, which essentially means a lack of concern for, and empathy towards, others. The other component is manipulation closely related to lying, derogating others and, too often, remorseless self seeking. When both features are embodied in one individual, it results in a "dark personality". Beyond these common features, however, all three members of the Dark Triad possess specific traits that are built on the basic structure. Machiavellians are primarily characterised by strategic planning, psychopaths by extreme antisociality, and narcissists by an egocentric outlook on life.

I think Machiavellianism, on the one hand, has basic traits in common with other members of Dark Triad. On the other hand, it also shows specific or typical features such as a rational mode of thinking, flexible decision-making, and cost/benefit calculation concerning behavioural output. From this perspective, the Dark Triad concept has in my view a rather poor explanatory power. It does not provide a distinct and unified dimension of personality which may serve to predict specific forms of human behaviour. On the contrary, it represents a loose structure of the three actually existing components but does not constitute a unique and separate personality trait. The Dark Triad is mostly useful for the purposes of description and categorisation insofar as it provides a framework in which the major features of human malevolence and evil may be integrated. However, this is only a wide and weakly integrated conceptual framework which may by no means replace the explanations about Machiavellianism, psychopathy and narcissism as distinct entities.

5

DEVELOPMENT, SOCIALISATION, LIFE HISTORY

How do some people become Machiavellians? What events occur in their lives that make them selfish, manipulative and deceitful to others? Or, alternatively, are they perhaps born to be Machiavellians, whose self-seeking behaviour is prescribed by their genes?

1. Genetics

Few studies have been devoted to the heritability of Machiavellianism. Philip Vernon and colleagues (2008) compared identical and fraternal twins according to their scores on the Mach-IV test. The authors found that Machiavellianism shows relatively low heritability (0.31), which means that only 31% of the individual variance on the Mach scales can be explained by genetic factors while the remaining 69% is due to environmental influence. This is particularly interesting because substantially higher heritability was found for both of the other two Dark Triad members: the value was 0.69 for psychopathy and 0.59 for narcissism. Even so, genetic factors do also contribute to Machiavellianism, as a recent study has revealed by means of molecular genetics (Montag et al. 2015). The study has found that a certain type of dopamine receptor gene is frequently carried by subjects scoring high on the Mach test. Dopamine has been known to play an important role in processing and predicting positive, pleasurable and rewarding events, whereas no particular knowledge is available concerning what specific physiological and psychological mechanisms mediate between this genetic effect and Machiavellianism.

BOX 5.1 TWIN STUDIES AND HERITABILITY

An examination of the genetic background of a behavioural or mental trait requires the environmental and hereditary effects on individual phenotype to be separated. This separation is a relatively common and accepted approach to animal behaviour, one has only to mention inbreeding, for example. However, the scope of such experiments in humans is highly restricted due to obvious ethical considerations. Nevertheless, there do exist ethically acceptable ways to analyse genetic factors of human behaviour. One way is the comparative study of twins. It is common knowledge that there are two types of twins: identical (monozygotic; MZ) twins carry the same sets of genes while fraternal (dizygotic; DZ) twins only carry 50% of each other's genes. If identical twins as compared to fraternal twins are found to show greater similarity in a behavioural, mental or personality characteristic, then the higher correlation may be explained by genetic influence. If, for example, a study on emotional responsiveness involving hundreds of twins obtains a mean correlation value of 0.5 for identical twins while the value is only 0.2 for fraternal twins, then it is a well-founded conclusion that the greater similarity between identical twins originates, at least in part, in their identical genotypes (Plomin et al. 2005).

Twin studies, besides adoption studies, enable researchers to estimate the heritability of a given behaviour by means of specific calculations. In the above-mentioned example, the heritability of emotional responsiveness is about 0.6. Heritability theoretically ranges from 0 to 1, and the ratio shows the extent to which individual variance in the studied trait can be traced back to genetic factors. For example, if a heritability ratio of 0.55 is obtained for general intelligence, then it suggests that 55% of the individual variance found in IQ scores in the given population is due to genetic factors (while 45% is due to environmental effects).

Although such calculations provide a reliable picture of the degree of genetic influence, they should be used cautiously. Human geneticists agree that genetic influence on human behaviour and thinking is not to be understood in terms of rigid determinism. Genes rather canalise behaviour: they generate sensory structures, neural mechanisms and developmental paths that make certain personality types and mental skills likely to develop. Environment, however, also makes an important contribution since genetic dispositions are manifested in continuous interaction with changing environmental factors.

In recent decades, a new discipline in human behavioural research, molecular genetics, has been rapidly advancing. It focuses on the position, function and biochemical manifestation of the singular genes underlying specific behavioural and cognitive traits. Thousands of genes have so far been found to play an important role in the development of human thinking and behaviour, in areas such as intelligence, novelty-seeking and alcoholism, to name but a few (Benjamin, Ebstein, & Belmaker 2005).

These findings lead to the conclusion that although genetic factors may have a certain role in the development of the Machiavellian lifestyle and thinking, Machiavellianism is primarily a result of environmental effects. Additional studies have also pointed out that such external influences frequently come from the family environment, usually in the form of impressions and experience that roughly equally affect siblings who are reared together. Human genetics refers to this condition as "shared environment", which includes common effects in the family, such as parenting style, emotional atmosphere or financial status. As long as 40 years ago a study pointed out the possible importance of parental influence: positive correlation was found between the Mach scores of 12-year-olds and their fathers (Kraut & Price 1976). Likewise, a close relationship was found between parents' Mach scores and their children's success in a card game essentially based on bluff and deception.

2. Family environment

The question offering itself at this point is what family environment and, in particular, what parental behaviour "produces" Machiavellian individuals? András Láng and Béla Birkás (2014) asked secondary students to describe their family environment. The study primarily focused on family cohesion and communication between family members, which were assessed with a specifically designed questionnaire developed by the authors (Box 5.2). The results revealed that high Machs and low Machs differed in their perception of family functioning. Machiavellians perceived their families as more disengaged, more chaotic and less cohesive, with a lack of clear rules and stable ties. They also reported poorer communication within the family and less satisfaction with family life.

The authors suggest that under such circumstances, children cannot develop intimate relationships and have fewer opportunities to practice various social skills. They may become lonely and isolated in an uncertain family environment that may compel them to develop narcissistic self-defence: they regard themselves in an extremely positive light, whereas they derogate others as not worthy of their attention. Moreover, a chaotic family environment is likely to prevent children from developing the sense that they can trust others and that cooperation is beneficial. Unpredictable parental behaviour may cause them to experience the feeling that they can only rely on themselves, which is, in turn, harmful to the development of normal self-control. Children can perceive ambiguous or deceptive communication among family members as a form of involuntary lying that may be beneficial in subsequent social interactions. Considering all these, it is not surprising that adult Machiavellians show low empathic concern, cynicism and poor emotional intelligence. However, a reverse interpretation of the findings also offers itself: those adolescents who have high Mach scores may judge their parents negatively. If this is the case, then it is not disadvantageous family conditions that subsequently cause children to develop a Machiavellian way of thinking but children's Machiavellian attitude that leads them to form an unfavourable picture of their families.

BOX 5.2 THE FAMILY ADAPTABILITY AND COHESION SCALE (FACES-IV; SELECTED ITEMS)

Respondents are asked to indicate the extent to which each item applies to their family by choosing one from the following five response alternatives:

1. Does not describe our family at all; 2. Slightly describes our family; 3. Somewhat describes our family; 4. Generally describes our family; 5. Describes our family very well

1. Family members are involved in one another's lives.
2. Our family tries new ways of dealing with problems.
3. We get along better with people outside our family than inside.
4. We spend too much time together.
5. There are strict consequences for breaking the rules in our family.
6. We never seem to get organised in our family.
7. Family members feel very close to each other.
8. The parents check with the children before making important decisions.
9. Family members seem to avoid contact with one another when at home.
10. Family members feel pressured to spend most free time together.
11. There are severe consequences when a family member does something wrong.
12. We need more rules in our family.
13. Family members are supportive of one another during difficult times.
14. Children have a say in their discipline.
15. Family members feel closer to people outside the family than to other family members.
16. Family members are too dependent on one another.
17. This family has a rule for almost every possible situation.
18. Things do not get done in our family.
19. Family members consult other family members on personal decisions.
20. In solving problems, the children's suggestions are followed.
21. Family members are on their own when there is a problem to be solved.
22. Family members have little need for friends outside the family.
23. It is difficult to get a rule changed in our family.
24. It is unclear who is responsible for things (chores, activities) in our family.

Obviously, further research is needed to clarify how these variables are related. Very few studies have been conducted in the field but the available data suggest that attachment to one's parents plays a key role in the development of the Machiavellian personality. A study involving young people aged 16 to 18 years assessed their relationship with their parents before 12 years of age (by means of the Parental Behavior Inventory; Ojha 2007). A negative relationship was found between loving parental behaviour (both the father's and the mother's behaviour assessed separately) and children's Machiavellian orientation. Seemingly, parents' restrictive and rejective behaviour fosters the development of manipulative tendencies in children. A double-bind relationship between parents and children possibly underlies this process: children are angry because they are not given enough care while, at the same time, they are afraid that their parents will continue to neglect them. In order to break out of this trap, children may develop a behavioural style that is based on misleading and deceiving their parents, and then extend this strategy to others.

A recent study likewise focused on the relationship between young adults' experience of parental care that they received in childhood and their scores on measures of the Dark Triad, including Machiavellianism (Jonason, Lyons, & Bethell 2014). The authors of this study also used a retrospective self-report measure: the young adults involved were asked to use specific questions to recall and assess their parents' parenting style and the care they received during childhood (until 16 years of age). They used a scale ranging from 1 to 3 to rate statements such as "My mother seemed emotionally cold to me." Furthermore, subjects also completed an adult attachment measure assessing the quality of their current relationships with others. They rated statements such as "It is easy for me to become emotionally close to others." The study revealed that low-quality maternal care is one of the most important factors contributing to the development of a Machiavellian personality. Poor maternal care results in insecure adult attachment, primarily in a fearful-avoidant attachment style (see Box 5.3). People showing such an attachment pattern are characterised by an ambivalent perspective: they long for emotionally close relationships while, at the same time, they find it difficult to bear emotional intimacy. Such ambivalent emotions often lead them to form negative views about others, which is an essential characteristic of the Machiavellian.

Considering the above, it is not at all surprising that studies using the "Kiddie" Mach Test (Box 5.4) specifically designed for children have drawn similar conclusions. Students aged 9 to 13 who scored high on the test were found to show low levels of empathy as indicated by their teachers' responses to a questionnaire (Slaughter 2011). Their lack of empathy may be related to their poor mind-reading ability, that is, their deficit in inferring others' emotions and needs (Stellwagen & Kerig 2013). Other studies suggest that high Mach children aged 8 to 12 are generally distrustful towards others and that they lie more frequently than the average. They do not have confidence in others' benevolence and do not show concern for other children and adults (Sutton & Keogh 2000). These characteristics astonishingly resemble those of adult Machiavellians.

It is possible, however, that "Machiavellian" children initially do not deliberately seek to deceive and harm others. Moreover, children may even be unable to make a sharp distinction between manipulative and cooperative behaviour (Sutton & Keogh

BOX 5.3 ADULT ATTACHMENT STYLES

Conventionally, four adult attachment styles are distinguished:

1   *Secure*

   Securely attached adults usually agree with such statements as "I don't worry about being alone or having others not accept me" or "I am comfortable depending on others and having them depend on me". People of this type mostly judge themselves and their relationships positively. They are more satisfied and emotionally more stable than others. They have no difficulty with either intimate closeness or independence of others.

2   *Anxious-preoccupied*

   People of this attachment type tend to agree with statements such as "I am uncomfortable being without close relationships, but I sometimes worry that others don't value me as much as I value them". They expect high levels of approval from their partner while they underestimate themselves in the relationship. They become more and more dependent on their partner, which further increases their anxiety.

3   *Dismissive-avoidant*

   Such people agree with statements like "It is very important to me to feel independent and self-sufficient" or "I am comfortable without close emotional relationships". They often deny the need for close relationships and even view themselves invulnerable due to their living without intimate relationships. They desire complete independence, which also includes a tendency to suppress their feelings as well as viewing themselves more positively than others.

4   *Fearful-avoidant*

   People with such an attachment style tend to agree with the following statements: "I want emotionally close relationships, but I find it difficult to trust others completely" or "I sometimes worry that I will be hurt if I allow myself to become too close to others". A certain kind of ambivalence characterises people of this type. They long for emotionally close relationships while, at the same time, they find it difficult to bear emotional closeness, and they are even afraid of intimacy. They do not trust the intentions of their partner, about whom they often have negative views. They cannot express their emotions properly, and they do not expect affection from their partner.

BOX 5.4 KIDDIE MACH SCALE (SELECTED ITEMS)

This version of the Mach scale has been designed for children aged 8 to 16 years. Respondents are asked to indicate the extent to which they agree with each item by choosing one from the following five response alternatives:

1 = completely disagree; 2 = generally disagree; 3 = undecided; 4 = generally agree; 5 = completely agree

- Never tell anyone why you did something unless it will help you.
- Most people are good and kind.
- The best way to get along with people is to tell them things that make them happy.
- You should do something only when you are sure it is right.
- Sometimes you need to hurt other people to get what you want.
- It is better to tell someone why you want him to help you than to make up a good story to get him to do it.
- A criminal is just like other people except he is stupid enough to get caught.
- Most people are brave.
- It is smart to be nice to important people even if you don't really like them.
- Sometimes you have to cheat a little to get what you want.
- It is never right to tell a lie.
- It hurts more to lose money than to lose a friend.

2000). Adults scoring high on the Mach-IV scale agree with statements such as "The best way to handle people is to tell them what they want to hear." By contrast, children scoring high on the Kiddie Mach Scale agree with statements such as the following one: "The best way to get along with people is to tell them things that make them happy." Obviously, there is a great difference between the two statements in meaning; still, it is highly probable that the cynical and ruthless nature of the adult Machiavellians' has its developmental roots in childhood naïve influence and deception techniques.

If so, how does development occur? At this moment, only hypotheses can be proposed in this regard. Children may step by step develop those techniques and abilities that help them get along better in an essentially unfavourable social environment such as, for example, an uncertain family environment or insecure attachment to the parents. They may learn, for example, that restraining their emotional reactions elicited by frustration and deprivation may enable them to consider circumstances rationally and cold-mindedly. Those insecurely attached to their parents may become unable to develop emotional attachment to others. Their cold, unemotional attitudes may, in turn, prevent them from internalising such norms regulating cooperation as the norm of reciprocity. Furthermore, in an environment where they experience mutual distrust and ambiguous communication, they may learn to alertly monitor the behaviour of others so that they can immediately adapt to environmental expectations. They also develop a stubborn passion for reward seeking, and the desire to gain immediate rewards in an emotionally depriving and unpredictable environment. Likewise, they learn to inhibit their spontaneous altruistic or benevolent behavioural responses in order to avoid relationships that would impose disadvantages and distress on them.

3. Moral development

A disadvantageous family environment also has an influence on children's moral development. Based on a study involving more than two hundred adult identical and fraternal twins, Jennifer Campbell and her colleagues suggest that Machiavellians (and psychopaths) fall behind others in acquiring and applying moral norms (Campbell et al. 2009). High Mach scores are strongly correlated with low levels of moral development, which correspond to Stages 2 and 3 in Kohlberg's model (Box 5.5). Subjects' responses obtained by a questionnaire have revealed that Machiavellians are clearly aware of their own interests but that they cannot reconcile them with their group's expectations. They are able to judge the moral implications of an action by considering its consequences but they lack a sense of commitment and responsibility, especially regarding consistent compliance with the rules (this latter would correspond to Stage 4 in the Kohlberg model). They have no regard, or perhaps no concern, for the fact that people living in different parts of the world have different views, rights and values (Stage 5).

Involving twins in the above-mentioned study implied particular importance when the authors turned their attention to the causes of low levels of moral development. The authors have established that moral development is a result of a complex interaction between genetic and environmental factors. Both low and high levels of moral development can be traced back to the effects of the shared family environment. Thus, it seems that parenting principles and parents' emotional accessibility as well as distress and trust within the family have considerable influence on whether one reaches a given stage of moral development. Machiavellianism may likewise be explained in this theoretical framework. The results showed that the relationship between levels of moral development and scores on Machiavellianism originate in childhood impressions received in the family rather than in genetic factors, which have only little importance in this regard. This finding is consistent with the previously mentioned observations on Machiavellians' socialisation: deficient parental care, disrupted trust and disordered communication may become a hotbed of Machiavellianism.

BOX 5.5 KOHLBERG'S MODEL

Lawrence Kohlberg (1927–1987) was an outstanding psychologist of his time, who extended Jean Piaget's epoch-making theory of cognitive development to the field of moral development. According to his model, the development of moral judgement takes place through six successive stages, at each of which one gives increasingly mature and complex responses to moral dilemmas. The six stages are as follow:

1   Compliance with rules is driven by obedience to authority figures and by the fear of punishment. Authority figures are obeyed unconditionally; no distinction is made between interests of the environment and self-interest.
2   Actions are motivated by recognising others' and one's own interests. Compliance with rules is important only if they are in harmony with one's personal interests.
3   Compliance with rules becomes essential because they represent the expectations of the environment (family, friends). Primary importance is attributed to values such as trustworthiness, loyalty, acknowledgement and gratitude.
4   Besides a system of personal motives, social expectations also appear in moral decisions. Those actions are desirable that do not conflict with the prevailing social norms and obligations.
5   A period of recognising principles that are more important than the prevailing social norms. One becomes aware of the diversity of people's views and values as well as of the relativistic nature of rules and values. Fundamental values (e.g. rights to life and liberty) have priority but individuals can freely and democratically decide to change the rules if they no longer serve the welfare of society.
6   Moral reasoning is based on universal ethical principles; one recognises that legal systems of different societies are also based on such principles. One follows individually elaborated ethical principles; existing rules and social norms are only valid insofar as they are based on considerations of individual principles.

4. Neural changes

Remarkable research findings published in recent years suggest that the above-mentioned early experiences may change certain brain structures over years. This is not a novel idea: several studies point out that continuous interactions with the environment result in local changes in the structure of the nervous system (Box 5.6). New synaptic connections may develop between neurons; dendrites may grow in length and branch out, and even the metabolic activity of neurons may change (Kolb & Whishaw 1998). In a brain imaging study using the structural MRI technique (Box 2.2 in Chapter 2), several differences were found between the brain structures of high and low Mach subjects (Verbeke et al. 2011). It has to be emphasised that this study, as opposed to other MR studies, did not examine the brain during decision-making in various tasks. The authors rather measured the local changes in the volume of various brain areas in each adult subject at rest and then looked for differences between high and low Mach groups.

Differences were found in several brain areas. For example, Machiavellians were found to have larger basal ganglia, one part of which (the striatum, more specifically the caudate nucleus) plays an important part in processing reward-related stimuli. Likewise found to be larger in high Machs was the hippocampus, which is involved in formation and retrieval of memories, especially general declarative memory (memories that can be explicitly verbalised). A similar increase in volume was observed in the insula, whose main function is to regulate negative emotions (fear, disgust, anger etc.) and, more generally, to identify and monitor internal emotional processes. Likewise, larger volumes were measured in those brain regions of Machiavellians that other studies found to be particularly active during decision-making in social dilemma situations (see details in Chapter 11). Those brain areas whose functions include inhibiting socio-emotional responses (dorsolateral prefrontal cortex), inference processes and processing social cues (inferior frontal gyrus) as well as persistent goal-directedness and filtering information (middle frontal gyrus) were found to be of a larger size in high Machs than in their low-Mach counterparts. Structural brain imaging has revealed that beyond the intense activity of these brain areas during decision-making, their volume at rest is also larger in adult Machiavellians. It is reasonably assumed that the increased volume of these regions is due to their increased use in the course of an individual's life. Specifically, it is probably a result of the increasingly complex connections and networks developing between the related groups of neurons.

BOX 5.6 THE LONDON TAXI DRIVERS' CASE

Several research reports published in the past two decades point out that individuals possessing expertise in a certain area (e.g. musicians) have a brain structure different from that of laypeople. One of the most widely known structural MRI studies found that London taxi drivers had a larger volume of grey matter in the posterior region of the hippocampus (Maguire, Woolett, & Spiers 2006) than did non-professional car drivers. The hippocampus is known for its importance in memory functions and spatial orientation. A taxi driver's job usually involves difficult navigational tasks that require the development of a detailed cognitive map of the cabbie's environment including the street network, the position of various buildings, driving directions, etc. London taxi drivers need to acquire a particularly high level of expertise since they can only obtain a taxi driving licence after completing 3 to 4 years of training, as a result of which they can recall about 25,000 streets and 20,000 locations without using a map. According to the results of psychological examinations, they performed better in recalling visual information related to London whereas they showed poorer learning and memory for certain types of visual information they had never seen before (e.g. delayed recall of complex figures). This suggests that their advanced memory is related to a specific narrow-range cognitive process tied to the knowledge of the familiar environment.

Considering all this, the researchers concluded that expertise, spatial memory and hippocampus volume were closely related. Moreover, they suggested that the differences between the brain structures of taxi drivers and other car drivers were due to a long-term learning process that changed the number, connections and network of neurons involved in developing mental maps. However, an alternative explanation of the findings also offered itself. Namely, it seemed possible that those choosing to work as a taxi driver would, in the first place, have an enhanced ability to process spatial information, which was probably related to better hippocampus capacity.

In order to test this hypothesis, the same authors subsequently conducted a longitudinal study (Woolett & Maguire 2011). The brain of each taxi driver involved in the study was examined twice: first when they started preparation for the taxi drivers' exam and then several years later, when they already had a valid licence and had worked as a professional driver. The study found that volume of the posterior hippocampal grey matter had increased over the years of driving in those who passed the exam, while no volume change was found either in those who failed or in control subjects (non-professional drivers). This suggests, according to the authors, that the increased hippocampal volume most likely occurred as a result of acquiring the detailed spatial representation of London's layout. Regarding the exact causes of such volume increase, only animal experiments provide information at the moment. Studies on rodents and other mammals show that spatial learning processes result, among other things, in the recruitment of new neurons and increased numbers of synaptic connections and dendritic branches in the hippocampus.

In sum, it is reasonable to conclude that differences in brain structure between high and low Mach groups result from previous developmental processes shaped by recurrent interactions with the environment. Due to the above-mentioned parental and family influences, children build up an inner world that implies lying and deception as efficient means of goal achievement. They shape their relationship with the social environment in such a way that they can successfully use such abilities for manipulating others while this success, in turn, positively reinforces their way of thinking and worldview. The effective deception also reinforces those cognitive and emotional processes that support goal achievement, such as reward seeking, emotion regulation, prediction of others' behaviour, inhibition of responses hindering manipulation and task orientation. These cognitive processes when frequently practiced in everyday life may gradually strengthen and tone up their neural bases, which will then show specific activity patterns in adulthood.

While the development of Machiavellian personality and thinking is evidently related to the development of certain neural structures, little is known about the process itself. The Machiavellian character is likely to change gradually while passing from childhood to adulthood (and probably thereafter as well). One study found a close relationship between children's Mach scores and their age (Sutton & Keogh 2000). It seems that as children grow, they become more and more distrustful, pessimistic and cynical towards their environment. However, a deeper understanding of the mechanisms, the "schedule" and the main causes of such changes require more studies to be accomplished.

5. Life history strategies

A model based on the theory of evolution, or more specifically on behavioural ecology, may help researchers gain additional insight into Machiavellians' socialisation. One fundamental proposition of evolutionary behavioural ecology suggests that living organisms have been selected in such a way that they invest the acquired resources into increasing their genetic representation in their offspring (see also Chapter 12). Since resources are always limited both in amount and in possible ways of utilisation, pursuing one activity always reduces the amount of time and energy available for another activity. For example, the behaviours that make individuals successful in mating are often mutually exclusive of the behaviours that result in successful parenting. Therefore, natural selection has favoured those strategies that enable organisms to make decisions on the optimal utilisation of limited resources (Borgerhoff-Mulder 1992). This is the case with humans as well: information processing systems of the brain are sensitive to environmental changes and give alternative behavioural responses to different ecological and social challenges. They are able to assess costs and benefits in terms of survival and reproduction and develop behavioural responses that ensure optimal adaptation to the given environment.

One model having key importance in behavioural ecology is known as the Life History Theory, which proposes that living organisms have been selected for a capacity to adjust their developmental paths in response to different environmental conditions (Wilson 1975). Regarding humans, this means that experiences acquired during the sensitive period of early life may have a large effect on the individual's subsequent course of life. Accessibility of resources, quality of attachment to the parents, and predictability of the social environment during childhood crucially influence what kinds of strategies one develops and uses as an adult. Favourable and unfavourable family environments may generate different developmental pathways

(Belsky, Steinberg, & Draper 1991). Researchers have found that in families where material resources are scarce and unpredictable, where attachment between children and parents is insecure and where high levels of distress and a depriving emotional climate dominate, children show accelerated maturation, increased sexual activity and a preference for short-term relationships in adolescence and adulthood. Compared with others, they start sexual life and leave school earlier, and they more often engage in noncompliant behaviour (e.g. truancy; Bereczkei & Csanaky 2001). Girls growing up under such circumstances attain menarche six to ten months earlier than the average, and they give birth, get married and get divorced earlier (Ellis & Graber 2000; Kim & Smith 1998). By contrast, in families where resources are relatively abundant, family members have more stable relationships with others, and where parents and children are emotionally closely attached, children show a delayed sexual maturation, begin to show interesting the opposite sex and have their first sexual intercourse later, and more frequently engage in long-term intimate partner relationships as adults.

BOX 5.7 ALTERNATIVE LIFESTYLE AND EVOLUTION

These life-history strategies have evolutionary roots. In humans – as well as in other species – those behavioural programs were selected in the past that responded to environmental effects in an adaptive manner, that is, those that helped individuals' survival and reproduction in the specific situation. In an environment that did not provide suitable material and social conditions for child rearing (e.g. impoverished economy, depriving relationships, absent fathers etc.), a more beneficial strategy for women was to reach sexual maturity earlier, not to be particularly selective of partners and to give birth to many children so that some of them would survive. Under more favourable circumstances, however, our ancestors' lifestyle changed in such a way that greater emphasis was placed on intimate partner relationships and intense parental care. They reared a relatively small number of children who, however, had a greater chance of becoming successful in the competition for social resources (occupational status, wealth, advantageous marriage etc.).

It has to be emphasised that such differences between life history strategies do not simply lead to differences in children's cognitive processes. In fact, childhood experiences have a great influence on one's entire developmental path and maturational processes, resulting in particular behavioural styles in adulthood. Little is yet known about the processes directly shaping such life history strategies; that is, the processes mediating between early experiences and subsequently emerging behavioural patterns. Presumably, an important mediating role is played by developmental processes of the brain (especially of the frontal lobe), by hormonal changes elicited by distress (e.g. increased cortisol level) and by insecure attachment formed with a person joining the family relatively late (e.g. a stepfather; Graber, Brooks-Gunn, & Warren 1995; Ellis et al. 1999).

As was discussed previously, the Machiavellian's childhood is characterised by insecure attachments, low levels of parental care and poor communication. The Life History Theory predicts that such circumstances facilitate a "fast strategy", that is a developmental path characterised by accelerated maturational processes and short-term intimate partner relationships. Several studies support this idea (Figueredo et al. 2005; McDonald, Donellan, & Navarrete 2012). These studies have revealed that those scoring high on the Mach-IV scale exhibit in contrast with low Machs less restricted sexual behaviour; that is, they are more willing to engage in casual sex and in uncommitted partner relationships. They start sexual life earlier, have more sexual partners on average and report that they have had more sexual experience than others. The Machiavellians' short-term mating is frequently associated with the high number of miscarriages and a shorter cycle length in women (Jonason & Lavertu 2017). Taking social behaviour into consideration, Machiavellians start to exhibit various forms of sensation seeking, aggression and antisociality relatively early, compared to non-Machiavellians. These various characteristics may be well integrated in the framework of life-history theory.

However, it seems that this theoretical framework – as well as any theoretical framework – has certain limitations. Some studies analysed attitudes towards the future reported by members of the Dark Triad including Machiavellians. The authors assumed that those pursuing a fast life history strategy would usually be relatively unconcerned with future outcomes and would rarely make long-term plans. In one experiment, attitudes towards the future were measured in two ways (Jonason, Koenig, & Tost 2010). In one case, subjects were presented with the "larger-later" financial dilemma: "You can have 100 dollars now or 1,000 dollars in a year. Which would you prefer?" In the other case, the authors assessed subjects' willingness to engage in risk-taking behaviour, which may be closely related to future life expectancy. For this purpose, subjects were asked about the frequency and amount of their alcohol consumption, drug use and smoking. Contrary to the predictions, in most cases the study found no significant differences between the responses of high and low Mach subjects. Machiavellians did not choose immediate rewards more frequently than non-Machiavellians, nor did they prove more willing to take risks in terms of harmful habits (with the exception of a slight effect of alcohol consumption). Essentially, this is consistent with previous observations on the Machiavellian personality (Chapter 3): Machiavellians are not characterised by high impulsivity or risk taking. By contrast, risk taking is part of the other two Dark Triad members' personality structure. Subjects with high psychopathy showed strong addictive tendencies regarding either drug use, smoking or alcohol consumption. Alcohol consumption was also positively correlated with narcissism.

Again, these findings suggest that a Machiavellian's way of thinking is not necessarily characterised by short-term strategies, neither by blindness towards future risks. As has been discussed earlier in detail, Machiavellians rather prefer to pursue a wide variety of complex strategies (see Chapter 2). In some conditions, they gain benefit from short-term, quick and improvisational actions while in other conditions they also often choose to analyse others' decisions and their expectable consequences, and to inhibit their momentary motivations in order to yield benefits in the long term.

Perhaps this behavioural complexity is what produced controversial results in some studies. In the above-mentioned study, the researchers developed a question-naire that contained statements concerning the major indicators of life-history strat-egies (Jonason, Koenig, & Tost 2010). Their results provided a rather ambiguous picture. Responses to most of the twenty items revealed no difference between high and low Mach subjects. Machiavellians reported in some cases that they strove to predict future outcomes ("I can often tell how things will turn out") while in other cases, by contrast, they reported that they did not "make plans in advance". They did not report a desire to have several sexual relationships simultaneously, whereas they did indicate that they did not need to be closely attached to someone before having sex with them.

Such conflicting responses suggest that the Machiavellian way of thinking and behaviour are much more complex than to let themselves be fully explained within the narrow limits of one theoretical framework or another. Presumably, single models offer explanations only for some Machiavellian characteristics. A more realistic interpretation of Machiavellianism requires that predictions on specific behavioural tactics observable under specific environmental conditions be tested. Paper-and-pencil tests can hardly provide adequate data for such comprehensive understanding, however reliably they might describe a particular personality trait or behavioural attitude. A recurring idea in this book points out the continuous need for experiments that provide more or less accurate models of real-life events. Such experiments may include, among other matters, measures of physiological indicators of emotions, as well as the monitoring of neural responses to various environmental cues, or the analysis of decisions during interactions with partners, as represented in the social dilemma games (Chapters 2, 10, 11).

6

COMMUNICATION

Christie and Geis (1970) point out in one of their first works that Machiavellians are pronouncedly successful in "face-to-face" interactions. The authors suggest that one major cause of such success is that they can distance themselves from the emotional influences which emerge during personal communication with one's partner. At the same time, Machiavellians deploy all manner of tricks of communication in order to achieve success. In most cases, they use verbal communication to manipulate others while also often employing facial expression, looks and postures to reach their goals. Occasionally, Machiavellians' nonverbal communication backfires, and they expose themselves.

1. Persuasive lies

As was discussed in the Introduction, Machiavellians often lie when it serves their interests. In fact, they lie very persuasively; that is, they conceal their true intentions efficiently. This was demonstrated, among others, in a study in which the experimenter conducted a conversation of a few minutes with two participants: one was the actual experimental subject while the other was the experimenter's confederate (the subject's partner). They had to jointly solve a series of tasks of increasing difficulty. Meanwhile, other members of the research team hidden behind a one-way mirror video-recorded the subject's gaze direction and the duration of eye contact with the confederate (Exlinne et al. 1970). Suddenly, someone entered the room and told the experimenter that they had a phone call, and that they should come over to the other room where the phone was. Soon after the experimenter left, the partner invited the subject to have a look at the experimenter's notebook left in the room and to crib the correct solutions of the subsequent tasks. When coming back, the experimenter continued the interview in an increasingly impatient tone, expressed skepticism and even suspicion, and accused the pair of cheating. Then the participants were given two minutes to make a confession. One-half of the subjects answered the charges alone while the other half confessed together with the partner. Naturally the video recording continued during the confession.

The study found that among those subjects who were taken in by the confederate's invitation and cheated, high Machs made greater efforts to conceal their misdeed than did low Machs. This was reflected in the finding that they less frequently looked away, that is, less frequently broke eye contact with the experimenter sitting in front of them. Instead, they steadily endured the interrogator's gaze as if attempting to convey that they had had nothing to conceal. By contrast, low Machs often lowered their eyes or averted their head. Furthermore, Machiavellians talked more than others in order to avert suspicion from themselves. Relatively few of them admitted cheating. This suggests that they are well able to regulate their behaviour as a function of the others' presence or absence.

It was quite surprising to observe, however, that high Machs more often resisted the temptation to cheat than did low Machs. Many of them even tried to dissuade the partner from unethical behaviour. The authors suggest that Machiavellians were reluctant because they wanted to avoid being manipulated by others. That is, it was not their moral sense that prevented them from complicity but their self-seeking, cynical attitude which led them to refuse to be told whether or not they should cheat. Machiavellians want others to let them decide on their own.

In any case, Machiavellians' behaviour shows a peculiar duality. On the one hand, they first put up a strong resistance to the confederate's attempt to implicate them, but on the other, after the die had been cast despite all their efforts, they more strongly resisted the interrogator's attempts to elicit a confession from them. This suggests that Machiavellians manoeuvre quite cleverly in order to protect their self-interest.

And that is not all. Machiavellians not only lie frequently and successfully but also have advanced self-knowledge in this regard. In an experiment, researchers used a brief questionnaire which included items such as "Please rate how good you would be at lying in a resume without getting caught" (Giammarco et al. 2013). The results revealed that high Machs reported a better than average ability to deceive others. It is known that Machiavellians do not foster illusions about themselves. Of course, this is part of their general attitude to people: they think that everyone wants to harm others but not everyone has the courage and resolution. In this sense, successful lying is an efficient means to get ahead of others in the "who will dupe whom" contest. It is also possible, of course, that Machiavellians think of themselves as successful liars simply because they often practice this art. A previous study surprisingly found that American university students lied four times a week on average, according to a self-report measure. There is no quantitative data on how frequently Machiavellians lie but the number is probably greater. However, the most recent studies clearly underpin that the number of lies and Machiavellianism are closely related (Jonason et al. 2014). Since "practice makes the master", it is possible that lying becomes an efficient routine over time.

BOX 6.1 DO WE BELIEVE MACHIAVELLIANS?

The elegant experiment conducted by Exlinne and colleagues may lead to the general conclusion that one core of successful lying is persuasive power; that is, the efficient concealment of true intentions. However, this proposition needs to be examined with regard to the target as well: how willing are people to believe a liar? This question was examined in an experiment in which pairs of subjects played the Prisoner's Dilemma game and winners received financial reward at the end of the experiment (Geis & Moon 1981). After informing subjects about the rules, the experimenter left the room. During the game, the opponent pair followed a self-seeking strategy and thereby won the money. While winners were consulting the experimenter, one subject in the losing pair (a confeder-ate) began to consider revenge and suggested to the partner that they take away the money from the opponents' pile on the desk. They actually did so but then the experimenter, coming back and looking at the money, became angry and accused the confederate of theft. The confederate denied the accusation and asked the partner (the actual subject) to back their statement, thereby forcing them to decide whether to confess or deny. Meanwhile, another experimenter recorded the whole procedure with a hidden camera. Finally, thirty-two inde-pendent judges were requested to analyse the video recordings and to judge the credibility of each subject's denial. The results revealed that Machiavellians were found to be more credible than non-Machiavellians. When subjects were implicated in a theft and then accused by the victim, high Machs' false denials were less often tagged as lies than were low Machs' denials. This corroborates the observation that Machiavellians pursue a rational strategy: the more cred-ibly they lie, the better chance they have to achieve their goal.

The study did not clarify exactly what deceived the judges when they failed to detect the lie. It is possible that the secret lies in Machiavellians' well-known emotional control and cold-mindedness (see Chapter 7). Lying is in most cases accompanied by guilt and anxiety: at least this is the case with most people. Psychopaths are an exception, but this is the main point where Machiavellianism essentially differs from psychopathy. Machiavellians are able to feel anxious but distress mostly tries them. However, they also exhibit an excellent ability to control their emotions and to conceal their anxiety from others. Keeping emotions from being reflected by one's face or way of speak-ing may considerably increase the persuasiveness and credibility of lying.

---

2. Impression management

One important Machiavellian strategy based on lying is making a good impression on others. Machiavellians strive to make others believe how intelligent, competent and helpful they are. A study has found that they are able to form a good impression only by nonverbal communication, that is, by facial expression and gaze (Cherulnik et al. 1981). Individuals with various Mach scores were photographed and video-recorded. One group of subjects was presented with the pictures and recordings. These subjects were asked to categorise the presented individuals according to Machiavellian and non-Machiavellian characteristics drawn from a summary of the research literature (cold-minded, selfish versus sincere, empathetic, etc.). Categorisation was found significantly more accurate than one would expect by chance. The traits which were chosen to describe the stimulus persons were consistent with the common characterisation of high and low Machs. For the sake of clarity, it has to be noted that subjects did not know the presented individuals' Mach scores.

Following this, other subjects were asked to describe the individuals presented in the pictures and recordings by adjectives selected from a list including 24 items. High Machs were mostly described as "smart", "brave", "ambitious", "appealing", "dominant" and "talented". By contrast, low Machs were primarily described as "irresolute", "sentimental", "unintelligent", "credulous" and "indecisive". It is surprising in itself that naïve subjects are able to distinguish Machiavellians from non-Machiavellians on the basis of their appearance. What is more, the characteristics they attribute to them are those which may be critical in subsequent interpersonal relationships. It seems that Machiavellians communicate specific and elaborate impressions to those with whom they interact. They play roles in order to elicit a favourable opinion from others. Deception by communication may precede deception by behaviour. In this sense, they manipulate people's opinion before manipulating people themselves. Obviously, it is profitable to appear smart and compassionate rather than stupid and selfish. Once they succeed in making a favourable impression, cheating will be easier. It can be too late for the victim when they come to understand Machiavellians' true nature. It is well known that low Machs are much more characterised by true sincerity, trustworthiness and agreeableness while they possibly fail to communicate these traits appropriately.

These studies corroborate those research reports according to which people find Machiavellians charming and appealing. People rate them higher on a social attractiveness scale than they rate low Machs (Wilson, Near, & Miller 1996). Moreover, Machiavellians themselves often deploy their charming appearance, either consciously or unconsciously, in order to gain influence on others. They often employ the tactics of flattery and enticement (Jonason & Webster 2012).

3. Telling faces?

A study very similar in methodology but quite different in its aim and results was conducted by an American research team which used 10 male and 10 female faces to generate average faces (prototypes; Holtzman 2011). One-half of the portrayed individuals scored high on the Mach scale while the other half scored low. In this way, the researchers generated an average face from each set of high Mach and low Mach faces. They likewise generated prototypes of men and women with high and low narcissism and psychopathy. (As was discussed previously, Machiavellianism is commonly associated with narcissism and psychopathy as one of the three members of the Dark Triad). These emotionally neutral average faces were presented to uninformed subjects who were asked to indicate on a scale ranging from 0 to 7 how well several statements described each pictured individual. The Machiavellian personality was defined as "a person who is manipulative for personal gain". Surprisingly, many subjects associated this definition with the average face generated from high Mach faces (the subjects, of course, were unaware of this). They were likewise able to associate the average narcissistic face with the description of narcissism ("arrogant, vain pompous, self-absorbed and assertive"), and this was also the case with psychopathy ("reckless, antagonistic, assertive with others, angry at others"). In sum, psychological profiles of the Dark Triad personalities including Machiavellianism were found to be strongly correlated with facial structures. The author suggests that Machiavellianism may involve a physical phenotype, besides psychological characteristics and cultural traits.

BOX 6.2 AVERAGE MALE AND FEMALE FACES GENERATED FROM FACES OF INDIVIDUALS SCORING EITHER LOW OR HIGH ON THE DARK TRIAD

(1. low Mach female; 2. high Mach female; 3. low Mach male; 4. high Mach male)

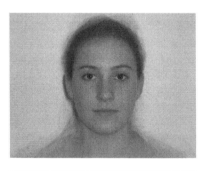

This is a very surprising finding that calls for an explanation. It is possible that physical features and personality traits are transmitted in a "genetic package" from one generation to another. An alternative and possibly more probable explanation suggests that Machiavellian personality traits are shaped by others' responses to the individual's physical features. The social perception of physical appearance may affect personality development. A hypothetical example may be a person with a narrow face who elicits aversion in others due to the negative attributions they may associate with this facial appearance. It is a different question regarding which sources and observations may lead to such prejudices that assign social values to various facial features (Keating 2003). If, however, there actually are such attributes, then it is theoretically possible that they canalise a certain course of personality development. It is possible that the individual judged on the basis of their physical features begins to behave according to others' expectations and gradually develops a character which is in turn reflected in consistently high Mach scores.

4. Telling behavioural features

Machiavellians may not only be betrayed by their facial appearance; they can be detected on the basis of their behavioural styles as well, especially in a closed group based on personal contact. Those who repeatedly contact Machiavellians gradually come to know their fundamental traits and become estranged from them. In a study, groups of subjects participated in a game in which they solved various tasks together (Rauthmann & Kolar 2013). They kept in contact with one another during the game and their personal impressions and experience enabled them to give a description of one another. They were asked to do so by filling brief questionnaires in which they rated their partners' personality and intellectual traits. Machiavellians were rated low on the dimension that included kindness, agreeableness and openness. Moreover, they were judged to have a negative effect on teamwork.

In a similar study, subjects were likewise asked to answer a few questions concerning the social and sexual attractiveness of Machiavellians (and other Dark Triad members; Rauthmann & Kolar 2013). Subjects did not find these people likeable, and they excluded the possibility of engaging in either a platonic or a long-term intimate partner relationship with them. They only saw a short-term relationship possible; they did not exclude the possibility of a casual relationship with Machiavellians. This is probably consistent with the nature of Machiavellian charm discussed earlier: many find them attractive eccentrics.

The previous descriptions suggest that Machiavellians strive to make a good impression upon others from the very beginning while, on the other hand, they are vulnerable in that their facial expressions and behavioural habits may betray them to the others. If Machiavellians are accepted by a group on the basis of the first impressions they make, but are excluded once group members gain more thorough knowledge of their personality and goals, this situation should impose a task on Machiavellians. They have to disguise themselves and ceaselessly change their tactics. Machiavellians are genuine chameleons, assuming diverse personalities in front of the public as they face diverse situations. They earn large profits in social dilemma games but once the experimenter enables players to punish free riders, they immediately restrain their profiteering ambitions and increase the sums offered to partners in order to avoid punishment (Spitzer et al. 2007). In most cases, they are unwilling to help others but when they are aware of being observed by other members of the community, they are at once ready to support even unknown individuals so that they maintain their prestige (or its illusion) in the group (Bereczkei, Birkas, & Kerekes 2010).

Another form of disguise is not so much related to Machiavellians' chameleon nature as it is to their quick escape when things are getting too hot. As was seen previously, the chance of being exposed increases when others come to know them thoroughly and become aware of their real nature. In this case, the successful strategy is to withdraw from the alert community in time and to look for other targets to exploit. Machiavellians like to fish in troubled waters when others appear fundamentally cooperative, but they instantly withdraw from profiteering when the prospective profit is not worth the risk. This is the case when, for example, all players enter into competition for limited resources that substantially reduces Machiavellians' scope for action (Bereczkei, Szabo, & Czibor 2015). Under this circumstance, they rather limit their egoism and wait for the more promising situations.

7

EMOTIONAL COLDNESS

From the beginning, researchers have considered Machiavellians' rational, cold and reserved behaviour as one of their fundamental characteristics. Geis and her colleagues have observed under laboratory conditions that high Machs exhibit an impersonal attitude towards their partners, detach themselves from the emotional atmosphere of personal relationships and are generally unconcerned with others' feelings and interests (Geis & Levy 1970; Geis, Weinheimer, & Berger 1970).

1. Emotional detachment

The authors proposed hypotheses concerning the effects of such emotional detachment on manipulation-related decisions. They start from the observation that although intense emotions may in general facilitate better performance, in many cases they inhibit learning in cognitive tasks involving analysis of complex stimuli (Zajonc 1965). Since high Machs are unconcerned with personal commitment and feelings, the emotional aspects of their relationships do not disturb their rational thinking. On the contrary, they devote full attention to the cognitive appraisal of the situation and only focus on the achievement of strategic objectives. Low Machs, by contrast, are unable to keep themselves from personal involvement and emotional implications that easily distract their attention and thought. This may explain those experimental findings (see Box 7.1) suggesting that Machiavellians primarily perform better than others in emotionally loaded situations such as, for example, when they have to engage in a debate on a subject involving matters of personal feelings and values (Geis, Weinheimer, & Berger 1970; Sullivan & Allen 1999).

BOX 7.1 THE CONGRESSMEN EXPERIMENT

In this thoroughly American experiment, the researchers informed subjects beforehand that the study focused on the psychological aspects of the legislative process (Geis, Weinheimer, & Berger 1970). Subjects were asked to imagine they were newly elected congressmen. Their goal was to make decisions which would represent the will of their constituents and which might help them ascend to the top levels of power (and possibly to presidency). They had to argue for or against issues which affected the masses. To that end, they drew five cards describing various issues. Some of the issues touched upon political issues which divided subjects and, in many cases, even compelled them to take a position on an emotional basis. Such issues concerned, for example, the revocation of previous civil rights legislation, the unilateral disarmament of the US army or the abolishment of the minimum age requirement for a driver's licence. There also were neutral or, so to say, trivial issues which attracted much less attention and presumably did not concern citizens personally. Such issues included, for example, approving the appointment of the chairman of the Rules Committee, changing the procedure for reporting committee actions or the relocation of the Bureau of Documents. Each subject was given a specific amount of time to argue either in favour of or against these issues in front of "fellow congressmen" whose roles were played, of course, by another group of subjects. Subjects had to address each issue in two ways: once they argued in favour of the issue, and another time against it. They were allowed to use any kind of rhetorical phrases, logical reasoning and any means of communication they preferred. After each proposal, fellow "congressmen" rated the persuasiveness and acceptability of the argumentation on a scale ranging from 1 to 5.

When neutral (trivial) issues were addressed, high and low Mach speakers obtained roughly identical scores. A great difference was found, however, in the evaluation of speeches on emotional issues: high Machs received higher voting points than lows. Machiavellians were judged the most capable debaters by fellow "congressmen" who were, of course, unaware of the speakers' Mach scores, nor did they even know that they had completed such a test. This was obviously not due to Machiavellians' being cleverer or having a better understanding of the task, since in that case a similar difference would have been found for neutral issues as well. It is more probable, although no relevant question was asked of the subjects, that Machiavellians argued more persuasively and more logically for or against the issue. The authors explained Machiavellians' better performance by suggesting that they kept separate their rational argumentation from the disturbing effects of emotions. They argued cold-mindedly, whereas low Machs' attention and concentration were often disturbed by affective influences. This explanation is supported by the finding that the greatest difference between the two groups was found in cases when they argued for their own personal position as opposed to cases when they argued against it. This finding strongly supports the idea that taking a stand for our convictions may elicit intense emotions in us, often at the expense of sober and clear reasoning.

2. Impulse control and communication of emotions

Subsequent research largely relied on these considerations. Several authors suggest that emotional coldness originates in strong impulse control that primarily elicits an unemotional analysis of the situation and indifference towards others (Jones & Paulhus 2009; Pilch 2008). Jones and Paulhus (2009, 2011) consider impulse control to be an essential Machiavellian characteristic from which several other characteristics ensuring successful manipulation originate. Namely, they are able to concentrate on a goal, to analyse data, to select from alternative tactical moves and to choose the optimal strategy in any given situation. Emotional coldness (impulse control) in this respect may be considered an adaptive characteristic, since indifference towards others may prevent emotional attunement to the target that in turn may facilitate their successful exploitation. Moreover, the lack of affective responsiveness to others reduces internal regulatory functions such as shame or guilt (McIllwain 2003). If one lacks these feelings, one hardly has a sense of the moral implications of one's actions, and this further paves the way for efficient manipulation.

The above-mentioned theoretical considerations, however, do not touch the cognitive mechanisms of cold-minded thinking. Is it possible that Machiavellians do not experience emotions at all or, alternatively, are they only unable or perhaps unwilling to express them? Current studies give contradictory answers to these questions. Certain findings suggest that Machiavellians poorly identify the negative emotions of others. One study found, for example, that in comparison with others, Machiavellians (and primary psychopaths) reported more positive emotions when presented with pictures of sad faces (Ali, Amorim, & Chamorro-Premuzic 2009; Wai & Tiliopoulos 2012). They possibly have difficulties in experiencing negative emotions, therefore the pain of others does not necessarily depress or distress them. The same studies showed that Machiavellians responded with negative emotions to happy (or neutral) faces. No clear explanation has yet been proposed to this latter finding although some authors (Wai & Tiliopoulos 2012) point out that dysregulation was found in psychopathic subjects' amygdala, which is involved in the coordination of emotional responses.

Other studies have revealed, however, that Machiavellians experience more intense negative emotions than average, especially in stressful situations. A study using a personality diagnostic questionnaire has found that high Machs are prone to emotional disturbance and explosiveness (McHoskey 2001). A more recent study using, among others, the five-factor BFI personality inventory found a certain kind of emotional instability among high Machs. They experience more negative emotions, lose their temper sooner and get upset more easily than low Machs (Szijjarto & Bereczkei 2015). In general, they are more tried by emotionally upsetting events and distress. These findings suggest that Machiavellians, albeit often described as cold-minded and rational, experience intense emotions and tension.

It is not by accident, however, that they appear to observers rather as sober and disciplined people guided by reason. Relevant studies clearly suggest that Machiavellians express their emotions rather poorly. They show a certain kind of restraint and seem to keep their emotional expressions under strict control (McHoskey 1999). The previously mentioned study using a questionnaire to measure various factors of emotional intelligence (see Box 8.1 in Chapter 8) has revealed that high Machs express emotions relatively poorly (Szijjarto & Bereczkei 2015). They report an inability to give accurate and refined expression to their own feelings and emotional impulses. Similar results were obtained in studies in which subjects were asked to recognise and identify the emotional expressions of strangers (Austin et al. 2007; Wai & Tiliopoulos 2012). Generally speaking, Machiavellians have difficulty both in communicating their own emotions and understanding those of others.

BOX 7.2 ALEXITHYMIA AND MACHIAVELLIANISM

The deficit in expressing and understanding emotions is related to alexithymia. This disorder is shown by patients treated with psychotherapy who have an inability to verbalise emotions and difficulty in identifying feelings, as well as distinguishing between various emotional states they experience (Sifenos 1973). The relationship between alexithymia and Machiavellianism seems obvious, and it is actually supported by empirical findings. Positive correlation was found between alexithymia (measured with a questionnaire specifically developed for this purpose) and Machiavellianism (Wastell & Booth 2003a). The authors suggest that high Machs lack an adequate emotional connection with the environment, thus they are not at all or are only slightly able to access their own emotional states and to identify those of others. As a consequence, they can only conceive of their environment in terms of self-interest, and they have a purely objectifying perspective on others. This leads Machiavellians to develop a pervasive instrumental attitude towards their relationships with others whom they consider as individuals to be exploited and manipulated in order to achieve their own goals. This is consistent with findings of a previous study which suggest that alexithymic patients treat others as instruments or easily replaceable objects and that they have an emotionally shallow and utilitarian attitude towards interpersonal relationships (Krystal 1988).

More recent studies have revealed a particularly close relationship between Machiavellianism and another essential characteristic of alexithymia besides the difficulties in emotional life, namely, externally-oriented thinking (Al Ain et al. 2013; Jonason & Krause 2013). This means that Machiavellians are rarely concerned with their internal life; they do not analyse their own thoughts and feelings, nor do they often rely on their imagination. The low levels of these two abilities – emotional deficit and external orientation – are not unrelated, of course. Those having difficulty identifying and processing their emotions rather rely on external influences to orient themselves in their environment. They develop a concrete and logical way of thinking in which emotional reactions hardly play any role. At the same time, externally-oriented thinking may be particularly useful for Machiavellians. They devote relatively little effort in analysing their internal life whereas they far more intensively seek to understand relationships and situations in the external environment. Machiavellians do not meditate; they do not ponder on their own feelings and thoughts. This may be advantageous when prompt action is needed. In fact, Machiavellians are masters of flexible adaptation (see Chapter 9) who quickly recognise the opportunities offered to themselves and mostly act immediately.

The authors also propose an alternative explanation, suggesting that it is in Machiavellians' own interest to conform their behaviour to external expectations to some extent so that others will accept them. Otherwise, they might easily become isolated and excluded from the group, which might prove fatal to them since thereby they would lose or substantially reduce their opportunities to manipulate others. Therefore, they show a certain kind of alertness and vigilance towards the external environment and strive to adapt to the shared values of the group.

3. Adaptive benefits

It is possible that the deficits discussed above may also be advantageous in terms of deception. Restrained emotional communication may facilitate successful manipulation since it deprives the potential target of such behavioural cues as might reveal the Machiavellian's intentions. The target cannot know what the Machiavellian's real intention is and often does not even suspect that the Machiavellian's indifferent attitude may foreshadow a potential attack.

However, it has so far been almost completely unknown whether such deficient emotional communication is intentional. It is possible that Machiavellians deliberately conceal their emotions in order to carry out a perfect deception. By exercising restrained emotional communication, they may acquire the ability to appear calm in any stressful situation, whatever emotions they experience. If this is the case, it is possible that certain inhibitory processes have developed during the evolution that serve Machiavellians' goals as a kind of proximate mechanism. However, an actual (non-deliberately) cognitive deficit which is interrelated with manipulative motivations is likewise possible. In this case, the disability or dysfunction of expressing emotions may similarly help Machiavellians hide their true intentions, and thus this mental deficit may become a means to influence others. An evolutionary approach readily offers itself in this case as well: although the inability to adequately express emotions entails several disadvantages in interpersonal relationships, the benefits of manipulative behaviour compensate for them, and these two components have co-evolved in a package in the course of evolution as an adaptive behavioural complex.

Regarding relevant empirical findings, a rather ambiguous picture presents itself. Both ideas are supported by experimental results. Intentional concealment of emotions is suggested by those previously discussed experimental findings which have revealed that Machiavellians efficiently disguise their lies and convincingly deny their acts of cheating (Exlinne et al. 1970; Harrell & Hartnagel 1976). Moreover, a study employing a brain imaging technique found an area in the dorsolateral part of prefrontal cortex (DLPFC) that showed particularly high activity in Machiavellians during decision-making (Bereczkei et al. 2015). One of the main functions of this region is to inhibit emotional responses and achieve cognitive control. DLPFC is typically engaged when individuals make decisions in which there is a conflict between social norms and personal interests or when individuals make decisions that may be counter to their own response tendencies (Rilling et al. 2008; Sanfey et al. 2003).

Another recent study, however, rather supports an alternative hypothesis. The results of this study suggest that Machiavellians show an actual deficit not only in expressing their emotions but also in identifying and distinguishing between them (Szijjarto & Bereczkei 2015). They have difficulty in "labelling" their emotions and understanding their true meaning, and they show poorer performance in perceiving the transitions between their emotional states. Obviously, further research is needed in order to gain a clearer insight into Machiavellians' emotion regulation.

4. Anxiety

The same ambiguity characterises the findings on Machiavellians' anxiety. Anxiety is a feeling of unpleasantness, uneasiness and worry over anticipated events, such as illness or death. Anxiety is not the same as fear, which is a response to a real or perceived immediate threat; anxiety is the expectation of future threat. Some of the related studies did not find any significant relationship between Machiavellianism and self-report measures of anxiety (e.g. STAI; Ali, Amorin, & Chamorro-Premuzic 2009). By contrast, other studies revealed a positive relationship between the two variables (Fehr et al. 1992; Al Ain et al. 2013). Besides controversy, this raises a paradox: the classic description of an emotionally cold personality is hardly reconcilable with the image of an anxious Machiavellian. The paradox may possibly be resolved by considering those previously mentioned research findings which suggest that while Machiavellians in fact experience intense emotions, they have difficulty identifying and expressing them. An early study found that when subjects were accused of theft, independent observers judged high Machs to be less distressed and anxious than were low Machs (Exlinne et al. 1970). It is worth considering that successful deception may in part depend on Machiavellians' ability to control the visible signs of their anxiety (Geis & Moon 1981). If lying and cheating are accompanied by anxiety (and usually this is the case), those will prove persuasive cheaters who are able to control the observable symptoms of their being anxious.

Insofar as Machiavellians are anxious, they may be aware that their behaviour leads to negative consequences or that their plans to deceive others would go against community norms. A recent study supports this idea (Birkás et al. 2015). This study employed a questionnaire which measured sensitivity to anxiety, that is, subjects' fears of anxiety-related symptoms, in three areas. One set of items concerns fears of anxiety-related bodily sensations (e.g. "When my stomach is upset, I worry that I might be seriously ill"). Other items are related to fears of cognitive disorganisation ("It scares me when I am unable to keep my mind on a task"). Finally, there are items assessing fears of negative social consequences connected to anxiety ("It is important for me not to appear nervous"). Machiavellianism is related to these latter fears; Machiavellians seem to be afraid of being rejected or negatively judged by others. This is probably due to Machiavellians' manipulative ambitions whose success partly depends on others' opinions of, and feelings towards, them. Successful deception inevitably requires that the target accepts and trusts the deceiver to some extent.

It is worth noting in this regard that psychopathy, which is closely related to Machiavellianism within the Dark Triad, is highly negatively correlated with various measures of anxiety (Ali, Amorim, & Chamorro-Premuzic 2009; Paulhus & Williams 2002). Psychopaths are well known for their lack of anxiety, and this is probably the most important difference between them and Machiavellians.

8

EMOTIONAL INTELLIGENCE AND EMPATHY

As early as 40 or 50 years ago, social psychological studies made it quite clear that Machiavellians as opposed to other types are less sensitive to their partners' expressions of nonverbal communication such as facial expressions, gestures, posture and movements. In an interesting study, subjects in pair combinations participated in a ball-and-spiral task (Durkin 1970). They used a tool that resembled a basin turned upside down in which a ball rolled around through passages and ramps. Two persons moved the tool, each holding one side. The goal of the game was to keep the ball in motion, to prevent it from falling out and to finally move it into the designated hole. Both subjects tried to jointly control the movement of the ball, something that obviously required remarkable coordination. They had to be alert to the partner's every subtle movement and signal. Every situation required quick responses without any chance to engage in prolonged consideration or reasoning. The study revealed that low Machs as opposed to high Machs gave more frequent and more efficient responses to their partners' movements. Low Machs more frequently corrected deviations of the ball by tilting the tool in the right direction. The author explained the difference by suggesting that high Machs in the given situation could not employ the rational decision-making abilities which usually made them successful under different circumstances. The game required immediate spontaneous reactions, which low Machs appeared to perform more efficiently. According to the author, the secret of their success lay in their better attunement to their partner and in their more refined perception of the partner's movements and the underlying intentions. By contrast, Machiavellians' reactions were characterised by a certain kind of objective attitude rather than by an interpersonal orientation.

1. The Machiavellians' shortage

This interpretation could be generalised: high Machs find it more difficult than average to understand the other's emotions, recognise the feelings or intentions reflected in the posture and facial expressions of others, and also to display difficulty in expressing and regulating their own emotions (Austin et al. 2007; Wai & Tilio-poulos 2012; Szijjarto & Bereczkei 2015; Pilch 2008; Vonk et al. 2015). In other words, Machiavellians have a relatively low emotional intelligence (EI). Emotional intelligence includes the abilities related to understanding and regulating both one's own and emotions and feelings and those of others. It not only includes accurate identification and recognition of emotions but also the ability to control our own emotions, that is, the ability to understand the relationships between our feelings, thoughts and actions. Individuals with high emotional intelligence are able to consciously reach an emotional state within themselves through which they can experience success and satisfaction in social relationships. Thus, emotional intelligence means a complex set of abilities characteristic of one's personality and measured by various tests and questionnaires (see Box 8.1). Such measures are used to calculate the emotional quotient (EQ), an index of one's ability to regulate and control one's emotions and to involve them in decision-making.

BOX 8.1 THE SCHUTTE SELF-REPORT EMOTIONAL INTELLIGENCE TEST

Subjects are instructed to indicate the extent to which each of the 28 items applies to them using the following scale: 1: strongly disagree; 2: disagree; 3: neither disagree nor agree; 4: agree; 5: strongly agree.

1 I know when to speak about my personal problems to others.
2 When I am faced with obstacles, I remember times when I faced similar obstacles and overcame them.
3 I expect that I will do well in most things I try.
4 Other people find it easy to confide in me.
5 I find it hard to understand the nonverbal messages of other people.
6 When my mood changes, I see new possibilities.
7 I am aware of my emotions as I experience them.
8 I expect good things to happen.
9 I like to share my emotions with others.
10 When I experience a positive emotion, I know how to make it last.
11 I arrange events others enjoy.
12 I seek out activities that make me happy.
13 I am aware of the non-verbal messages I send to others.
14 I present myself in a way that makes a good impression on others.
15 When I am in a positive mood, solving problems is easy for me.
16 By looking at their facial expressions, I recognise the emotions people are experiencing.
17 When I am in a positive mood, I am able to come up with new ideas.
18 I easily recognise my emotions as I experience them.
19 I motivate myself by imagining a good outcome to tasks I take on.
20 I compliment others when they have done something well.

21   I am aware of the nonverbal messages other people send.
22   When I feel a change in emotions, I tend to come up with new ideas.
23   When I am faced with a challenge, I give up because I believe I will fail.
24   I know what other people are feeling just by looking at them.
25   I help other people feel better when they are down.
26   I use good moods to help myself keep trying in the face of obstacles.
27   I can tell how people are feeling by listening to the tone of their voice.
28   It is difficult for me to understand why people feel the way they do.

Self-report measures invariably indicated that they have difficulty in understanding either their own or others' emotions, and that Machiavellians are less able than others to harmonise their thoughts and feelings. This is somewhat surprising since one might expect that manipulation and deception in fact require Machiavellians to survey their target's emotions and intentions as well as to turn this knowledge into action. Moreover, Machiavellianism is not only negatively related to emotional intelligence but also to the more broad construct of social intelligence that includes sensitivity to, and understanding and control of, social relationships (Box 8.2).

BOX 8.2 SOCIO-EMOTIONAL INTELLIGENCE AND MACHIAVELLIANISM

Recently, Austrian and German researchers have developed a test named the Social Skills Inventory whose 90 items cover two broad areas (Nagler et al. 2014). One of these, Emotional Intelligence, is further divided into three dimensions. Emotional expressivity assesses the accuracy of communicating emotional states ("I have been told that I have expressive eyes"). Emotional sensitivity is related to interpreting others' emotions ("I am often told that I am a sensitive, understanding person"). Emotional control is a measure of regulating emotional displays ("I am very good at maintaining a calm exterior even if I am upset").

The other broad area is Social Intelligence, which is likewise assessed by the same threefold measure. Social expressivity includes one's manner of verbal expression and engaging others in social discourse ("When telling a story, I usually use a lot of gestures to help get the point across"). Social sensitivity concerns adequate interpretation of others' communication and appropriate social behaviour ("I am generally concerned about the impression I am making on others"). Finally, social control assesses one's manner of self-presentation and playing roles ("I am not very good at mixing at parties").

Nagler and colleagues found that Machiavellianism was negatively correlated with two subscales of Emotional Intelligence (emotional expressivity and emotional sensitivity). Furthermore, in contrast with others, Machiavellians reported poorer skills on all three factors of Social Intelligence.

2. Manipulative intelligence

However, some authors point out problems with the conventional explanation for these findings (O'Conner & Athota 2013). These authors raise the possibility that Machiavellianism and emotional intelligence are negatively related just because EI measures focus almost exclusively on positive emotions. They concern traits such as "kind", "friendly" and "benevolent". Thus, it is not surprising that it is the low Machs, that is, those willing to cooperate and inclined to be empathetic, who produce high scores on EI scales. Machiavellians, by contrast, are less likely to possess such traits, therefore they cannot score high on EI measures. It is obvious, as the authors point out, that personality factors mediate the relationship between Machiavellianism and emotional intelligence. For example, those scoring high on the Agreeableness scale encompassing characteristics such as "kind", "polite", "understanding" and "good-natured" (see Box 3.1 in Chapter 3) usually also have a good understanding of their personal relationships and have a regard for the emotional states of others. By contrast, those who possess the opposite personality characteristics, that is, those who are less friendly and understanding, are more prone to cheat and exploit others. Confirming this expectation, the author eliminated (controlled for) the effect of the Agreeableness factor, and indeed the negative relationship between Machiavellianism and emotional intelligence disappeared.

Even more importantly, the authors devised a scale named Perceived Emotional Competence (PEC). "Neutral" items on this subscale measured the actual ability to understand and control emotions without involving positive traits such as "optimism", "sense of community" or "willingness to help". It is not a surprise that a positive relationship was found between this alternative construct of emotional competence and Machiavellianism, even for those scoring low on Agreeableness. This means that Machiavellians may be able to understand others' emotions and control their own feelings at a high level but that essentially they employ these abilities to serve their self-interest. In the light of the above findings, the relationship between Machiavellianism and emotional intelligence is mediated by a certain personality type, and those with such a personality character are in fact inclined to use their emotional abilities for manipulative purposes.

This observation is highly consistent with findings of several other studies which have also demonstrated that Machiavellians, who generally show poorer abilities on EI measures, are in fact better than others in certain dimensions (Austin et al. 2007; Grieve 2011; Nagler et al. 2014). Elizabeth Austin and her colleagues (2007) developed a 41-item scale based on different measures of emotional intelligence. The test, which was named the "Emotional Manipulation Scale", comprises items which imply communicative strategies aimed at deceiving others. Such strategies are largely based on emotional blackmail, on guilt-based manipulation and various influence tactics (Box 8.3). Subjects were asked to indicate the extent to which they agreed or disagreed with each item. High Machs reported substantially more frequently that they were willing to employ strategies aimed at deceiving, confusing or influencing others according to their own goals.

BOX 8.3 THE EMOTIONAL MANIPULATION SCALE (SELECTED ITEMS)

- I know how to embarrass someone to stop them behaving in a particular way.
- I know how to make another person feel uneasy.
- I know how to play two people off against each other.
- I can make someone feel anxious so that they will act in a particular way.
- I am good at reassuring people so that they're more likely to go along with what I say.
- I sometimes pretend to be angrier than I really am about someone's behaviour in order to induce them to behave differently in future.
- I can simulate emotions like pain and hurt to make others feel guilty.
- If someone has done something to upset me I think it is acceptable to make them feel guilty about it.
- I can offer words of encouragement and reassurance to a friend to get them to do something I want.
- When someone has made me upset or angry, I often conceal my feelings.

This finding invites several alternative explanations. One of them suggests that Machiavellians still do not have high emotional intelligence. They simply approve deploying emotional manipulation against others as reflected in their responses to the items of the scale. A "stronger" explanation for the above finding may be that Machiavellians actually exhibit above average emotional intelligence in certain situations. When they have the opportunity to deceive others either verbally or nonverbally, they immediately deploy tactics of emotional manipulation. Specific cues related to manipulative opportunities may elicit a response in which they tend to take advantage of the emotions of others in the hope of successful deception. By contrast, in situations where there is no chance to exploit others, they remain blind to the feelings of others as disturbing factors for which they find no use/profit.

3. Emotional intelligence in realistic situations

The studies presented so far used so-called paper and pencil tests which provided a measure of emotional intelligence based on responses to self-report items. This method gives a relatively accurate picture of one's view on one's own abilities and experience related to understanding and dealing with emotions. This is important information but not objective enough since there is a slight risk that some of the respondents do not adhere to reality when judging themselves. A more reliable picture may be obtained by observing subjects' behaviour in certain situations. For this reason, some researchers have used methods which provide a measure of performance-based emotional intelligence (Austin et al. 2007; Ali et al. 2009). They have studied, for example, how people read others' facial expressions in pictures or video recordings. Subjects are asked to interpret the feelings and emotions of those showing a certain facial expression or gaze. One study used the Multimodal Emotion Recognition Test (MERT), which involves several sensory modes and provides a complex measure of emotional intelligence. Subjects were presented with a randomised series of photographs, short videos, silent films and sound recordings of speech without visual stimuli. They were asked to name the emotions expressed by the actors in different ways (Box 8.4).

This study produced findings similar to those obtained in previous research. Subjects with higher Mach scores showed poorer performance than those with low scores. They were less likely to associate the face seen or the speech heard with the respective emotion. Again, the study offers the conclusion that Machiavellians' global emotional intelligence is lower than average, even if measured by employing sophisticated techniques.

However, this study also had a questionable aspect, namely that although the method they used was complex, the stimulus material modelled social interactions in a rather static manner that was far from realistic. The face captured in a photograph is not the same as the face in a real interaction when muscle movements are also visible: lips stretching into a smile, a nod of the head, eyebrows raised quickly or slowly. Nor does a portrait reveal the gestures accompanying facial expressions: arms outstretched or folded, the body turning to or away from the partner. The observer cannot hear the vocal emotional expressions accompanying the experience of satisfaction, sadness or joy. And vice versa: the listener of a voice recording is completely deprived of the sight of the speaker, a quite unrealistic situation in most cases.

BOX 8.4 PICTURES OF THE MULTIMODAL EMOTION RECOGNITION TEST (MERT)

Besides portraits such as the ones below, the test contains short videos, silent films and sound recordings of (unintelligible) speech without visual stimuli. In each case, subjects have to identify the emotions reflected in the pictures, videos and sound recordings.

This is the reason why one may argue that the experimental techniques employed in most previous studies modelled interpersonal relationships in a rather unrealistic manner. In fact, the case is not much better with those more "dynamic" stimulus materials which present observed individuals' (actors') behaviour and speech in a short motion picture. Even such materials fail to overcome the essential problem, namely, that subjects have to understand others' emotional expressions without being actively involved in the interaction. The question then is how Machiavellians behave in a real world of personal relationships where they are involved in real social events; that is, in situations where the way they interpret and respond to the emotions of others as well as the way in which they control their own have consequences for their own and others' future behaviour.

One study created an opportunity to examine how people express, conceal and recognise emotions in a realistic situation (Orosz & Bereczkei 2015). The experiment was based on the well-known Cheat card game, played in groups of three, each of which included a low, a medium and a high Mach subject. Besides ensuring personal interaction, another advantage of the game is that players are compelled to deceive their partners since those players win who are better at concealing their true intention through a false claim. Furthermore, success can also be achieved by those who are better at detecting their partners' attempts at deception, that is, those who efficiently read the opponents' subtle movements, facial expressions, gestures, tone and other nonverbal cues (Box 8.5).

BOX 8.5 THE CHEAT CARD GAME

The three players take seats at a round table at an equal distance from each other so that they can see each other equally well. The researchers select 72 cards from an Uno deck consisting of 108 cards so that the selected deck contains eight cards of each rank from 1 to 9. Each player has 8 cards at the start. In the present study each group of players included a low, a medium and a high Mach subject as measured by the Mach-IV scale. Each group played a total of 10 rounds, the first of which was a trial round enabling players to learn the rules. Each round included 15 turns and lasted approximately 5 minutes.

Subjects had to place their cards face down onto the middle of the table in numerical order from 1 to 9, in such a way that when it was their turn each player had to play a card exactly one number higher than that played by the previous player (e.g. number 6 had to be followed by number 7). Each player had to announce the number of the card they were playing that turn. If the player whose turn it was did not have a card of the required number, they were compelled to make a false announcement (since it was a rule that the required number should be announced at each turn). If either of the opponents suspected that the player was making a false announcement, they were allowed to call out "Cheat!". In such a case, the card was turned over to check its number. If a false announcement was exposed, that is, if the actual number of the card was different from the claim made by the player whose turn it was, the player had to take all previously played cards from the table. If the claim proved true, however, the stack of cards on the table had to be taken by the opponent who had called out "Cheat!". The winner of the game was the first player who succeeded in emptying their hand or the player with the fewest cards in their hand at the end of the round. The winner could take their winnings home. The real money reward made the experiment more realistic and serious since all subjects tried to employ the most expedient tactics possible in the hope of taking home the greatest winnings.

The researchers recorded the number of times each player called out "Cheat!" as well as the number of times each player gained a point by calling out "Cheat!" (i.e. when a lie was revealed). In order to obtain an accurate statistical measure, the C-index was introduced (C standing for cheat) that was calculated as a quotient obtained by dividing the number of effective cheat calls by the number of all cheat calls. In this way, the C-index showed the rate of correct detections within the total number of "accusations".

One interesting result of the experiment was that high Machs cried out, "Cheat!" more frequently than low Machs and also scored a higher number of effective cheat calls. In other words, high Machs were more likely than low Machs to detect their partners' lying. Their performance was also found better in terms of the rate of correct detections compared to the total number of cheat calls, as indicated by the C-index. In turn, the rate of correct detections showed a close correlation with the winnings gained: it was the subjects who made more points through successfully detecting lies whose winnings were greater. Moreover, the results also suggest that Machiavellians concealed their emotions more efficiently, since their partners made fewer points by calling out "Cheat!".

Although the experiment supports the theory that Machiavellians are successful in a system of personal relationships, it has not revealed what exactly happens during the game. What is it that Machiavellians are more likely to detect than others? Is it changes in others' facial expressions? Does it lie with telling movements or subtle postural changes? Is it perhaps changes in breathing or voice? This is yet to be revealed, while it seems reasonable to conclude, as the authors do, that in a realistic experimental setting which involves subjects as active participants with the prospect of earning a reward, Machiavellians exhibit above average abilities to read certain nonverbal cues as well as to conceal their own emotions.

It is possible that the success of Machiavellians at the game was in part due to the increasing tension or distress that might gradually overwhelm subjects. A self-report questionnaire administered at the end of the game revealed that high Machs had experienced more intense distress during the game than subjects with lower Mach scores. They were more distressed than others, primarily when telling a lie. This finding is consistent with those discussed previously: Machiavellians experience intense emotions but they are able to conceal them.

Of course, alternative explanations may be raised as well. It is possible, for example, that Machiavellians simply think rationally during the game rather than read and conceal emotions. They may keep the partners' movements, calculate and estimate how likely various numbers are to be played in the subsequent rounds. However, such a strategy is rather unlikely to work due to the relatively large number and variety of cards used in the game. Moreover, subjects reported at the end of the game that they had not resorted to such "rational" tactics. In any case, future experiments will need to monitor the game more efficiently by means of hidden cameras or computer simulation in order to gain reliable insight into Machiavellian strategies.

4. Empathy

Emotional intelligence is closely related to empathy. Empathy generally refers to one's ability to understand and conceive another individual's mental state as well as to have a capacity to place oneself in another's position (Batson 2009). This latter is the more important aspect: empathy essentially means that one experiences someone else's joy and pain, shares these feelings and personally experiences them. Various empathy tests currently available usually measure how much one is concerned with others' feelings, how much one can put oneself in someone else's shoes and to what extent one can personally experience others' feelings and impressions (Box 8.6). It has to be noted that empathic ability in itself does not imply positive concern for others since empathy may remain at the "theoretical" level of pity that is not followed by action. It is a fact, however, that those scoring high on empathy scales are usually more willing to cooperate with and help others.

BOX 8.6 THE INTERPERSONAL REACTIVITY INDEX (IRI; SELECTED ITEMS)

- I often have tender, concerned feelings for people less fortunate than me.
- I sometimes find it difficult to see things from the "other guy's" point of view.
- Sometimes I don't feel very sorry for other people when they are having problems.
- I really get involved with the feelings of the characters in a novel.
- I try to look at everybody's side of a disagreement before I make a decision.
- I sometimes try to understand my friends better by imagining how things look from their perspective.
- Other people's misfortunes do not usually disturb me a great deal.
- If I'm sure I'm right about something, I don't waste much time listening to other people's arguments.
- When I see someone being treated unfairly, I sometimes don't feel very much pity for them.
- When I'm upset at someone, I usually try to "put myself in his shoes" for a while.
- Before criticising somebody, I try to imagine how I would feel if I were in their place.

If reconsidering at this point the relationship between emotional intelligence and empathy, one may conclude that they overlap to a great extent. An essential aspect of both is detecting others' emotional states, being sensitive to others' verbal and nonverbal communication as well as controlling and regulating one's own emotional states. However, empathy means more in two regards. First, beyond recognising and identifying emotions, empathy also includes understanding the contents of others' mental states such as thoughts, desires and goals. This is termed as mindreading ability, something discussed in detail in the next chapter. Second, a highly empathetic person not only understands others' emotions but also share emotions with the observed person. This difference is often referred to by the dichotomy of "cold" and "hot" empathy (Box 8.7).

BOX 8.7 COLD AND HOT EMPATHY

In recent years, the difference between cold and hot empathy has received much attention in the related literature (McIllwain 2003). Cold empathy fundamentally involves cognitive processes: it enables one to recognise someone else's mental state and feelings as well as to understand the deprivation, loss or disappointment leading to their current situation. However, cold empathy does not enable one to share others' emotions. Instead, it is based on a certain kind of perspective taking and attribution of mental states without the resulting emotional experience. Presumably, cold empathy does not necessarily elicit the intention to help the partner; in fact, understanding the partner's thoughts and intentions may equally as well enable one to take advantage of them (Davies & Stone 2003). Cold empathy basically covers the mind-reading ability discussed in detail in the next chapter.

The concept of "hot" empathy is essentially synonymous with the conventional notion of empathy. It refers to the ability to experience the observed individual's emotional state that motivates the observer to help them. The difference between the two types of empathy may be illustrated by two statements. People with high cold empathy agree with the following statement: "I find out easily what others want to talk about." People showing hot empathy identify with the following statement: "I try to emotionally identify with my friends' problems." While cold empathy is not necessarily accompanied by hot empathy, hot empathy could hardly be functional without cold empathy, that is, without the ability to infer others' thoughts and feelings by taking their perspectives. However, experiencing others' emotions and needs requires one to be aware of one's independent individual existence, which implies a different perspective from that of the partner (Keenan 2003). In other words, hot empathy does not mean complete identification or merging with the partner.

It is not by accident that cold and hot empathy scales are relatively weakly correlated (Al Ain et al. 2013). They are likely based on different cognitive processes and different neural structures.

Not surprisingly, Machiavellians usually show a low level of empathic concern. Using various paper and pencil tests, researchers found strong negative correlation between Mach scores and global empathy scores (Ali & Chamorro-Premuzic 2010; Wai & Tiliopoulos 2012; Wastell & Booth 2003b). Moreover, Machiavellianism showed a similar inverse relationship with each of the different components of empathy such as perspective-taking, emotional responsiveness and emotional attunement. This suggests that Machiavellians have difficulty in understanding and especially experiencing others' emotional states as well as identifying with the feelings and thoughts of a person independent of them. At this point, it is worth recalling a Machiavellian characteristic discussed in more detail in previous chapters, namely externally-oriented thinking. This means that Machiavellians are rarely concerned with their internal life, whereas they much more interested in getting valuable things from the external environment (Jonason & Krause 2013). This is closely related to a lack of empathy, since instead of being concerned with the personal aspects of their social relationships, they are concerned with the material benefits that they can take from them.

Considering all this, it is not surprising that Machiavellians' low empathy is accompanied by low willingness to exhibit cooperative or altruistic behaviour. They are not willing to show benevolence to others and are not even willing to cooperate. A study suggests that they show a certain kind of social indifference, impatience towards others, a lack of helpfulness and in some cases even vengefulness (Paal & Bereczkei 2007).

9
MIND READING

Since as early as the beginning of research on Machiavellianism, Machiavellians have been considered as skilled observers of human nature who readily employ their experience and impressions of people to deceive and manipulate them. When the concept of mind reading (theory of mind, mental state attribution) became dominant in cognitive psychology, researchers predicted that Machiavellians would prove excellent mind readers having the ability to infer others' mental states. They would efficiently predict others' thoughts, feelings, intentions, knowledge or lack of knowledge (see Box 9.1).

1. Hypotheses and falsifications

The assumption made that Machiavellians were good mind readers followed directly from the apparently well-grounded hypothesis that manipulation and deception by necessity require one to take the target's mental perspective. Without a well-developed theory of mind, it would hardly be possible to successfully manipulate others and to recognise the targets' weak points, of which sometimes they themselves may be unaware (Paal & Bereczkei 2007). Those who can more easily take on others' points of view and understand their intentions, beliefs and knowledge can more efficiently employ this knowledge to achieve their goals than those having a poorer mind-reading ability. This does not necessarily contradict the phenomenon of emotional detachment discussed previously; it is possible to understand the goals and knowledge of others without identifying with their emotions. In this way, one can assess others' mental states, feelings and thoughts, but this is done in a purely cognitive, rational manner (McIllwain 2003). This may be quite beneficial to Machiavellians since in this way they gain clear insight into others' beliefs, their intentions, and even their entire complicated internal life whereas they themselves

---

BOX 9.1 MIND READING

Studies in recent years have confirmed that in developing an interpersonal relationship one must largely rely on a complex cognitive ability, namely, what is referred to as the "theory of mind" or "mind-reading" ability. The term theory of mind refers to one's ability to attribute to others mental states and contents such as desires, beliefs, intentions and emotions that may be different from one's own mental states. Theory of mind enables people to view others as individuals who have an internal life guiding their behaviour not directly perceptible by the physical senses. Lack of this ability would substantially weaken one's orientation in the social environment, since thus one could then only rely on external physical cues when trying to understand others' behaviour (Perner 1991; Paal & Bereczkei 2007).

Most experts agree that only humans have a fully developed theory of mind, and that it emerged at a relatively late stage of human evolution (Mithen 2000). Its development was crucially shaped by the requirement of adaptation to large, constantly changing human groups. The adaptive benefit of mind-reading ability in such an environment was that it improved individuals' ability to understand and predict others' behaviour. This, in turn, resulted in the development of complex and sophisticated tactics of cooperation and competition with fellow group members. The more accurate and refined an understanding of others' emotions and thoughts our ancestors could gain, the more efficiently they could orient themselves in the complicated world of interpersonal relationships (Dunbar 2002).

This evolutionary development resulted in special abilities to understand the mental states of other people, which seem to be largely independent of other cognitive functions (e.g. intelligence or memory). Brain imaging studies on healthy people as well as on people with brain injury and those with certain mental disorders (e.g. autism) localised these abilities in specific brain areas (Apperly 2011). Among these, one of the most important areas is the medial prefrontal cortex that shows increased activity during handling and taking different mental perspectives. This area is functionally connected to another area (temporo-parietal junction) in the posterior region of the brain, which is involved in the identification of different mental states.

---

do not become depressed or confused by sharing others' emotions. All this is consistent with the conclusion proposed at the end of the previous chapter: researchers distinguish the two types of "cold" and "hot" empathy. While Machiavellians, on the one hand, do not show empathic attunement to others' thoughts and emotions, it is highly probable, on the other hand, that they can easily read and understand these thoughts and emotions.

There have been instances of complete falsifications in science (albeit possibly not as often as would be desirable) when experimental findings clearly contradict the proposed hypotheses. This has been the case as regards the ability of Machiavellians to read minds. Research has found that Machiavellians do not have an above average ability to attribute various mental states to others. In the first related experiment (Paal & Bereczkei 2007), subjects were presented with various stories and then were asked to answer questions concerning the characters' presumable beliefs, goals and thoughts (see Box 9.2). In light of the theoretical predictions, it was a surprising finding that high Mach subjects did not at all perform better in this mind-reading task than their low Mach counterparts. That is, the hypothesis that those more willing to manipulate, deceive and exploit others have a better ability to attribute mental states has not been supported.

BOX 9.2 A NARRATIVE-BASED MEASURE OF
THE THEORY OF MIND

The measurement of adults' mind-reading ability is most often based on narrative comprehension. Subjects listen to or read short stories which present life situations, personal relationships and conflicts differing in complexity. Each story is followed by paired statements, each pair including a true and a false statement, from which subjects select the correct response of the alternatives. The following story is an example (Paal & Bereczkei 2007):

Simon and Andrew had been best friends for years. They had had no disagreement for a long time but everything changed when Andrew began to go out with Melinda. The girl soon became jealous of Simon. She felt that Andrew spent too much time with his friend and talked to him about things that he should in fact have shared with his girlfriend. Simon also felt that Melinda did not like him, and so he tried to spend as little time as possible together with her. One day Simon approached Melinda with a bunch of CDs in his hand and asked her to take them to Andrew. "I'd not ask you but today I can't come over to see Andrew; he didn't come to school either, and I have to deliver these to him urgently," Simon said. "And what makes you think I'll see Andrew today? Anyway, there's not enough room in my bag for so many CDs," Melinda answered. "Sure, of course," Simon replied. When that evening Andrew asked if Simon had sent him a couple of CDs, Melinda said: "No, he didn't. He just came to me and asked if you'd come to school because he should give you a couple of CDs. When I told him I'd take them with pleasure he said he'd rather not leave that to me." Andrew got awfully furious. He said he had always felt that Simon was not pleased about his relationship with Melinda and that maybe it was time to think that friendship over. "Just as you please, Andrew," Melinda said.

1   A)   Simon was Melinda's boyfriend who became jealous of Andrew.
    B)   Andrew was Melinda's boyfriend who became jealous of Simon.

2   A)   Simon felt that Melinda did not sympathise with him.

       B)   Simon felt that Melinda sympathised with him but hid her feelings.

3   A)   Melinda did not like Simon because she felt that Andrew spent too much time with him.

       B)   Melinda did not like Simon because she thought that the boy wanted to estrange Andrew from her.

4   A)   Simon thought Melinda did not want to take the CDs to Andrew because there was not enough room in her bag.

       B)   Simon thought Melinda did not want to take the CDs to Andrew because she hoped to thereby show him in a bad light in front of Andrew.

5   A)   Andrew asked as early as next morning if Simon had sent him a couple of CDs.

       B)   Andrew asked as early as that evening if Simon had sent him a couple of CDs.

6   A)   Andrew suspected that Melinda wanted to set him against Simon.

       B)   Andrew did not suspect that Melinda wanted to set him against Simon.

7   A)   Melinda thought that Andrew thought that Simon was against his relationship with Melinda.

       B)   Melinda thought that Andrew thought that Simon was not against his relationship with Melinda.

Subsequent studies clearly found a negative relationship between Machiavellianism and the mind-reading ability. Results obtained by the most diverse methods invariably show that Machiavellians perform below average in understanding others' mental states. They also show relatively poor performance in narrative comprehension and score low on the "Reading the Mind in the Eyes" test (see Box 9.3) in which subjects presented with pictures of individuals' eye regions have to infer the observed individuals' mental states, feelings or emotions (Lyons, Caldwell, & Schultz 2010; Ali et al. 2009). Likewise, a negative relationship was revealed between Machiavellianism and mind reading by a test in which subjects had to read faces showing neutral, negative or positive emotions (Ali et al. 2009). Moreover, high Machs as opposed to low Machs showed a poorer performance on the Reading the Mind in the Voice Test (RMVT) that requires subjects to identify the emotions of speakers reading out a short unfamiliar text (Ali et al. 2010). They had difficulty even in judging whether the speakers communicated neutral, negative or positive emotions. In light of this, it is not surprising that Machiavellians, as has previously been discussed, showed poor performance on tests measuring emotional intelligence and empathy (Paal & Bereczkei 2017; Ali et al. 2010; Austin et al. 2007; Vonk et al. 2015).

BOX 9.3 THE READING THE MIND IN THE EYES TEST (BARON-COHEN)

The test consists of 34 pictures of the eye region of different individuals' faces. Four adjectives describing different emotions are presented at each corner of each picture. Subjects are asked to select the appropriate emotion which the eyes reflect in each picture.

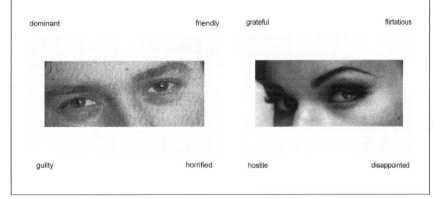

dominant   friendly   grateful   flirtatious

guilty   horrified   hostile   disappointed

2. Adaptive deficits

The big question, then, is how one showing below average ability to recognise others' knowledge, goals and emotional states can successfully manipulate people. This is a difficult question, and it has not yet been decisively answered. One possible answer is that the measures conducted so far provide a valid and accurate picture of individual differences; that is, Machiavellians actually show deficits in a wide area of social cognition. If that is the case, then one may argue – making a virtue of necessity – that such deficits may in fact serve manipulation and deception, similarly to the way in which difficulties in expressing emotions may help them carry out their schemes (see Chapter 7). Specifically, if they cannot understand the causes of others' pain, then their manipulative ambitions will not be substantially affected by bad feelings or an ill conscience.

However, there is a serious problem with this idea, namely, that the disadvantages of social incompetence stemming from a poor mind-reading ability most probably exceed the potential advantages of this mental blindness. That is, one's lack of guilt does not help when one is unable to understand others; in such a case, attempts at manipulation will probably fail. A poor mind-reading ability may prevent successful manipulation before emotional blindness could eliminate moral inhibitions.

3. New methods: narratives of manipulation

Another possible explanation for the negative relationship between Machiavellianism and mind reading suggests that the mind reading tests currently in use are far from being perfect: they are not capable of tapping individual differences in responses to subtle cues of social behaviour. It is possible that Machiavellians can appropriately interpret the emotions and thoughts of others in certain social situations and attitudes, primarily in those required for manipulation. In a recent experiment, subjects had to undersand stories in the same way as in previous studies discussed above. In this case, however, the stories were presented in two different forms. One group of them included "conventional" stories of the same type as presented in Box 9.2. These may be called "narrative stories", since each story describes an event from a narrator's perspective. The authors pointed out that the problem with this kind of stories, among others, is that they contain several mentalisation terms (e.g. "Melinda *felt* that Andrew spent too much time with his friend"). Such mental state attributions in the narratives may interfere with the subjects' own interpretations and thereby disturb the comprehension of the story.

For that reason, the authors devised another type of stories that do not contain descriptions of the characters' thoughts and desires (Szabo, Jones, & Bereczkei under publication). With the exception of short descriptions of scenes and characters, such stories only contain dialogues. The narrative unfolds through these dialogues, played by amateur actors and presented as sound recordings. Dialogues inform subjects about what characters say and do without a narrator suggesting how to interpret their behaviour. Such so-called "dialogical stories" well reflect everyday interactions in which partners communicate with each other and tend to infer each others' feelings and thoughts.

Finally, the third group of stories comprises so-called "manipulative-tactical" accounts. These are also presented in a dialogical form but an element unique to them and so not found in dialogical accounts is a salient and deliberate deceptive tactic. Such tactics include, for example, flattery, the principle of "the best defense is a good offense", playing the victim, and the most diverse ways of cheating, an example of which is presented in Box 9.4. The dialogical and manipulative-tactical stories are also followed by paired statements, from which subjects select the correct response alternative.

The experiment yielded several interesting results. It was revealed that subjects made many fewer mistakes (i.e. much more frequently selected the correct response alternatives from paired statements) when interpreting dialogical accounts than when presented with narrative accounts. This is probably because dialogues realistically model everyday social interactions, which provide well interpretable and familiar cues for mind reading.

As regards the current subject specifically, a negative relationship was found between Machiavellianism and the ability to understand narrative stories. This is not a surprising finding in the light of results obtained in previous studies that had also used the same type of stories. Furthermore, no significant relationship was found between Mach scores and the number of correct answers given to dialogical stories. However, a positive relationship was measured between Machiavellianism and mind-reading performance in the manipulative-tactical accounts: high Machs made fewer mistakes than low Machs in such tasks. This suggests that Machiavellians show a remarkable sensitivity to social cues indicating situations and interpersonal

---

BOX 9.4 MANIPULATIVE-TACTICAL NARRATIVES

(*Displayed on a screen*) In a clothing store, the shop assistant and the shop-keeper are talking quietly, turning their back to the entrance. The entrance door opens and a fine melodious chime heralds the arrival of a customer. Both turn back at once, then the shop assistant comes to see the customer while the shopkeeper disappears into the stockroom at the back of the store.

(*Sound clip*) **Shop assistant**: Good morning! Can I help you?

Customer: Good morning! There are beautiful coats in the shop-window. I'd take a closer look at them. I'm looking for an elegant cloth coat which is also suitable as casual wear.

Shop assistant: A coat? Pardon me, my hearing is a bit . . . impaired.

Customer: Yes, a coat. (*Shouting*:) A c-l-o-t-h c-o-a-t!

Shop assistant: This way then, please. Here we have the cloth coats.

The customer is perusing and trying on the coats while the shop assistant is eagerly praising them. The customer turns back and forth among the coats for a long time, then finally starts to look for the price tag on the coat he tried last. He finds the tag but it only shows general information without the price. He turns to the shop assistant.

Customer: I can't find the price. How much does this coat cost?

Shop assistant: Pa . . . pardon? Speak a bit louder, please.

Customer: There's no price shown on the coat. H-o-w m-u-c-h d-o-e-s i-t c-o-s-t?

The shop assistant *turns toward the stockroom*: Lizzie! How much does this coat cost?

The shopkeeper *sticks out her head from the stockroom*: That beautiful cashmere coat? Six hundred fifty.

The shop assistant *cupping hands behind his ears*: How much?

Shopkeeper: S-i-x-h-u-n-d-r-e-d f-i-f-t-y.

The shop assistant *turns to the customer*: She says it's 350.

Customer: All right, I'll buy it.

Both move forward to the counter, the customer pays down 32,000 forints and leaves with the coat. As soon as the entrance door is closed, the shopkeeper comes out of the stockroom and pats the shop assistant on the back with a smile on her face.

Shopkeeper: Today we got a good deal again . . .

---

relationships that imply ample opportunity to deceive and exploit others. This finding, in turn, apparently supports the formerly assumed close relationship between mind reading and manipulation: those who are more successful in understanding others' intentions can also more effectively utilise this ability to reach their own goals. It seems that Machiavellians in fact recognise very accurately when others (characters in the stories in the study) manipulate or are being manipulated. This sensitivity possibly originates in their past experience. More specifically, it is highly probable that one who is willing to use various deceptive tactics in one's own life also recognises them easily when used by others. Answering the original question raised above, there is probably a specific aspect of mind reading in which Machiavellians are more successful than others.

In sum, it is possible that Machiavellians are in general average or poor mind readers, whereas they show above-average cognitive abilities in situations offering the opportunity to manipulate others. This conclusion is consistent with the findings of previously discussed studies which have revealed that although Machiavellians exhibit low emotional intelligence, they show excellent performance on the so-called Emotional Manipulation Scale (see Box 8.3 in Chapter 8). Therefore, while Machiavellians generally show deficits in mind reading and emotional intelligence, they may have superior abilities to employ emotional and cognitive manipulation when the situation allows deceptive tactics and provides the prospect of profit. This conclusion points to another one which is discussed in detail in the next chapter: Machiavellians flexibly adapt their behaviour to, and optimise their profits in, the situations they face.

4. Types of mind reading

Some authors propose a theoretical framework which is closely related to the issues discussed above while at the same time placing them in a broader theoretical perspective. Namely, these authors distinguish between the so-called idiographic and nomothetic forms of the theory of mind (McIllwain 2003; Paál 2011). The concept of idiographic mind reading focuses on individual differences and refers to one's ability to infer and predict another person's current mental state. This covers the concept of the theory of mind in its classic sense, and this is the subject of most related studies. Much less scientific attention is devoted to nomothetic mind reading despite its being an important mental operation presumably often used in everyday life. Nomothetic mind reading is not aimed at revealing the observed individual's specific mental states but is an attempt at categorising the individual into a general "type" based on previous experience. The observer is not concerned with the particular partner's current knowledge, thoughts and desires but with the ways similar people in similar situations usually think and act. It is possible that Machiavellians take a nomothetic view when inferring others' motives and expectable actions. Thus, they use their previous experience collected since childhood to generate types that they apply to new situations in order to make decisions on the possible forms and outcomes of manipulation.

A good example of Machiavellians' generalising and categorising ability is provided by an experiment of Philip Zimbardo and colleagues (1970) in which each subject solved various tasks with a partner. As shown in Chapter 2, confederates (informed persons) tried to persuade subjects to cheat. Machiavellians resisted temptation when their partner was previously depreciated by the experimenters. By contrast, many more Machiavellian subjects agreed to cheat when they were told that their partner was a popular and intelligent person. This difference suggests that in a low-dissonance condition (where a high-prestige person initiated the deception of the exprimenter), subjects had good justification for accepting cheating. The authors concluded that Machiavellians' decision whether or not to cheat was most influenced by the cognitive labels used to describe their partner. That is, their decision was not guided either by moral considerations or by the partner's behaviour but by their impression of the partner formed prior to personal contact. Low Machs, by contrast, did not show sensitivity to such labels. Their decision on cheating was primarily influenced by their feelings towards, and impressions of, the partner which developed in the face-to-face interaction between them.

In sum, the experiment revealed that high Machs' future behaviour was primarily guided by their general judgment of the partner (as suggested by the experimenter). In everyday situations, of course, such labels develop in continuous interaction with the social environment during socialisation and personality development. Machiavellians rely on their general impression of the potential target as well as on the specific situation when deciding to what extent they will rely on a deceptive strategy. On the basis of their previous experiences they also shape an opinion on whether the potential target is an appropriate person to be manipulated. Some people are easy to persuade because they lack self-confidence. Some are susceptible to being set against others since they are generally distrustful of people. Some are found to have a skeleton in the closet, thus their guilt can be used to compel them to do something that essentially serves the manipulator's interest. Machiavellians make use of the potential target's weak points – as is discussed below.

5. The target's vulnerability

It clearly seems that people are often exposed to the danger of manipulation by their own weakness and vulnerability. As Doris McIllwain (2003) pointed out, one could hardly conceive how crucial a role human weakness plays in victimisation. We foster several illusions and false beliefs about ourselves which may deprive us of the ability to defend ourselves. We believe ourselves to be better than we really are, judge our attitudes and ambitions more favourably than is actually reflected in our behaviour, and we often explain our actions by giving reasons different from their real purposes. Moreover, several human qualities may be added to the list that help others successfully manipulate us: fear, guilt, vanity, supertitiousness, wishful thinking and so on. In certain situations, such self-deceptions and frailties make us vulnerable to manipulation (McIllwain 2003). Machiavellians efficiently make use of such opportunities inasfar as they know by experience how people "work" as opposed to people holding common views on this subject.

One strategy they use to achieve their goals is to create mental states in people who can then be manipulated successfully. An example of this strategy is guilt induction, which Machiavellians efficiently use to exploit others (Vangelisti, Daly, & Rudnick 1991). It includes tactics such as "reminding others what obligations they have in a relationship", "referring to the partner's responsibility in a situation", "enumerating past actions one undertook to help the partner ", and so on. While, of course, many people resort to guilt induction either consciously or unconsciously, Machiavellians frequently and readily exploit this psychological effect. They are more likely than others to agree with statements such as "When I'm angry at someone or hurt by them I often respond by trying to make them feel guilty", or "I can easily make others feel guilty".

That is, in accordance with the above, Machiavellians are able to understand and strategically exploit human qualities that make their target potentially vulnerable. This does not necessarily require them to infer the target's specific and current mental states but it does require the ability to elicit cognitive or emotional cues related to the target's behaviour and thought that serve their goals in a specific situation. Machiavellians frequently choose their target purposefully: for example, they try to manipulate those whom they judge to be willing to cooperate and to have concern for others (see Chapter 11). Their choice is based on the view that such people embody the type of dupe who is relatively easily exploited.

6. Spontaneous mentalisation

Based on diverse experimental findings, we have so far pointed out that Machiavellians show above average performance in certain forms or components of mind reading (nomothetic mind reading, guilt induction, emotional manipulation etc.). Another issue ignored so far concerns *motivation* rather than ability. Specifically, do Machiavellians positively strive to understand others? Is it possible that their interest in successful manipulation provides them with unusually strong motivation to predict others' behaviour? In a study, the researchers used a collection of twelve pictures as the stimulus material and asked subjects to describe each picture freely, mentioning everything that came into their mind. The study was aimed at revealing what subjects would pay more attention to in the pictures presenting everyday situations: whether they focus on the situations themselves and the objective circumstances or on the possible thoughts and emotions of the people in the picture. The authors assumed that the setting enabled subjects to spontaneously use their mind-reading ability, which would be reflected in their responses given to the pictures. They termed this phenomenon "spontaneous mentalisation" and defined it as the disposition or motivation to conceive others' mental states by taking their perspectives.

The results revealed essential individual differences in such dispositional mind reading: subjects showed substantial differences in whether and how frequently they used mentalisation terms referring to the supposed thoughts, feelings and intentions of the people in the pictures (see Box 9.5). Importantly, a marked difference was found between low and high Machs in this regard. The latter gave significantly more spontaneous descriptions of the presented people's mental states than the former. This finding was not affected by the size of the texts written by the subjects. According to the authors, the finding shows that Machiavellians are more motivated than others to assess others' mental states, even though they do not show a better mind-reading ability in general. Machiavellians seem to be strongly inclined to take others' mental perspectives, and such spontaneous willingness possibly increases their chance to deceive and exploit others in certain situations. In accordance with the idea of nomothetic mind reading, it is possible that this motivation focuses on the understanding of others as a representative of a character or personality type.

BOX 9.5 SPONTANEOUS MIND READING

Subjects were presented with pictures such as the examples below:

They were asked to write down what the pictures made them think of, that is, no restriction was applied to the contents of their responses. The resulting written accounts were transcribed into digital texts, which were then analysed by means of a software specifically designed to conduct psychological content analysis.

The texts were coded for words referring to the presented people's perception, emotions and thoughts, such as those in the examples below:

Focus on perception: "two kids are each peeping through a hole"; "the little child is watching a blazing fire"; "a man is watching the landscape"; "a boy is passing by a girl without looking at her".

Focus on emotions: "there is no particular sign of happiness"; "the little boy looks lonely"; "it is clear she is not pleased"; "I fancy I can see a worried girl"; "the little boy is standing timidly".

Focus on thoughts: "pondering people"; "the man in the picture is also meditating on this"; "she is staring at the landscape and is thinking"; "she cannot think of anything else"; "he is walking broodingly".

Finally, the below examples are four responses given by four different subjects to the same picture. The first two responses do not contain any spontaneous mentalisations while the other two do.

1 "There is a train in the picture with a girl standing in it. She is leaning out of the window. It is a black-and-white picture."

2 "Travelling is important to everyone. The condition of trains in our country is not really suitable for travelling. Still, many use this means of transport."

3 "A careless moment before departure. The girl is travelling far away but not into the unknown. She knows whatever awaits her at the end of the journey, it will be something new and interesting. She casually thinks, for the last time, of all she is leaving behind."

4 "A lady is travelling far away from her loved ones. She is staring in front of her with glassy eyes. Leaving makes her sad."

10
FLEXIBILITY

Hopefully, the previous chapters have made it clear that Machiavellians are not characterised by rigid thought patterns; they do not act according to some pre-existing schema, to which they would adhere at any price. Research findings reported in the past few years have clearly shown that the uniqueness of the Machiavellian character lies in tactical skills and flexible decision-making. Under certain circumstances they are motivated by momentary inspirations and improvisation, but Machiavellians are first of all strategists who efficiently adapt to changing circumstances. Long-term strategic planning is perhaps their most important characteristic, which at the same time distinguishes them from the other two members of the Dark Triad, that is, from psychopaths and narcissists.

1. Rational decisions

As early as 40 or 50 years ago, social psychological experiments conducted by Richard Christie and his colleagues revealed that in comparison with others, Machiavellians showed better performance in a number of tasks requiring versatile problem-solving skills. In one such experiment, subjects played a game in groups of three (called the "Con Game"), in which three players were seated around a game board (Geis 1978). A player could advance on the board simply by forming a coalition with an opponent. Players were required to make deals with each other. Deals could primarily be made through persuasive verbal communication in which players could make propositions regarding when and with whom they wished to form alliances and how they wanted to share profits. The winners were those who were most successful in getting others to cooperate, that is, those who talked one or the other of their two opponents into forming a coalition. In return, they agreed to give the partner a little more of the prize at the end of the game – at their own expense. The game was played in either of two bargaining conditions. In the "ambiguous" condition, players "conventionally" showed the back of their cards to their partners so that they could not see their value. In the "unambiguous" condition, players laid their cards face up on the table. Machiavellian players were significantly more successful than others in the ambiguous condition in which players could not see each other's cards. This is because in the course of the game they were efficient at persuading one of their partners to ally with them rather than with the third party. To that end, they frequently offered money to their partner from their winnings.

An alternative version of the experiment was also conducted: here the experimenters controlled the distribution of the cards so that each player only had cards of low, medium or high value in their hand (Geis 1978). The seemingly successful tactic for players with cards of low value was to offer their potential ally a relatively large sum from their prospective profits while making do with smaller sums offered by their partners. According to the majority, this was their only chance to form an alliance with either partner. In this case too, however, Machiavellians followed a different strategy. Even in a weak position, when they had low cards in their hand, they offered and claimed sums as large as those negotiated when they had medium- or high-value cards. They seemed to be confident that they would be able to convince their partners and control the situation. Indeed, they behaved as dominant members of the groups, and others somehow viewed them as the best coalition partners worth allying with. Accordingly, Machiavellians frequently rejected the offers of players with low-value cards and turned their attention to players in a better position, evidently hoping to form a stronger alliance.

The authors concluded from these findings that high Machs treated the situation rationally, in a cognitive perspective, whereas low Machs were rather guided by their emotions. The former gave more consideration to situational demands and efficiently exploited the rules – without violating them. The latter also knew the rules well but they chose rather to follow their feelings. All this is consistent with observations on the individual differences in emotional intelligence and emotional coldness discussed in the previous chapters. However, the authors themselves point out that there is much more than simple emotional detachment involved. They suggest that Machiavellians have above average social skills. Indeed, they are better understood if it is considered that they take the initiative and skillfully handle social relationships than if it is merely pointed out that they lack a sense of morality or that they are emotionally uninvolved.

In another social psychological study, subjects were asked to imagine they were owners of a relatively small company (Grams & Rogers 1990). The company had an urgent need for oil in order to continue operation. One version of the experiment modelled a dramatic situation: economic collapse could only be prevented by an emergency fuel purchase at any price (high motivation condition). In another version, the crisis was not insurmountable, but the company would have no prospects for development without further energy supplies (moderate motivation condition). Subjects were informed that their partner, who in fact was the experimenters' confederate (subjects, of course, were unaware of this), would represent the interests of the oil company. Subjects were also told that the oil company had a very strict business policy and frequently had refused to do business with their company in the past. The company owners played by the subjects were told that their job was to get the other person to supply them with the required amount of oil. To that end, they could resort to various tactics that they considered necessary for achieving their goal (see details in Box 10.1).

The study found that Machiavellians, that is, those scoring high on the Mach scale prior to the experiment, preferred first non-rational tactics to rational ones as well as indirect to direct tactics. For example, they often resorted to deceptive tactics and tried to plant their ideas in the minds of their target. They also often appealed to emotions, when trying to elicit compassion, responsibility or "humane" feelings from the partner. The most interesting finding, however, was that high Machs adapted more flexibly to the changing situation than did low Machs. When the situation was aggravated and there was a vital need for oil (high motivation

---

BOX 10.1 INFLUENCE TACTICS

- *Rational tactics:*
    - Compromise: Both parties give up part of their desired goals to obtain some of them.
    - Bargaining: Offering to reciprocate favours or make two-way exchanges.
    - Reason: Use of logic or rational arguments.
- *Non-rational tactics:*
    - Deceit: Attempting to trick the target into compliance by using lies.
    - Emotion-Target: Influencer tries to flatter target or put him or her in a good mood.
    - Thought manipulation: Making the target think that the influencer's way is the target's own idea.
- *Direct tactics:*
    - Reward: Stating that positive consequences will occur if the target agrees.
    - Threat: Stating that negative consequences will occur if the target does not agree.
    - Assertion: Voicing one's wishes loudly or forcefully.
- *Indirect tactics:*
    - Hinting: Attempting influence without openly stating what one wants; subtle attempts to bring up the point.
    - Emotion-Agent: Influencer tries to make him or herself appear sincere and kind.
    - Expertise: Claiming to have superior knowledge or experience.

condition), Machiavellians tried out several different tactics. As conditions worsened, they increasingly frequently resorted to rational tactics, which resulted in decisions that were profitable in the long run. Such tactics were expensive (since the oil company had to be paid) but at the same time could ensure the deal. For example, one subject made the following proposal: "If you fulfil my request, you will come off very well. Think logically. You will make a lot of money with the business and you have my appreciation. There is no way you can lose."

2. Pretended altruism

Subsequent studies have confirmed and further elaborated the conclusions of social psychological studies conducted in the past decades. Wilson, Near, and Miller (1996) explain Machiavellians' flexible behaviour by considering Machiavellianism as a "master strategy" that includes both deceptive and cooperative tactics. They argue that a central regulatory system controls both selfish and unselfish subsystems and judges which of them is more expedient in any given situation. Apart from the difficulty with theoretical modelling, let alone empirical verification of such an omniscient central regulatory system, the idea is very much worth considering. It is because Machiavellians seem to be actually able to shift from one strategy to the other when their interests so require. They adapt to the changing challenges in their social environment by continuously changing their behaviour.

In a real-life study, the researchers examined the conditions under which university students would be inclined to volunteer for charity work (Bereczkei, Birkas, & Kerekes 2010) (Box 10.2). The study revealed that 40% of the students were willing to help strangers in need (old people, homeless people, mentally disordered children, etc.). This is not a surprising finding, nor is it a surprise that Machiavellians showed much lower willingness to perform charitable activities. It was also revealed, however, that they behaved in different ways in different situations. When other group members did not know of their decision (anonymous condition), very few Machiavellians were willing to offer charity work. By contrast, when offers were made in front of the group, three times as many Machiavellians volunteered as those in the anonymous condition. The authors suggest that this finding reflects "pretended altruism" aimed at making a good impression on others and maintaining influence within the group. In consistence with this explanation, results of a sociometric questionnaire administered both before and after the experiments show that sympathy for individuals appearing to be altruistic generally increased in the group. Such individuals were judged to be more reliable and friendly than previously. However, pretended altruism was unnecessary when group members had no knowledge of each other's decision. In that case, Machiavellians "showed their true colours"; that is, they did not join the charitable initiative.

This result is consistent with research findings suggesting that Machiavellians in the long term try to avoid being exposed. When they have to face the possibility that their deceptive and manipulative behaviour may negatively affect their

BOX 10.2 VOLUNTEERING, REPUTATION, MACHIAVELLIANISM

The experimenters visited students at a seminar where they administered several personality tests, sociometric and other questionnaires without informing the students about the aim of the study. About one month later, the authors invited a representative of a real operating charitable organisation to visit the seminar groups involved in the study and to invite them to support people in need on a voluntary basis. The representative distributed sheets in the group that listed seven target groups associated with the respective forms of support. The list included, among others, organising a one-day blood donation program, charitable fundraising, cleaning up a retirement home, supporting children with intellectual disabilities, etc. Subjects could choose one or more of the listed charitable activities targeted at different groups. Each action involved one single occasion of about 6 hours' duration. Besides selecting their preferred action, the students were also asked to choose the date and time when they wanted to carry out the action. For that reason, they maintained phone contact with the representative of the charitable organisation.

However, charitable offers were made under different conditions in different seminar groups. Seminar groups were divided into two sets. In some groups, offers were made in the presence of the group members who, however, did not know of each other's offers (anonymous group). After the representative of the charitable organisation informed the students about the conditions of voluntary work, each student used the previously received sheet to indicate what kind of support, to whom and when they wanted to give it. In the other set of groups, offers were made openly, in such a way that each prospective volunteer loudly declared their undertaking in front of other group members (public group). The declared offers and the planned conditions of their accomplishment were recorded by the representative of the charitable organisation. At the last stage of the experiment, the representative contacted the students by phone to agree upon the date and time of the action.

A sociometric questionnaire was administered both in the initial and final stages of the experiment, which assessed sympathy-based relationships in the group as well as group members' views on each other. This measure includes questions such as whom the respondent would prefer to make friends with, whom they regard as the most popular in the group, or whom they would have asked for help in hardship. Differences between the results of the two sociometric measures could reveal whether the charitable action improves the judgment and reputation of a group member within the group.

reputation in the group, they choose to keep themselves from direct cheating, and even begin to play the altruist. At other times, they choose to cooperate in order to avoid punishment – which is discussed below.

3. Punishment

In a Swiss study subjects played the Trust game (see Box 2.1 in Chapter 2) in which the subjects were not informed that the first player was a computer (Spitzer et al. 2007). They had to decide what portion they would return from the sum they had received from the "first player" (after this had been doubled by the experimenter). This procedure lasted for five rounds, as a result of which various sums accumulated in the players' accounts. Beginning from the sixth round, the experimenters informed subjects that they would allow the first player (i.e. the computer) to punish the second player if that player returned an unfairly small portion of the sum they received. Specifically, the computer was programmed in such a way that it withdrew a certain sum from the second player's account after she or he had made an unfair offer. The smaller the amount the second player offered, the larger sum the computer withdrew.

The results revealed that high Mach players had earned substantially more money than had low Machs by the end of the game. They did so because they had employed a dual strategy. At the first, non-punitive stage of the game, they returned relatively small sums to the first player, thereby accumulating a larger amount in their accounts than had the others. At the second, punitive stage of the game, however, they strove to keep their gains by increasing the offered sums in order to avoid punishment or at least severe punishment. This combination of selfishness and opportunism made Machiavellians successful in terms of financial reward.

These findings may lead to several conclusions. One is that Machiavellians were able to successfully adapt to the changing circumstances by making flexible decisions. The other conclusion is that they are highly sensitive to the threat posed by possible punishment. Anticipated punishment and subsequent actual sanctions signaled to them that they would lose their money if they continued to follow their selfish tactics. Presumably, this is another example of pretended norm fulfilment since their apparent efforts to obey the norm of reciprocity clearly reflects their pursuit of self-interest.

However, this is not where the experiment ended. Using an fMRI brain imaging technique (see Box 2.2 in Chapter 2), the researchers attempted to reveal the neural processes underlying Machiavellians' decisions. The experimental procedure was the same as that described above except that the subjects lay in the MR equipment throughout the game. They could see each offer made by their partner (the computer), and they could use buttons placed in their hands to set the amount they wanted to offer in return. Meanwhile, the MR equipment measured changes in brain activity during decision-making. The experiment found that Mach scores were positively correlated with brain activations in the left anterior orbitofrontal cortex (OCF); the higher the Mach scores were, the larger the increase in activity that the mentioned brain area showed. It had been known from previous studies that the OFC is involved, among other things, in processing and evaluating cues of punishment and reward (Kringelbach 2005). At the same time, it has an important role in behavioural responses to unpredictable situations. A social dilemma situation such as the Trust game precisely represents the kind of task that involves fundamental uncertainty since the partner's response may not be foreseen. This suggests that Machiavellians' increased sensitivity to cues of punishment also manifests itself in the underlying neural processes, especially in situations whose outcome is uncertain.

Machiavellians also showed increased activity in the right insula. This is interesting because the insula has long been known for its important role in processing negative emotions such as anger, fear, pain and sadness (Rilling et al. 2008). It is possible that punishment elicited more intense negative emotions in Machiavellians as compared to others, which in turn had an effect on their behavioural responses. More specifically, Machiavellians were likely to be afraid of retaliation, that is, of the material loss they might suffer if they transferred too small an amount of money to the partner. In turn, this apprehensive reaction could make them sensitive to punishment, which they then tried to evade by increasing their offers.

There is moreover another interesting finding obtained in this experiment. The researchers not only applied the "social" form of punishment (as mentioned above) but also a non-social form. Non-social punishment was applied in such a way that subjects were informed that their partner's responses were generated by a computer and were not given by a real person. In this case, no increased activity was found in the insula, which suggests that the circumstances of punishment strongly influence changes in neural activity. Generally speaking, the characteristics of Machiavellian thought are related to brain areas involved in the regulation of social relationships. This will be discussed in detail later.

4. Adaptation to the social environment

Machiavellians not only consider the possible consequences of external punishment when changing their behaviour. They also take interpersonal relationships into account They take into consideration the composition of the group, how individual group members behave during interactions and what processes operate within the group.

In an experiment (Bereczkei & Czibor 2014), subjects played the Public Goods Game (Box 10.3). During five rounds, all players were allowed to decide how much they would contribute to the public pool and how much they would keep for themselves. No punishment was allowed. All players knew of the others' decisions in each round. The aim of the study was to reveal whether any player's behaviour would be influenced by the altruistic or selfish behaviour of the other three players. An altruistic player was a subject who transferred at least 80% of their private funds to the group's account. A selfish player was defined as one who contributed 20% or less to the group's account. The study found that high and low Machs showed different styles of play. The decisions of the former were largely influenced by the presence and number of altruists in the group. By contrast, low Machs' decisions were primarily influenced by personality factors and not so much by the presence of altruists. This suggests that the behaviour of Machiavellians is primarily influenced by situational factors, as they are likely to adjust their decisions to the composition of the group.

BOX 10.3 THE PUBLIC GOODS GAME

Similarly to other experimental games (see Box 2.1 in Chapter 2), players are usually seated in separate rooms, each player in front of a computer, the computers being connected to one another. Each player uses a keyboard to enter the sum they offer, which is also displayed on the other players' screens. The contributing player is only identified by a pseudonym or number displayed beside the offered sum. The experimenter monitors all moves in front of a central computer. The screens display either real currencies or points that are subsequently converted to real money. In both cases, players actually receive and take home the sum of money that they win in the game.

The Public Goods Game comprises several rounds – usually ten. Subjects are informed in advance of the number of rounds and a few other conditions of the game. The game usually involves four or five subjects, all of whom starts the game with equal sums in their private accounts. The players decide in each round what proportion of their funds they will contribute to the public pool. The offered sums are added to the group's account while the remaining funds are kept in the players' private accounts. At the end of each round, the experimenter increases (e.g. doubles) the total amount contributed to the group's account and *returns equal sums* to all players. Thus, for example, if five players start with 1,000 tokens each, and they contribute, for example, 300, 400, 500, 600, and 700 tokens to the public pool, the total contribution will be 2,500 tokens. Then (after doubling this sum), each player receives 1,000 tokens at the end of the round, which are added to their private funds kept after their public contributions. Then the second round begins, in which all players decide again on the sum they offer, and so on. At the end of the game, each player receives the amount of money accumulated in their private accounts.

The sums contributed to the public pool practically indicate the degree of cooperation. The social dilemma lies in that individual interests often come into conflict with the common interest of the group. Under the given conditions (rules) of the game, the players' personalities and motivations determine what decisions they make in the successive rounds.

The option of punishment may also be included in the conditions of the public goods game. In such a case, players are allowed at the end of certain rounds to impose a fine on those whom they judge to be defectors according to their previous play.

It is worth noting that Machiavellians, on average, contribute less to the public pool (group account) than others. This was also the case in the presented study, and the researchers expected with good reason that Machiavellians' profiteering ambitions would be further heightened by the presence of altruists, whom they consider dupes. However, this is not what happened: when Machiavellians saw on the screen that one or more altruists were playing in the group, they also increased their contributions. Seemingly, this is not a rational decision since thereby they keep less in their private account. Machiavellians might calculate that if they contributed small amounts to the group account, altruists might easily change their minds and reduce their public contributions, which would have been an unfavourable turn of events for Machiavellians. They could think it would have been a mistake to lose out on the contributions of those who offered 80% of their private funds. This is yet another example of pretended altruism, for unselfish behaviour served to increase private gains in this case as well. Indeed, the results confirmed the expectation: Machiavellians earned larger sums at the end of the five rounds than did others.

As opposed to altruists, the presence of defectors (selfish players who contributed 20% or less of their funds to the group's account) influenced the behaviour of both low and high Machs. Both groups substantially reduced their contributions in the presence of defectors. The reason for this is that defectors pose a serious danger to all players since they make money from the others' public contributions. Therefore, defection in most cases elicits counteraction and, in a way, provides justification for other players, even for altruists, to shift away from their initial cooperative attitude to a selfish strategy. This is especially true when there is no external punishment to restrain defection. In such a case, there is no other option than to withdraw cooperation.

5. The protean character

The findings presented so far fundamentally question the formerly reiterated assumption that Machiavellians are only successful in the short term. Several authors have suggested that the underlying factors of Machiavellians' success are their highly reward-driven behaviour and their simultaneous disregard for possible long-term costs and risks (Wilson, Near, & Miller 1996). In other words, they act according to the principle of the "first strike": they immediately take advantage of their target's weakness while being unconcerned with the negative consequences their actions have for them in the long run. This is in part true, of course; it was previously discussed that Machiavellians frequently focus on immediate rewards and disregard future risks and others' expectations (see Chapter 2). Obviously, such behaviour has its price: among other things, they lose their money and fail in social relationships in the long term, face punitive sanctions or become socially isolated.

All things considered, however, Machiavellians are not short-term strategists. They act in more sophisticated ways. They assess possible advantages and disadvantages in every situation and make decisions optimal in terms of benefits. Immediate gain is the most profitable in some cases while long-term planning is expedient in others. The previous chapters have provided several examples of situations in which Machiavellians adjusted their decisions to the behaviour of others, alternating between selfish and unselfish tactics. For this reason, Machiavellians may also be referred to, using a conventional term, as opportunists: they switch between behavioural tactics as the situation requires and present themselves in a way that best meets their self-interest.

Peter Jonason and Gregory Webster (2012) describe this attitude as a protean character. Proteus is a well-known figure from Greek mythology; he is able to constantly transform his appearance, adopting the shape of a lion, a snake, a bull, or a bird and then transforming into fire, water or a tree whenever he wants to avoid being compelled to foretell the future to others. Regarding Machiavellians, their protean nature lies in that they do not adhere to one single strategy, even if it has proved reliable, and thereby they can avoid detection. Accordingly, the authors have found that Machiavellians use a wide variety of manipulative strategies, which they often change as circumstances require (Box 10.4). The authors have concluded from the results that social influence tactics provide a versatile and diverse set of manipulative means. If one tactic fails, the next one will work. What matters is that one should always find an effective course of action that yields benefits.

Choosing the most fruitful influence tactic in a given social environment is a crucial step towards success. However, deploying a diverse set of manipulative tactics has another advantage for cheaters: they may be able to avoid detection. Changing strategies from situation to situation generates unpredictable conditions, making detection difficult. Machiavellians do not rely on one single strategy but continuously create new faces and new behaviours that are likely to reduce to the likelihood of others predicting their behaviour. This, in turn, enables them to avoid detection even in recurrent, lasting situations where Machiavellians seem familiar to others.

BOX 10.4 PROTEAN TACTICS (JONASON & WEBSTER 2012)

In the experiment, subjects with different scores on Machiavellianism (as well as on narcissism and psychopathy) were asked to report how frequently they used certain tactics in order to achieve success in social interactions. Machiavellianism was closely correlated with charm, playing hardball, striving for monetary reward, debasement, self-serving social comparisons, seduction and coercion. Subjects were then asked what types of tactics they used when attempting to get help from four different types of individuals such as family members, opposite-sex friends, same-sex friends or strangers. Mach scores were closely correlated with almost all forms of social influence in all four social categories: coercion, responsibility invocation, reason, pleasure induction, debasement, charm. Finally, subjects were asked to select one strategy that they judged particularly efficient in social relationships such as coalition formation, self-protection, status seeking, mate-acquisition/retention. Machiavellians primarily used charm to build coalitions among same-sex friends; they reported high willingness to employ affability, a pleasing demeanour and a charming tone towards their friends.

In summary, this chapter might reveal that Machiavellianism is related to strategic thinking and flexible long-term planning rather than to a short-term perspective and risk taking. This Machiavellian ability is particularly outstanding when compared to psychopathy. People with a high level of psychopathy are usually extremely inflexible. In an experiment, subjects played a gambling game that involved high risk of loss but where players were allowed to quit at any time. Despite these conditions, psychopaths continued playing persistently and lost everything (Jones 2014). Machiavellians, by contrast, did not take unnecessary risks but rather chose to restrain themselves and thus profited from the game.

BOX 10.5 FLEXIBLE SEXUAL BEHAVIOUR

The strategic thinking and flexible lifestyle of Machiavellians is also reflected in their sexual behaviour. Recent studies that primarily approach this phenomenon from the comprehensive theoretical perspective of the Dark Triad (embracing psychopathy, narcissism and Machiavellianism) confirm the earlier research finding that Machiavellians prefer short-term relationships (see Box 1.5 in Chapter 1). At the same time, these studies also refine the picture. They have revealed that Machiavellians by no means refuse to enter into long-term relationships as strongly as the other two members of the Dark Triad do (Jonason, Luevano, & Adams 2012). It has also been found that Machiavellians are not concerned with the specific form of casual relationships. Those with high psychopathy find the most pleasure in instant sex with a booty-call partner, who phones them with the expressed or implied purpose of sex. Besides this form of relationship, narcissists also have a preference for regular sexual contacts with a "friend" of the opposite sex without being involved in a romantic relationship. Machiavellians have no preference for any specific form of casual relationships, which is completely consistent with their opportunistic thinking, that is, with their choosing the form of intimate partner relationship that best meets their current individual interest.

All three members of the Dark Triad show high willingness to lie to their partner in an intimate relationship. A difference between psychopaths and Machiavellians is that the former enjoy lying (i.e. report positive emotions after the act of lying) whereas the latter purposefully devise their lies (Baughman et al. 2014). Machiavellians' responses show that they focus on tactics and impression management rather than on emotions when trying to captivate a member of the opposite sex. In general, their behaviour is based on the assumption that their partner will believe their lies. Obviously, Machiavellians' previously mentioned charm and deceptive communication play an important part in their success.

11

DECISION RULES AND NEURAL MECHANISMS

The previous chapter has concluded that Machiavellians are flexible strategists who are often able to follow long-term plans and thereby successfully manipulate others. In order to achieve their goals, they have to adequately assess the most important characteristics of the social situation and the partner, and then they have to select the most expedient influence technique. The question offers itself again: how is it possible that Machiavellians perform so well in social life? If they do not exhibit an outstanding performance in tasks involving high-level cognitive functions that generally play a crucial role in the regulation of interpersonal relationships (mind reading, emotional intelligence, empathy), then what is their advantage that makes them successful?

I propose that Machiavellians possess unique mental and neural equipment that distinguishes them from others. Their way of thinking is based on specific decision-making and problem-solving mechanisms that help them process stimuli they receive in a changing social environment. These can be revealed not only by assessing psychological characteristics but also by analysing neural processes, as the recent findings suggest. Below, I enumerate the most important domains of Machiavellian intelligence.

1. Monitoring

Although Machiavellians do not appear to have an above average ability to accurately infer others' individual thoughts and emotions (see Chapter 7), they are highly efficient in monitoring others' behaviour. A set of experiments aimed to establish to what extent individuals' decisions in a social dilemma situation would be influenced by their partners' behaviour (Czibor & Bereczkei 2012; Bereczkei, Szabo, & Czibor 2015). Groups of four subjects played the so-called Public Goods Game, in which players could either cooperate with or deceive others (see Box 8.3 in Chapter 8). Each player could see on a screen how much money the others contributed to the public pool and how much they kept for themselves. Regression analyses of the data led the authors to the conclusion that high Machs were more likely than low Machs to base their decisions on their partners' behaviour. More specifically, the partners' contributions to the public pool in a specific round significantly influenced the Machiavellians' contributions in the next round in such a way that they tended to offer lower amounts of money. By contrast, low Machs' offers were most influenced by the personality factor of Cooperativeness and not so much by their partners' previous decisions. That is, Machiavellians appear to continuously monitor their partners and to adjust their behaviour to their own as if they acted according to the following scheme: "Begin with a medium investment, see what the others do and always offer less than they do." This suggests that when making decisions in competitive situations, Machiavellians rely on fellow group members' behavioural cues whereas non-Machiavellians (cooperators) rather follow internalised norms.

Some studies, using brain imaging techniques (see Box 2.2 in Chapter 2), associated this algorithm with specific neural functions. Differences were found between high and low Machs' neural activity patterns in various social situations. During the decision-making phase ("How should I respond to my partner's offer?"), specific brain areas were found to show increased activity in Machiavellians but not in others. In one study (Bereczkei et al. 2013) involving subjects in the Trust Game (Box 2.1 in Chapter 2), increased activity was measured in the right inferior frontal gyrus (IFG) of high Machs (see Box 11.2). Located in the dorsal part of the frontal lobe, this area is primarily involved in making inferences and predictions in various tasks (Liakakis, Nickel, & Seitz 2011). In an experiment, for example, in which subjects had to resolve a conflict, activity of the IFG was found to be related to reward anticipation required in social competition as the participants played in order to win. The authors suggest that this neural activity implied the subjects' effort to observe the competitors' actions

BOX 11.1 THE REGIONS OF THE MAIN FUNCTIONS IN THE HUMAN BRAIN

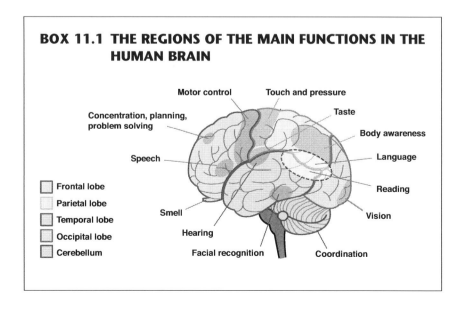

(Polosan et al. 2011). Since making inferences plays a crucial role in complex social relationships, the inferior frontal gyrus has an important function in processing subtle cues providing information about the partners. It may enable Machiavellians to monitor a partner's behaviour step-by-step and to adjust their responses accordingly.

2. Task orientation

It has clearly appeared since as early as the first studies that a typical Machiavellian is task-oriented rather than person-oriented (Geis 1970). This means that above all they focus on the goal and do not let their attention be distracted by circumstances irrelevant to this goal. They are not concerned with either the partner's mood or their own emotions. They consistently follow their own way and strive to make the most of the situation. They are probably guided by the following decision-making rule: "Choose the strategy that is probably the most effective one and keep to it against any disturbing or hindering environmental influence." It is worth noting that psychopaths presumably do not follow this rule since they are driven rather by immediate gratification, impulsivity and short-term thinking (Jones & Paulhus 2011).

It is not by accident that Persistence is the very personality trait that has the strongest influence on Machiavellians' decisions in the successive rounds of the Public Goods Game (Bereczkei & Czibor 2014). Individuals scoring high on the Persistence scale are generally characterised by ambition, steadfastness and perfectionism (Box 3.2 in Chapter 3). They manage frustration efficiently and mobilise great efforts for the reward they have set out to gain. In the above-mentioned experiment, Machiavellians consistently transferred small sums to the group's account during five rounds and earned the most money at the end. Their high level of Persistence helps them consistently keep to their strategy based on rational principles. Due to the excess of cognitive orientation over the emotional orientation, a Machiavellian is able to fully control a situation: to concentrate on a goal, analyse data, select strategy in order to fully exploit available resources and to not be distracted by the presence of a partner. Non-Machiavellians, by contrast, are more focused on the relation and its ethical aspects, showing lesser vigilance and determinism in attaining their own aspirations. This gives a Machiavellian an advantage in taking every opportunity to gain benefits (Pilch 2008).

Task orientation is closely related to persistent goal-directedness which, in turn, requires one to filter out all information irrelevant to the goal and to inhibit all actions uninvolved in goal achievement. Accordingly, increased activity was found in high Mach subjects' left middle frontal gyrus (Box 11.2) in response to a social dilemma situation (Bereczkei et al. 2013). This area plays a crucial role in cognitive controls in the processing of logical relationships and in the manipulation and the active maintenance of information in working memory as required for high level planning. (Liu et al. 2012). It is also related to inhibitory control in terms of impeding a tendency to do something and filtering irrelevant information (Polosan et al. 2011). It is possible that Machiavellians, as opposed to others, are more willing and inclined to inhibit previously tried inefficient decisions and plans in order to replace

BOX 11.2 THE INFERIOR AND MIDDLE FRONTAL GYRI

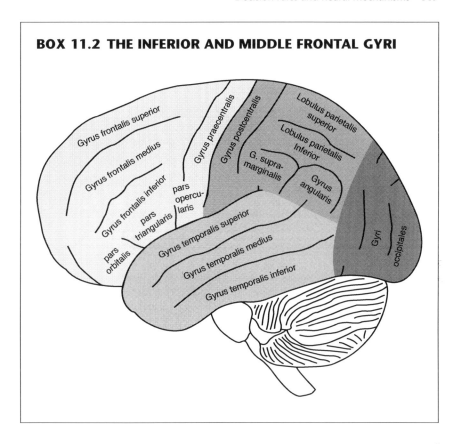

them with more expedient solutions. In a social dilemma situation, they can easily ignore social rules concerning fairness and equity in order to increase their payoff.

3. Reward seeking

It has been established since almost as early as the beginning of psychological research on Machiavellianism that Machiavellians are reward-oriented: their attention and interest are oriented towards gaining external resources (money, prestige, status). As was set out in detail in Chapter 2, Machiavellians strive to be the winner in almost all situations and try to gain the largest profit possible. In some cases, they judge striving for immediate rewards to be the most expedient strategy while in other cases they use indirect tactics, taking roundabout ways (e.g. pretended altruism) in order to gain benefits. Particularly complex long-term adaptation processes are demanded from Machiavellians in an environment where the behaviour of others is unpredictable, therefore the outcome of struggling for rewards is uncertain and even involves risk (see Chapter 10). In sum, Machiavellians may be guided by the following algorithm in such activity: "Strive to gain rewards in every situation in which the benefits deriving from your actions exceed the accompanying costs and losses."

These experimental observations are closely related to the finding that high Mach subjects as compared to low Machs showed increased activity in the right thalamus (Bereczkei et al. 2013). Moreover, the more money Machiavellians had won by the end of the game, the larger the activity increase that was measured in this brain area. It has been known for a relatively long time that the thalamus is involved, among other matters, in processing rewards, including material rewards. A meta-analysis embracing more than a dozen studies points out that this area may be particularly important in predicting rewards (Liu et al. 2011). On the one hand, the thalamus has been found to be involved in subjects' adequate assessment of risks related to winning or losing money. On the other hand, the thalamus may be one of the brain areas regulating active avoidance of external influences involving risk. It plays a role in error detection and in processing cues informing about uncertain rewards (Winkler, Hu, & Li 2013).

The above observations offer the view that the neural processes underlying Machiavellians' decisions are related to the evaluation of the partner's expectable behaviour and to the consideration of alternative tactics to gain rewards. Most social dilemma situations such as the Trust Game always have an element of low predictability and high risk, especially when players cannot influence each other's decisions (e.g. they are not allowed to impose penalties). These conditions may compel players to make probability estimates of future rewards and to assess the benefits and potential risks associated with the rewards. It is highly probable that Machiavellians, who are well known as permanently searching for short-term benefits, show a higher

BOX 11.3 THE THALAMUS

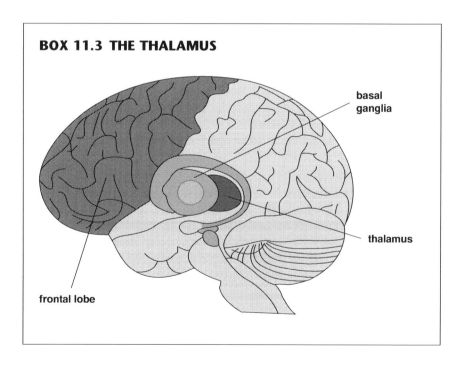

basal ganglia

thalamus

frontal lobe

skill at reward-related decisions. The increased thalamus activity in high Machs may relate to the anticipation of success following a risky decision. That is, it is possibly related to successful action plans that they devise while monitoring their partners' behaviour in order to gain rewards. This explanation was supported by the other result of this study, which showed a close relationship between thalamus activity and the size of rewards gained by Machiavellians. It is indeed possible, therefore, that the neural processes involved in processing material rewards influence their success.

4. Inhibition of cooperation

The studies examining subjects' decisions in social dilemma situations suggest that Machiavellians often inhibit quick and spontaneous responses. They are able to control their emotions, which can prevent them from winning (Box 11.4). They usually disregard the cooperative efforts and expectations of others, and overcome their feelings and impulses facilitating trust towards their partners. They seem to act according to the following decision-making rule: "Do not be rash in following those impressions and feelings that would prevent you from gaining the largest profit possible."

BOX 11.4 EVEN A SMALL REWARD IS A REWARD

In an experiment, subjects played the Ultimatum Game (see Box 2.1 in Chapter 2). The basic rule of the game is that if the second player accepts the amount of money offered by the first player, they split the funds accordingly, whereas if the second player rejects the sum, neither of them receives any money. Rational self-interest would suggest that even the smallest sum is worth accepting since it is still more than nothing. Nevertheless, previous studies uniformly found that a large number of people were unwilling to accept a sum that they considered unfairly small (Gintis et al. 2003). These people reported negative emotions towards those who tried to shortchange them. Their anger led them to retaliate to unfairness even at the price of also depriving themselves of gain.

High Mach players, however, acted according to their self-interest: they not only transferred small sums as first players but also accepted almost any sum, however small, as second players (Meyer 1992). When the experimenters asked subjects to indicate the minimum amount they considered acceptable (i.e. the "resistance point"), Machiavellians were found to be willing to accept an offer making less than 50% of the funds available to the first player. By contrast, low Machs adhered to the 50-50 split and considered any offer below that point unfair. Machiavellians had no such moral objections; they accepted everything that increased their profits. They seemed to overcome their negative feelings elicited by unfair splits in order to gain benefit.

An important related finding is that high Mach subjects involved in a social dilemma task showed increased activity in a brain area that plays an important role in conflict management and emotion regulation. This area is the dorsolateral prefrontal cortex (DLPFC), more specifically, a part of it lying in the middle and inferior frontal gyri (Box 11.5), which is involved in processing conflicts between personal interests and social norms (Sanfey et al. 2003). It was found to show increased activity when, for example, subjects broke their promise to take their partners' requests into account during joint task solution (Baumgartner et al. 2009). Other findings suggest that the DLPFC played an important role in abstract reasoning processes in favour of utilitarian judgments. Such processes come into play when one approves of violating ethical norms such as, for example, the norm prescribing avoidance of causing harm to fellow human beings. The personal moral violations may elicit prepotent, negative social-emotional responses that drive people to deem such actions as inappropriate. In order to judge a personal moral violation to be appropriate one must overcome a prepotent response. This utilitarian function is fulfilled by the dorsolateral prefrontal cortex (and by the anterior cingulate cortex). For example, the right DLPFC showed an elevated activity in subjects who were willing to accept unfair offers in the Ultimatum Game (Knoch et al. 2006).

BOX 11.5 THE DORSOLATERAL PREFRONTAL CORTEX (DLPFC)

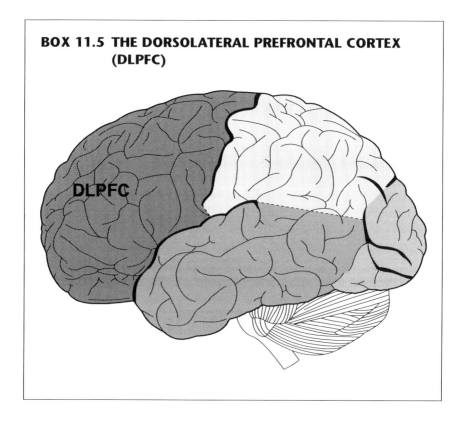

This quite clearly shows parallelism with Machiavellianism. As has been discussed earlier, Machiavellians do not adhere to ethical principles, and they are ready to violate norms if their interests so require. They are likely to judge moral violations to be appropriate, especially in situations that offer material reward for breaking norms (Christie & Geis 1970). For gaining benefits, they may use cognitive control over emotions in accordance with their goals. Relying on abstract reasoning processes, they can overcome prepotent social-emotional responses and handle moral dilemmas in a utilitarian manner. Therefore, the increased activity in the DLPFC of high Machs may be associated with the inhibition of the reciprocal answer to the partner's cooperative initiative. Machiavellian individuals may override their "spontaneous" reaction to the cooperative initiation of others and maintain their self-oriented impulses.

5. Generalisation

The chapter on mind reading has already presented the hypothesis that Machiavellians' social success is based on their ability to sort people into types, which they efficiently use to decide whether and by what tactical means someone can be manipulated. Previously, this hypothesis was discussed in relation to the theory of mind: Machiavellians do not infer their partner's specific mental states but form a general judgment of them based on generalised previous experience. In fact, a cognitive rule is in play in this case as well: "Categorise this person according to your previous experience and recall those behavioural tactics that yielded benefits when you dealt with people of this type."

In my view, Machiavellians are remarkably smart observers of human nature. They efficiently recognise those traits in people that once offered an opportunity to exploit others. Some appear sincere while others prove forgetful or extremely introverted. There are people who are preoccupied with a personal relationship or their job to the extent that they show no concern for anything else, therefore they are easy to deceive. Other behaviour reflects emotional instability: sometimes they feel knocked down, at other times they fly high, and such strong emotional involvement may also offer a good opportunity for manipulation. And one might continue the list, of course.

Several studies suggest that the ability to make general inferences and judgments about people is related to working memory capacity. Working memory consists of a central executive system and several subsystems storing and analysing visual and verbal information. The central executive is responsible for processing and integrating information received through different sensory channels, for coordinating different functions and for controlling cognitive processes (attention, inferences). Those scoring high on working memory tests have a rational thinking style and a high-level ability to make inferences.

All these may be important, because a recent study has found a close positive relationship between Mach scores and scores on a working memory scale (Bereczkei & Birkas 2014; Box 11.6). This finding shows that Machiavellians are characterised by good argumentative skills and an above-average preference for using logical rules

---

BOX 11.6 WORKING MEMORY (WECHSLER ADULT INTELLIGENCE SCALE; WAIS)

This intelligence test comprises four scales: verbal comprehension, working memory, perceptual organisation and processing speed. The working memory scale assesses the abilities to store and recall information, to concentrate attention and to process the received information. It includes two subscales: arithmetic and digit span.

The arithmetic subtest measures the abilities related to memory, attention, mental operations and processing numerical sequences. It comprises ten arithmetic problems, all of which can be solved by only using the four basic operations.

An easier problem: How long does it take to walk 24 kilometres for a person walking at a speed of 3 kilometres per hour?

A more difficult problem: A certain job takes 6 days for 8 workers to finish. How many workers are needed to finish the same job in a half-day?

The digit span subtest consists of three parts. First, subjects are asked to repeat a sequence of digits in the same order as the experimenter presents to them. The easiest sequence contains 3 digits and the most difficult one includes 9 digits; there is no logical relationship between the digits. Second, subjects have to repeat the presented digits in reverse order. Third and finally, subjects have to repeat the digits in ascending order according to their values.

---

which, in turn, suggests that they are able to quickly process and efficiently organise information. This view is consistent with the finding that within working memory capacity, Machiavellianism shows a relationship with arithmetic rather than digit span (see Box 11.6). More specifically, the former is used to measure the ability to make inferences, to solve problems and to devise new operations while the latter reflects the ability to store and reproduce information. Consequently, Machiavellians are not simply efficient in memorising and recalling information but much rather in using the so-called computational operations, that is, on the basis of their previous experience they infer others' personality type and emotional life.

6. Target selection

Machiavellians often achieve success by selecting the person who creates the optimal target under the given circumstances, that is, the individual or individuals whose deception involves the lowest cost and risks while yielding the highest benefits possible. "Choose those from whom you can expect the greatest reward."

This strategy may be implemented in several ways. One study found that Machiavellians mostly tried to profiteer when they could expect others to propose cooperation under the given circumstances (Bereczkei, Szabo, & Czibor 2015).

Subjects played the Public Goods experimental game (Box 8.3 in Chapter 8) in either of two conditions. In one condition, subjects played the game in the classic mode, in which cooperation was theoretically profitable and most players earned some money depending on the tactics they used. In the other condition, the rules of the Public Goods Game were modified so that it modelled open competition. Specifically, only the winner and no one else received financial reward, that is, the player who had collected the most money by the end of the game. The study found that Machiavellians followed the typical exploitative strategy in the cooperative condition: as compared to others, they contributed less to the public pool and earned more at the end of the game. In the competitive condition, however, they were not more selfish than others. Essentially, the sums they contributed to the group's account were similar to those transferred by their partners.

The researchers concluded that Machiavellians were most successful in cooperative situations because the circumstances enabled them to exploit the generous offers of their partners. In this condition, the others were supposed to contribute a substantial amount to the public account, following the norm of cooperation. Machiavellians are not bound by this norm, which makes exploitation relatively easy. "If everyone is cooperative but me, the profit is mine." The altruist is the best dupe, the optimal target. By contrast, in a situation where everyone is competing for a limited amount of profit, exploitation does not appear to be effective. Everybody wants to achieve the same thing: obtain the money of the others. Since relatively small amounts of money could be redistributed among players, Machiavellians were unable to make good use of their selfish tactics.

It is possible that certain brain areas play an important role in the selection of the potential victims. Several studies have revealed that the inferior frontal gyrus (Box 11.2) is involved in goal directed cognition, e.g. making predictive inferences during various tasks. This brain area plays a role in analysing the intentionality of the partner's behaviour during social interaction, and in rational reasoning during decision-making (Liakakis, Nickel, & Seitz 2011; Steinmann et al. 2014). Hence, it may contribute to the Machiavellians' skill at analysing and anticipating their partners' decisions in social dilemma situations. This idea was supported by the results of a recent brain-imaging study, in which each subject playing the Trust Game alternately received fair and unfair offers from their partner (from a computer; Bereczkei et al. 2015). A fair offer reflected a cooperative partner's behaviour whereas an unfair offer represented a competitive or even hostile partner (Box 11.7). The study found IFR especially active when high Mach individuals received a large amount of money (fair condition) from the partner (computer), whereas no stronger activity was found in this neural circuit if the other player transferred a very low sum (unfair condition). In other words, Machiavellians showed elevated activities in this brain area when they played with a cooperative partner. By contrast, no activity increase was observable when the partner did not show willingness to cooperate but rather competed for the expectable reward.

Obviously, Machiavellians considered their cooperative partner as a potential target, and the norms of cooperation provided great opportunities for exploiting others. Machiavellian people with strong self-oriented motivations and rational decisions may take advantage of the others' cooperative intentions. It is not surprising, then, that in this game they gained significantly higher profits when their partners were willing to cooperate than in the case where the partners engaged in rivalry. Machiavellian behaviour may reflect the following algorithm: "Pick the dupe and then adjust your decisions to their behaviour". In accordance with this consideration, a recent study found that those persons are highly vulnerable to social manipulation who possess personality traits such as low extraversion, high neuroticism and high agreeableness (Chung & Charles 2016). Implying trustfulness, forgiveness and temperate manner, these traits on the Big Five scale (Chapter 3) may make people especially good target of exploitation.

BOX 11.7 FAIR AND UNFAIR OFFERS

Subjects played a two-round version of the Trust Game (Box 2.1 in Chapter 2) while lying in the MRI scanner. In the first round, they were asked, in accordance with the usual rules of the game, to offer a part of their funds to the second player (simulated by a computer without the subject's knowledge). After the experimenter tripled the offered sum, the second "player" responded in either of two ways. In the present study, participants played a set of two-round Trust games. In the first round, the subject as player 1 offered an amount of money, and player 2 (the computer) reciprocated in two possible ways. In one case, it returned about the same amount of money that it had received (fair condition). In the other case, however, it only returned 30% of the sum initially offered by the first player, that is, an insignificant part of the tripled sum it had received (unfair condition). In the second round, the computer began the game as the first player by offering an average sum, and the subject (player 2) made a decision as to the amount in return. In general, second players were more motivated to reciprocate when the first player proved to be cooperative and reciprocated an average or above average amount of money in the first round. Indeed, this is how low Machs acted: they offered a large sum (at least as large as that which they had received before) when their partner had proved generous, whereas they transferred a small sum when their partner had been unfair in the previous round. Machiavellians also punished unfair partners but they chose to exploit those who had previously been willing to cooperate. That is, they did not even try to reciprocate fair offers and returned a sum one third less on average than that they had received.

Both fair and unfair games were played 12 times by each subject during fMRI scanning. Given that each game included 2 rounds, the study included a total of 48 rounds, that is, each subject made a total of 48 decisions. Behavioural data were provided by a statistical analysis of these decisions while the underlying neural processes were inferred from the mean activity changes in specific brain areas.

12

EVOLUTIONARY ORIGINS

The previous chapters of this book have focused on Machiavellians' cognitive abilities, personality traits and family background. These factors are responsible for the emergence of a specific attitude and behaviour peculiar to Machiavellianism. They are also referred to as "proximate causes" because they are the direct determinants of decision-making processes and behavioural tactics that make people Machiavellians.

However, there is another set of causes which do not form the immediate background of behaviour but so to speak regulate people's actions and thoughts from a distance. These are referred to as "ultimate causes", which prescribe the function or purpose of a behaviour (see Box 12.1). During evolution, our ancestors developed physical and mental abilities that helped them adapt to environmental conditions, primarily to the conditions of their social environment. The evolutionary emergence of Machiavellian qualities was presumably due to the successful manipulative techniques that might contribute to their ancestors' survival and reproductive success. In other words, Machiavellianism as a behavioural strategy has often proved beneficial in a complex system of social relationships, and so the underlying psychological mechanisms have been maintained over time and continue to influence people's lives.

1. The social intelligence hypothesis

Interestingly, proximate and ultimate approaches to Machiavellianism were first proposed roughly at the same time. As is discussed in Chapter 1, Richard Christie and Florence Geis began social psychological research in this field in the 1960s; they were then joined by an increasing number researchers in various parts of the world, and their work done during the subsequent half-century resulted in a comprehensive description of the nature of Machiavellianism. The previous chapters have enumerated our recent knowledge of the proximate processes related to manipulative attitude, lifestyle and thinking, and of their underlying motives.

BOX 12.1 PROXIMATE AND ULTIMATE CAUSES

Behaviour may – and should – be explained at several levels, two of which have particular importance. Proximate explanations reveal the direct causes underlying behaviour, such as motivational states, environmental stimuli or hormonal processes. Much is known, for example, about such essential influencing factors of human sexual behaviour as the secretion of certain hormones (e.g. testosterone), the function of specific neural regions (e.g. hypothalamus), the effects of one's childhood environment and social norms regulating sexual relationships.

Evolutionists, by contrast, are interested in the so-called "ultimate" explanations of behaviour, which refer to the adaptive mechanisms brought about by natural selection. They strive to understand those evolutionary causes that provide the fundamental functions of specific behavioural outcomes (Cosmides & Tooby 1992). According to the evolutionary approach, those behavioural strategies were favoured by positive selection that proved beneficial for our ancestors' survival and reproduction. To take another example from the field of sexuality, people today still have an evolved preference for several morphological and behavioural traits that once contributed to successful mate choice and, therefore, to an increased number of offspring. They include physical characteristics signaling an individual's fertility and resistance to disease, such as a woman's low waist-to-hip ratio or a man's facial testosterone markers. They also imply adaptive sexual strategies that help one assess a potential partner's commitment, physical fitness or parenting capacity. For example, jealous reactions to the threat of actual or suspected infidelity may increase the probability of having a biological child and decrease the risk of the partner's withdrawing investments from the family (Buss 2005).

In an evolutionary psychological perspective, the knowledge of evolutionary strategies enables one to predict specific (proximate) forms of behavioural and cognitive processes. It is predictable, for example, that young adults (especially men) are more likely than women to exhibit noncompliant and risk-taking behaviour, since over human history young males were especially interested in obtaining resources required for reproduction at any price. An adaptive-ultimate analysis of behaviour can integrate specific psychological explanations to a broader theoretical framework, and contributes to clarifying what factors are the primary causes and what their consequences may be (Crawford 1998). As a consequence, evolutionary psychology broadens the understanding of the causes underlying behaviour and provides an explanatory framework that enables one to study the universal laws of human nature.

In parallel with – and completely independently of – the advancement of this line of research, the ultimate approach was also becoming dominant in research on Machiavellianism. The story goes back to what is known as the social intelligence hypothesis, described first by Nicholas Humphrey (1976), which suggests that humans' unique high-level intelligence has been a result of adaptation to the social environment rather than having developed in response to challenges posed by the natural environment as had been proposed by many authors at that time. Human uniqueness was not primarily due to hunting and/or tool use aimed at acquiring the necessary food but much rather to an increased demand for meeting the group's changing needs. Humphrey started from the observation that social animals live in a social environment that is more complex – and hence less stable and less pre-dictable – than their natural-ecological environment, thus posing greater demands for adaptation. Social life comprises behavioural strategies that require high-level mental abilities – creative intelligence in Humphrey's terminology. Individuals have to be able to foresee the consequences of their actions, others' expectable reactions and the costs and benefits of their subsequent behavioural responses. They have to do all this in an environment where the social stimuli they respond to are transient, changeable and often ambiguous. The more complex a group is and the more multi-faceted interpersonal relationships it comprises, the larger number of and more complicated the social challenges individuals have to deal with. They have to coordinate their activities with those of others and ward off attacks and schemes against them while striving to come off well in their relationships. In other words, they have to make decisions that enable them to take advantageous positions in a web of conflicting interests while leaving integration of the group intact and thereby preserving the benefits provided by social life. In sum, the fundamental proposition of the social intelligence hypothesis suggests that complexity and variability of the social environment generated those selection pressures that led to a rapid develop-ment of intelligence. Apes' large brains and cognitive abilities primarily developed to serve social problem solving and only secondarily as a result of adaptation to the natural-ecological environment. We are not so much intelligent tool users but rather shrewd strategists of social relationships. Social skills, however, provide means for solving a variety of problems, some of them clearly being non-social in nature. Humphrey suggests that technical skills (e.g. tool use) are later developments in evolution; moreover, their emergence was in many cases due to high-level social skills (e.g. imitation).

Evidently, one central domain of the social intelligence of primates and humans comprises manipulative-deceptive strategies. Richard Dawkins and John Krebs (1978) explain in their pioneer study that organisms often communicate honest signals to one another. When, for example, a dominant animal signals its superior strength and aggressive intention by its posture and facial expression, it is beneficial for both parties involved in the interaction. It is beneficial for the signaler, who can maintain its dominant position without risking physical fight. Similarly, it is also beneficial for the receiver, who is reliably informed by the communicative signal about the physical fitness and emotional state of the dominant individual. Thus,

BOX 12.2 THE SOCIAL BRAIN HYPOTHESIS

The social intelligence hypothesis was extended by new theories during the late 1980s and the 1990s, as a result of which the hypothesis developed into a more accurate explanatory model with predictive power. One of the new theories, the social brain hypothesis proposed by the English researcher Robin Dunbar, was to become dominant (1992, 1998, 2002). It has been known for a relatively long time that primates have a neocortex disproportionately larger than those of other animals. This neocortex, which controls high-level cognitive processes, may be two or three times as large as other, more ancient regions of their brain. It is the advancement of the neocortex that has been mainly responsible for the rapid large-scale increase in brain size during primate evolution, which reached its peak with the emergence of apes and humans. In a comparative study across a range of primate taxa (including modern humans) Dunbar found a close correlation between group size – which he considered the most reliable measure of group complexity – and the neocortex ratio (i.e. the ratio of the size of the neocortex to the rest of the brain). Average group size is the highest in those primate species that have the highest neocortex ratio. As regards humans, the volume of the neocortex is four times as large as other parts of the brain (e.g. midbrain, cerebellum, medulla) taken together. This is consistent with the fact that humans, even including hunter-gatherer societies, live in unusually large groups in contrast to other animal species.

Dunbar has concluded from this observation that the limits of group size are prescribed by the information processing capacity of the brain. The extent to which animals can develop complex social relationships depends closely on the cognitive equipment they have available to make the necessary social judgments and inferences. Looking at the other side of the coin: large and complex groups emerging as a result of certain evolutionary forces (e.g. the "pressure" imposed by powerful predators) created an environment where individuals possessing outstanding social skills had an advantageous position in the competition for resources. The demands of adaptation to changing relations within the group positively selected for those cognitive abilities that generally resulted in increased brain size and intelligence (Byrne 1997).

Regarding the specific abilities in question, Dunbar pointed out four areas. One area includes visual abilities serving, among others, differentiation among group members based on their appearance and behaviour. Another area is memory capacity, which plays an important role in storing and recalling images of previous relationships and in keeping an account of others' altruistic and deceptive behaviour. The third is emotion regulation, which has crucial importance in developing long-lasting relationships and in resolving conflicts with fellow group members. Finally, the most important area includes cognitive abilities regulating social relationships in terms of both manipulation and cooperation, such as mind reading, computation and mental simulation.

the submissive individual can weigh up the circumstances and make an adequate decision (to back down or to meet the challenge).

In this case, signaling is honest and reliable since it serves the interest of both parties. In many other cases, however, natural selection has favoured deceptive signals that enable individuals to manipulate and exploit others. The signaler is often interested in misleading the receiver if the fake message can improve its chances for survival and reproduction. There is a host of experimentally verified cases of such non-cooperative signals, which fulfil various functions from ensnaring prey (e.g. anglerfish) to misleading rivals in mating competition (Andrews 2002).

The authors suggest that deceptive communication could in turn create a selection pressure for animals on the receiving end of the manipulation to evolve a retaliatory strategy. The improvement of manipulative behavioural techniques on one side has facilitated the development of sophisticated defense mechanisms on the other side, which, in turn, has exerted selection pressure on even more efficient manipulative skills, and so on. An arms race of deception and contra-deception has emerged that has resulted in an expansion of brain size and improved cognitive abilities.

2. The Machiavellian intelligence hypothesis

These theoretical considerations have been supported by studies on primates. Beginning from the 1970s, field work has been conducted with the aim of revealing the frequency and specific forms of intentional deception among individuals of various primate species (Byrne 1995). Primates have been found to use a wide variety of manipulative and deceptive tactics. Sometimes they distract conspecifics' attention, while at other times they try to prevent others from noticing something. The most sophisticated form of manipulation that primates exhibit – and the one most resembling human behaviour – is the way they use others as means to achieving their own goals. Such cases are presented in Box 12.3.

Currently, there are several hundreds of reported observations of deceptive behaviour among primates similar to those presented in Box 12.3. They are termed "tactical deception", which refers to cases when one individual manipulates another by sending an intentionally misleading signal which in turn elicits a response from the latter that enables the manipulator to take advantage of the situation.

Such studies led researchers to develop the "Machiavellian intelligence hypothesis" in the mid-1980s (Byrne & Whiten 1988). The theory was based on the idea that the skillful manipulation of others conferred a significant evolutionary advantage. Successful deception and exploitation of rivals exerted selection pressure on the development of an increasingly more complex social intelligence. In other words, primates' – and especially humans' – intellectual abilities evolved because over a long time successful manipulation improved the deceiver's chances of survival and reproduction. Successful manipulation, in turn, required more and more sophisticated mental abilities. In this way, Machiavellian strategies, improved intellectual abilities and increased reproductive success facilitated each other in a positive feedback loop.

BOX 12.3 INTENTIONAL DECEPTION AMONG PRIMATES

In a field study of baboons, researchers observed that a young male repeatedly duped adult group members (Byrne 1995). The young male under observation noticed an adult female digging out nutritious roots from the earth. This activity is hard and tiresome work even for adults, especially during the dry season. The youngster waited until the female had finished digging out the root, then looked around to see that nobody was around and suddenly burst out in a cry of pain. In response to the loud cry, its mother immediately appeared on the scene and chased away the female, who was lower ranking than the mother in the dominance hierarchy. When both females had left, the youngster consumed the food peacefully. The researchers concluded that they had witnessed a case of intentional deception, in which the young used its mother as a social instrument, so to speak, for removing an obstacle (adult female) and obtaining food. This explanation was supported by the observation that the youngster only resorted to this trick when its mother was out of sight and hence could not become aware of the obvious deception.

Even more complicated cases have been recorded among apes. Chimpanzees observed in the Gombe reservation were fed from a box placed in a clearing in a forest. One chimp walking nearby noticed that the box was open and that the food was freely accessible. It was just about to take the food when it noticed another chimp approaching who was stronger and dominant, and which never shared food with others. The former then hastily looked away in order to distract the newcomer's attention from the food. However, this had the effect of raising suspicion and the latter simply made its way onward, pretending disinterest. It then stopped behind a nearby tree, waited until the other chimp had taken the food out of the box, and then suddenly appeared and took the food away. This combination of deception and counter-deception suggests that the latter chimp might have recognised its conspecific's intention, which enabled it to prevent itself from being duped.

The Machiavellian intelligence hypothesis has been confirmed by several studies on primates. A comparative study has concluded that the frequency of deceptive behaviour is closely related to the relative volume of the neocortex: species with a larger neocortex more frequently engage in manipulative activities (Byrne 1995). This suggests, on the one hand, that manipulation has been an essential selective force in the evolution of a highly developed brain and creative intelligence. On the other hand, one may argue that successful manipulation demands considerable cognitive capacity: only those species are able to intentionally deceive others that possess advanced mental equipment. This subject has been discussed in detail in Chapter 9 with regard to humans.

A study of polygynous primate species has found that the larger the neocortex volume, the weaker the relationship between the rank of individual males in the hierarchy and their reproductive success, as expressed in the number of matings (Pawlowski, Dunbar, & Lowen 1998). In most species of mammals, the rank of any male in the dominance hierarchy highly influences the likelihood of its access to females: the dominant male usually mates with more females. It has long been known that there are several exceptions, especially among primates. However, exceptions may only occur under very restricted conditions in terms of cognitive abilities: inferior males only have a chance to mate if they are able to deceive and evade dominant males who alertly control their females. This is primarily possible in species that exhibit complex mental abilities used to distract rivals' attention and to send misleading signals. Observations have revealed that female baboons groom low ranking males hidden behind a rock, and inferior male chimps cover their erected penis with their hands in front of dominant males. Such observations may lead to the conclusion that socially skillful animals – which have a large neocortex – can use subtle behavioural tactics in order to find a mate even if they have a low position in the dominance hierarchy.

3. Machiavellianism: evolutionary and psychological approaches

The Machiavellian intelligence hypothesis suggests that people may obtain various benefits from successfully exploiting others. Although the theory was originally applied to the order of primates which, of course, includes Homo sapiens as well; researchers have agreed that manipulative and deceptive strategies have made an essential contribution to the emergence of humans' uniquely large brain and intelligence.

This evolutionary explanation appears consistent with the psychological explanation discussed in the previous chapters. As seen previously, several studies have demonstrated since the first publication of the classic book of Christie and Geis (1970) that people are able and willing to mislead and deceive others. It has also been revealed that there are great individual differences of degree in Machiavellianism: people differ in their willingness to deploy various manipulative tactics in order to gain benefits. In this respect, the Machiavellian intelligence hypothesis may be applied to humans as well: members of our species use various forms of deception and cheating as specific means of adaptation to the social environment.

In a different respect, however, a substantial gap has emerged between the evolutionary and psychological approaches to Machiavellianism. Research findings of the past decade have not completely fulfilled the expectation that the Machiavellian intelligence hypothesis would fully explain humans' Machiavellian behaviour. Previous chapters, especially the findings presented in Chapters 11 and 12, have shown that people scoring high on Machiavellianism have relatively poor emotional intelligence and mind-reading ability. This invites the following question: how are Machiavellians able to successfully manipulate others when they show deficits in

BOX 12.4 AN OUTLINE OF SYNTHESIS

So far, very few authors have attempted a synthesis of the evolutionary and psychological approaches to Machiavellianism. One of the exceptions is the comprehensive work of David Sloan Wilson and his colleagues (Wilson, Near, & Miller 1996), which was the first to integrate the two approaches. The authors establish that the theory of evolution provides an excellent conceptual framework for a uniform explanation to an incredibly wide range of Machiavellian behaviours. Moreover, it also enables researchers to make predictions on those phenomena of Machiavellianism that have not yet been studied.

The authors consider Machiavellianism to be a form of social intelligence exhibited by several primate species, especially by apes. In this regard as well, humans are characterised by unique qualities since their incomparable intellectual abilities enable them to manipulate others in an extremely complex and sophisticated manner. Interestingly, however, previous studies have not found a close relationship between Mach scores and IQ scores (i.e. general intelligence; O'Boyle et al. 2013). Machiavellians do not seem to outdo others in general intelligence. The authors point out, however, that this was not necessarily the case in our ancestors' environment. Furthermore, it is worth noting from an evolutionary point of view that successful manipulation does not necessarily require global intellectual superiority from Machiavellians but far rather demands certain specific mental abilities. Such abilities enable one to deceive others without considerable risk of detection.

The evolutionary success of Machiavellianism is further supported by the fact that Machiavellians often take leadership positions in companies and institutions. Moreover, their charming appearance and assertiveness often lead others to place them in leadership roles (see in detail in Chapter 2). If this was also the case in the past, then they presumably achieved high status and respect within their group, which might not only yield social success but reproductive success as well. More specifically, men with higher statuses as opposed to those with lower ranks have more biological children in almost all pre-industrial societies (Bereczkei 2015). More biological children, in turn, might provide the guarantee for the survival and spreading of Machiavellianism during evolution.

Likewise, evolutionary principles may explain sex differences in Machiavellianism. While distributions of men's and women's Mach scores largely overlap, women's mean scores are somewhat lower than men's. This is probably due to men's stronger competitive tendency, which is a "product" of evolution. Men generally take greater risks and more often exhibit noncompliant behaviour in order to gain resources. The authors point out, however, that differences between sexes lie not so much in the frequency of manipulation but rather in its style. It is possible that men prefer more overt, assertive and violent forms of manipulation while women rather resort to covert, restrained and concealed deceptive tactics such as casual rumours and gossiping. Further research may establish whether the evolutionary hypothesis matches reality.

qualities essentially required for manipulation? How can they achieve success when they have worse-than-average abilities in recognising the emotions of others and in understanding what others feel, think or want? Our answer to this question has been that Machiavellians show unique cognitive and social characteristics, which enable them to achieve their goals. On the one hand, their emotional intelligence and mind reading ability are not in all respects worse than others'. In specific environments – mostly in interpersonal relationships providing suitable conditions for deception – they definitely prove sensitive to others' emotions and inner life (see Chapters 8 and 9). On the other hand, research has revealed that Machiavellians have special skills and abilities. In certain areas, they outdo people with lower Mach scores. For example, they show an excellent aptitude in monitoring the behaviour of others. They exhibit persistent task orientation, which is related to their working memory capacity. Under uncertain and unpredictable conditions, they efficiently assess possible ways and costs of gaining rewards. They have above average ability in inhibiting spontaneous emotions and in selecting potential targets (see Chapters 10 and 11). Generally speaking, it may be established that their thinking and behaviour are characterising by outstanding flexibility. Their behaviour shows a certain chameleon nature: they alter their attitudes towards others depending on their own interests and the given circumstances, and they are even willing to go so far as to "play" the altruist in order to deceive others.

All these recent findings of psychological research are consistent with the evolutionary model of Machiavellianism. However, further questions arise, of course. In what forms and through what mediation processes do evolutionary strategies of Machiavellianism contribute to modern humans' thinking and behaviour? From a different perspective: in what ways do evolutionary motives manifest themselves in the actions of the modern Machiavellian? Essentially, these questions concern the extent to which the Machiavellian intelligence hypothesis may, according to our current knowledge, contribute to a valid understanding of human nature. Certain respects of this issue are worth considering.

4. Demands of the social environment

One basic proposition of the Machiavellian intelligence hypothesis – as well as of explanations based on the social intelligence hypothesis in general – is that the social environment as compared to the natural environment poses a greater challenge to primates since it is more complex, diverse and variable. Continuously changing and rearranged relationships between group members impose substantial demands on individual adaptation such as, for example, persuading others to form coalitions, warding off attacks by others, reconciling former enemies if necessary and so on. Accordingly, dynamic adaptation to social life has exerted selection pressure on special and sophisticated abilities and qualities that has enabled group members to use both cooperative and deceptive strategies within the group (Whiten & Byrne 1997).

Diverse and changing social environments, however, may provide different conditions, which require specific responses from individuals. Those having above average manipulative abilities may equally have to deal with either cooperative or deceptive partners in different situations. It clearly seems that Machiavellians are challenged more by a cooperative social environment while a non-cooperative environment imposes greater demands on non-Machiavellians. This is because Machiavellians, having a cynical worldview and amoral attitude, are more likely to approve of various forms of betrayal, perfidy and deception. In many cases, they even consider antisocial behaviour as a norm, assuming that everyone is essentially malevolent and immoral. Therefore, they may find themselves in an unexpected and confusing situation when confronted with unselfish and cooperative behaviour on the part of others. They see such situations as challenges that must be dealt with in some way. Such situations presumably require them to exert additional efforts in order to assert their self-interest. At the same time, partners proposing cooperation are ideal targets of manipulation. They are easy to deceive and they usually yield large profits since manipulation mostly finds them unprepared.

Hence, Machiavellians are reasonably expected to find cooperative situations both burdening and profitable. In terms of the Machiavellian intelligence hypothesis, this means that the evolution of their social and cognitive abilities was primarily driven by the selection pressure on efficiently managed exploitation of cooperative partners. Machiavellians have to assess all costs, benefits and risks associated with either rejecting or exploiting cooperation. Non-Machiavellians, by contrast, who are more willing to trust others and to comply with social norms, have an easier job in making decisions: they cooperate when others cooperate while they deny cooperation when others deceive them.

Available experimental findings support this idea. In the Public Goods Game, Machiavellians offer the smallest sums from their private funds to the group when their partners prove cooperative (Bereczkei & Czibor 2015). If, however, others also show competitive behaviour, they see no point in meeting the challenge since there is no available dupe to exploit. A brain imaging study using the fMRI technique revealed that high Machs' brain activity increased when they had to respond to a fair offer in the Trust Game. By contrast, no activity increase was found when they were offered an unfairly small sum (Bereczkei et al. 2015). Low Machs responded in the opposite manner: they showed the highest brain activity when playing with defectors, who offered little or nothing as first players. A possible explanation to these findings is that Machiavellians find cooperative situations the greatest challenge, as they require intense analysis from them. It is not by accident that one of the brain areas that showed increased activity in them during the experiment (the dorsolateral prefrontal cortex) plays an important role in inhibiting spontaneous emotional responses and in making utilitarian decisions (see Chapter 11). This finding presumably reflects that a sense of reciprocity elicited by the partner's fair offer – which is an extremely strong social norm – is repressed and replaced with the much more profitable "give little" algorithm by the mentioned brain area. By contrast, individuals with lower Machiavellianism and higher ethical expectations find dealing with defectors a problem, one which they have to solve in order to avoid being exploited.

These studies demonstrate that high Machs use their cognitive abilities to assess their partners' cooperative intentions and to pursue exploitative tactics when the benefit exceeds the expected costs. Presumably, it was the advantages derived from continuous exploitation of potential targets that exerted selection pressure on Machiavellian intelligence during evolution. In other words, it was not the social environment in general but some of its specific conditions that contributed to the evolution of manipulative skills. These conditions comprise interpersonal relationships that enable profiteering from others' cooperation. This is consistent with one important basic proposition of social intelligence theories: complex and changing social environments generate the ability to develop solutions to multi-faceted situational problems (Crook 1988).

5. The individual and the group

As has already been discussed, a complex social environment facilitates the development of manipulative tactics. Such tactics serve individual benefits usually gained at the expense of fellow group members. Such exploitation, however, has a limit in an evolutionary sense: others' losses may not reach an extent that would endanger group cohesion. This is because disintegration of the group would also harm the self-interest of the Machiavellian: if there is no group, there is no target to exploit. Moreover, if too many fellow group members fall prey to the manipulator's tactics, or if exploitation exceeds their tolerance, then manipulation becomes too "costly" for the manipulator. This means that the group responds with countermeasures and punitive sanctions. Unrestrained manipulation is easy to detect, hence the community can impose sanctions on the manipulator. Thus, Machiavellians have to maintain a sensitive balance in most cases. The evolutionary pressure on adaptation has kept manipulation at a level where it is still profitable but not harmful to group cohesion.

Present-day Machiavellians seem to be subject to this constraint as well. In one experiment, subjects played a game in which they could win various sums of money (Geis 1970). An alliance made by two players substantially improved their chances of winning, which of course entailed having to share the winnings at the end of the game. Allied players had to make a promise that they would not break the alliance. If they did break it, however, they did not have to face any sanction, and they could take the profit individually. Not surprisingly, Machiavellians as opposed to others more often broke their alliances during the game, from which they derived profit in most cases. If, however, they initially promised not to break the alliance, they kept their word until the end. These findings suggest that although Machiavellians often go against the group's expectations, they do not break the rules when it entails dissolution of an alliance. They do not because they may incur serious long-term consequences by doing so. Breaking their promise would discredit and disparage them in front of others to the extent that in the future, perhaps as soon as in the next game, they would be rejected as unreliable partners.

Machiavellians, of course, also try other ways to gain reputation in their community. One such peculiar way is reflected in the previously presented experimental finding (Chapter 8) that Machiavellians are even willing to help strangers when fellow group members are there to observe them (but not in other cases; Bereczkei, Birkas, & Kerekes 2010). At other times, they put up with making a good impression on others (Chapter 2). In such cases, Machiavellians positively seek opportunities to improve their reputation and to achieve the group's approval. This may on the one hand improve the efficiency of their subsequently used deceptive tactics, while on the other it may also protect group cohesion. Others perhaps see the Machiavellian as a contradictory person: "you have to be cautious with him but he's not a bad guy after all."

6. Evolutionary mechanisms

The idea of a possible synthesis of the evolutionary and psychological approaches to Machiavellianism invite further considerations. In an evolutionary perspective – more specifically, regarding ultimate explanations – an important question is what evolutionary processes have developed the cognitive and social skills underlying manipulation (Bereczkei 2017). What factors of the social environment have affected the development of Machiavellianism? What selection forces have shaped the evolution of manipulative strategies? Let us consider the possible answers.

6.1. Arms race

Many species exhibit deceptive behaviour in the form of automatic and stereotypical responses to specific situations. Saturniid moths bear large colourful eyespots on their wings, which resemble the large staring eyes of raptors (e.g. owls and hawks). When a natural enemy (e.g. a blue jay) appears, the moth stretches out its wings and shows its eyespots, which elicits fear in their enemies. The momentary resulting petrification of the predator is enough for the moth to escape.

Manipulative behaviours exhibited by higher-order animals – and by humans, of course – mostly involve some form of intentionality. Such tactical deception occurs under conditions that enable individuals to adjust their behaviours to subtle influences and changes in their social environment (Hauser 1997). As was discussed previously (Chapter 10), one fundamental characteristic of Machiavellianism is behavioural flexibility and variability, which some refer to as a protean character or chameleon nature. Behavioural plasticity in general is an essential mechanism that enables individuals to adapt to changing environmental conditions. When complexity and variability of the environment increases, it is of critical importance to be able to continuously change reactions according to previous experience and external conditions (Taborsky & Oliveira 2012).

In an evolutionary perspective, Machiavellian intelligence is a special type of social intelligence that enables higher-order animals to continuously change their deceptive tactics in harmony with changes in their social environment. Evolutionists suggest that Machiavellian intelligence comprises innovative and creative forms of social problem solving, which are crucial for successful deception (Strum, Forster, &

BOX 12.5 LEVELS OF DECEPTION

Animals, including humans, engage in various forms of deception, which may show substantial differences depending on the nature of the underlying cognitive processes. Differences are primarily determined by the intention motivating the specific deceptive behaviour and by the extent to which the behaviour serves the acquisition of resources. Philosopher Daniel Dennett (1998) distinguishes between several levels of intentionality, which may have importance in deception, among other things. This "zero-order intentionality" does not involve any form of intentionality but is simply based on a stimulus-response schema generated by natural selection in order to improve the chances of survival and reproduction. Anglerfish bear a moving – and, in some cases, even luminous – lure to attract other fish swimming nearby. These latter expect to catch prey but, eventually, themselves fall prey to the anglerfish. The so-called "first-order intentionality" differs from the former level in that the animal carries out an action that is aimed at deceiving another individual. This level may be exemplified by the case when a cat is painfully meowing outside the entrance door; when its owner gets up and lets it in, the cat immediately occupies its owner's place in the armchair situated in front of the warm fireplace. Despite its apparent complexity and purposefulness, this behaviour presumably is the result of a relatively simple associative learning process. During this process, the cat associates two previous events – the response elicited by its meowing and the comfort of the vacant armchair – in a new situation. Explanation of the behaviour does not require the assumption that the cat has intentions.

The simplest form of intentional deception is based on "second-order intentionality". This can be formalised as follows: "X wants Y to think Z while X knows that not-Z." In other words, one individual manipulates another by implanting a false belief in them in order to achieve their own goal. An adequate example of this level is the young baboon's behaviour described above. Humans, of course, exhibit substantially higher levels; they are able to apply fourth and fifth-order intentionality: "Peter wants Helene to believe that John did not want to explain to Martha why Stephen had been late."

Hutchins 1997; Hauser 1997). Among these, one important element is concealment of intention: the efficiency of manipulative tactics largely depends on whether the target detects the deceptive intention. Concealing manipulative intentions and thereby achieving success are considerably facilitated by a protean attitude; that is, using diverse and continuously altering tactics, which makes deception unpredictable. Due to the benefits of behavioural flexibility, natural selection may have favoured the ability to develop alternative tactics, which in turn may have facilitated the evolution of more and more sophisticated manipulative strategies (Miller 1997).

This process is closely related to the evolutionary "arms race" (see Box 12.6). More and more sophisticated deceptive tactics may have led to gradual development of the psychological mechanisms of deception detection which, in turn, exerted selection pressure on ever more improved manipulation skills and so on. The evolution of Machiavellian intelligence may be represented by a spiral ascending in space and time: the more complex the manipulative skills developed, the more efficient did counteractions against deception evolve (Goody 1997). This arms race has resulted in accelerating development of several cognitive abilities. It has led to the emergence of a form of manipulative flexibility one of the essential functions of which is to improve the unpredictability of deception and thereby to prevent detection.

It has to be noted that while manipulative behaviours of a chameleon nature leave the target uncertain regarding the outcome of the event, cooperative behaviour is based on predictable rather than unpredictable actions. More specifically, cooperation requires partners to be attuned to one another, to recognise one another's intentions and to plan their next move in accordance with their partner's current behaviours. In other words, predictability of the partner's behaviour is beneficial under conditions that have contributed to the evolution of empathy, trustworthiness and honesty (Miller 1997).

BOX 12.6 ARMS RACE

Evolutionary transformations are often driven by processes that follow the logic of an arms race. For example, predators are successful if they are strong and fast enough to take down prey. In response to predator success, prey species undergo an evolutionary transformation that further improves their physical skills and speed. This, in turn, exerts selection pressure on the physique of predators, further enhancing their capacity. Parallel selection processes with opposite effects come into play, in which advantages gained on one side provide the basis for advantageous changes on the other.

Such races often appear in an extremely complex form and last for a long period (Krebs & Davies 1981). Ancestors of the cuckoo presumably selected "naïve" targets initially, that is, individuals of a bird species (the "host") that could not distinguish a cuckoo's eggs in their nests. As a result of mutation, however, the ability to recognise eggs emerged in the host species and gradually improved, increasing the host's reproductive success. In turn, cuckoos laid eggs that became more and more similar to the host's own eggs. Effects brought about by one species were always followed by a delayed counter-effect on the other species' side. After a while, cuckoos reached the limit of egg imitation, forcing them to change hosts: they chose another unsuspicious bird species to hatch their eggs. It may actually be reconstructed whether various bird species (e.g. red-backed shrike, robin) were exposed to cuckoos' brood parasitism in the past, and if yes, whether their ability to recognise eggs improved.

The arms race has played an important role in human evolution as well. To bring an example related to Machiavellianism: sophisticated abilities to deceive others and to detect deception probably developed during a coevolutionary process (Trivers 1985). At the beginning of this process, a primitive form of deception – based on complete denial of cooperation and reciprocity – was eliminated by natural selection since it was relatively easy to detect, hence the group applied vigorous sanctions against such behaviour. However, more moderate forms of deception – which involved reciprocation although this always remained below the profit gained – continued to be practiced, including the most diverse forms of perfidy, hypocrisy and swindles. From that time on, a complicated evolutionary game started in our ancestors' social environment. Natural selection favoured more sophisticated and more covert forms of deception while, at the same time, it also facilitated the emergence of perceptual and cognitive processes serving quick and efficient detection of deceivers. These, in turn, exerted selection pressure on even more sophisticated forms of deception, which resulted in more and more complicated detection techniques and so on. The current situation is that people show high performance in both. Even if disregarding speech and only considering nonverbal communication, people are found to exhibit an incredibly sophisticated repertoire of lying and deception techniques. People are able to conceal emotional facial expressions that they do not want to publicly communicate (Ekman 1991). However, studies of the past 15 years have clearly demonstrated that sophisticated psychological mechanisms serve deception detection as well: most people are able to decide who deceived whom in a previous situation, merely on the basis of the deceiver's facial expression (Balint-Kovacs, Hernadi, & Bereczkei 2013; Verplaetse et al. 2007).

6.2. Frequency-dependent selection

Besides the arms race, another evolutionary mechanism may also have contributed to the development of Machiavellian behavioural flexibility. This is known as frequency-dependent selection, and is driven by very peculiar dynamics (see Box 12.7). Since, as was discussed earlier, Machiavellianism proved a profitable strategy under certain conditions during evolution, Machiavellians improved their chances of survival and reproduction, hence their number began to increase in the population. However, the greater their number was in a given community, the greater the challenges they had to face. The probability of being detected increased as well as the risk that Machiavellians would encounter, and try to take advantage of, each other. In parallel with its spreading, the Machiavellian strategy demanded more and more investment whereas it became less and less profitable, which resulted in a continuous decrease in the number of Machiavellians. This process, however, reached a certain point after which Machiavellianism became profitable again. Specifically, a decreasing number of Machiavellians combined with an increasing number of cooperators resulted in more and more potential targets, hence larger profits could be gained by less investment. Such continuous fluctuation may have led to the development of a wide variety of manipulative techniques. Some of them support adaptation in times when ample resources are available while others serve survival under adverse circumstances.

BOX 12.7 FREQUENCY-DEPENDENT SELECTION

Rarely occurring types in many cases are in an advantageous position in terms of adaptation to the environment, but only as long as their number remains below a certain limit. In parallel with their increasing number, their advantage gradually decays. Large male bullfrogs occupy territories providing ample food and try to attract females by loud croaking. Small young males, which are not strong enough to acquire a territory, follow an alternative strategy. Their appearance deceives territory owners, which do not consider them rivals. Satellites wait in silence near dominant males until females arrive, with which they try to mate. While their chances of mating are substantially lower than those of dominant males (only 4 or 5 out of 73 matings involve young males), this strategy still offers them an opportunity of reproduction despite their physical underdevelopment. However, the more satellites – and the fewer large territory owners – there are, the less chance the former have to join in the competition for mates.

The 50-50 distribution of sexes among animals and humans is considered to be a result of frequency-dependent selection (Trivers 1985). It is a well-known fact that the vast majority of species have roughly equal numbers of male and female offspring. Earlier, this was explained by a group selection theory that suggested it was in the reproductive "interest" of each of these species that every individual find a mate, and thereby the species reach the highest possible number of offspring. However, several issues were raised concerning the validity of this explanation, meaning that individual frequency-dependent selection has recently been dominantly considered responsible for the emergence of parity. The argument for this hypothesis is as follows. Suppose that there is a population in which substantially fewer males are born than females. The males, who easily find a partner (or partners) among a large number of females, have more biological children, among whom the male issue likewise have an advantageous position in terms of having biological children and so on. However, the initial advantage of males decays over time since an increasing number of boys have less and less chance to find a partner in the population. Moreover, after a certain point, parents come off better if they have girls, who gain an advantage in mate choice and reproduction due to the male majority. This continuous process of oscillatory evolution reaches equilibrium in the long term: roughly equal numbers of boys and girls are born.

No experiment or computer simulation has yet been devised to model the role of frequency-dependent selection in the evolution of Machiavellianism. There are research findings, however, suggesting that this evolutionary mechanism may have contributed to the diversity of Machiavellian tactics. Researchers revealed relatively early that the success or unsuccess of deception – and, consequently, the frequency of Machiavellians in a population – largely depends on the probability of detection and on the associated costs and disadvantages imposed on detected Machiavellians (Dunbar 1998; Hauser 1997). In a different perspective, one may suggest that the frequency of manipulation also depends on what strategies potential targets use and to what degree Machiavellians profit in a given situation. When the benefits of manipulation decrease, people expectably are less willing to pursue a strategy that serves to exploit others. In a study, young adults played the Public Goods Game (Box 8.3 in Chapter 8). A subject's behaviour was categorised as a defector strategy if the average sum they transferred to the group's account did not exceed 20% of their private funds. A subject's strategy was considered altruistic if their average contribution to the public pool amounted to at least 80% of their funds. It is not surprising that a substantial difference was found between defectors' and altruists' Mach scores (108 and 97, respectively). The study found that the number of defectors was the highest when many players followed an altruistic strategy. This mostly occurred early in the game. When altruism decreased – usually around the third round – the number of those thriving on defection also decreased. Unfortunately, the experiment did not offer an opportunity to observe the opposite tendency. Therefore, the question remains whether preference for a defector strategy becomes more frequent when the number of altruists begins to increase again for any reason.

7. Summary: The costs and benefits of Machiavellianism

Both arms-race and frequency-dependent selection are closely related to the fact that any population shows large variance in Mach scores. All related studies show that the degree of Machiavellianism – irrespective of the specific scale or test used – varies from individual to individual. Some show a complete lack of a cynical worldview, ruthlessness and manipulative intentions whereas others exhibit high levels of such characteristics. Most people, of course, occupy an intermediate position between the two extremes: they usually seek to cooperate while sometimes they are also willing to take advantage of others.

So far, this behavioural diversity has been considered self-evident: any population, society or group shows a roughly normal distribution of Machiavellianism as well as of any other personality trait or intellectual ability. At this point, the question is why this immense diversity has evolved. Daniel Nettle (2006, 2007) argues that differences between individuals and groups have developed in the course of evolution so that organisms can adapt to specific ranges of environmental conditions. Thus, the question requires one to identify diverse manifestations of a universal behavioural strategy (Machiavellianism in this case) and the conditions under which these have evolved. Nettle suggests that behavioural and genetic variability is best explained by considering evolutionary costs and benefits of the given behaviour in order to identify the optimal forms of adaptation by matching the two sides against one another.

The studies presented here clearly show that a high level of Machiavellianism often proves beneficial. Machiavellians usually successfully take advantage of others, especially in an unpredictable environment (e.g. in a social dilemma situation) and under conditions lacking strict and clear rules (e.g. no punishment is applied). Those with high Mach scores, however, have to pay the price for their success. They are easily recognised and detected in a close-knit community based on personal acquaintances (e.g. a company of friends or a workplace community). In the long term, they may lose the social capital previously acquired through a charming demeanour. Such a loss may have substantial consequences for them in present-day societies, but it might be even more so in an evolutionary environment where – as studies of current hunter-gatherer societies have revealed – an individual who lost the approval of their community was condemned to death, both in the social sense (ostracised), and often biologically as well (Bereczkei 2009).

Considering now the other side of the spectrum, that is, the consequences of low Mach individuals' behaviour, the picture likewise offers many diverse forms of costs and benefits. People showing low levels of Machiavellianism outdo Machiavellians in most social situations that require coordinated actions. Cooperation usually requires some form of empathy, mutual attunement and understanding, which Machiavellians generally lack. Moreover, low Machs may also gain advantages in environments where social norms are observed and noncompliance is sanctioned. By contrast, low Machs are often disadvantaged in social situations that involve intense emotions. This book has presented several experiments that demonstrate that low Machs are rarely able to detach themselves from the emotional influences and value-related aspects of the situation, and their emotional involvement often hinders discernment and rational thinking.

In light of this, Machiavellianism may be considered a continuum encompassing various combinations of costs and benefits of varying degrees. Therefore, it is presumable that the optimal outcome is to be found in the middle of this spectrum: individuals positioned in this range are manipulative enough to acquire sufficient resources but not so much as to risk losing them. Nevertheless, such strategies do not eliminate the diversity of Machiavellianism, particularly because changes in the environment make shifts in the momentary optimal balance between costs and benefits, which continuously changes in space and time. As we have seen, in an environment where manipulation is easy to detect, Machiavellians expect to profit somewhat from pretended cooperation until conditions of the social environment enable them to make use of their much more profitable manipulative tactics. Moreover, the profits enjoyed by Machiavellians also depend on what the most frequently used behavioural strategies in the population are, which brings frequency-dependent selection into play. In an environment where most individuals in the population are altruists, and therefore make "easy" targets, Machiavellians can efficiently assert their self-interest. These evolutionary processes result in a wide spectrum of Machiavellianism in the population, each of whose points represents adaptation to a specific social situation.

BIBLIOGRAPHY

Al Ain, S., Carré, A., Fantini-Hauwel, C., Baudouin, J., & Besche-Richard, C. (2013). What is the emotional core of the multidimensional Machiavellian personality trait? *Frontiers in Psychology*, *4*, 454. DOI: 10.3389/fpsyg.2013.00454.

Ali, F., Amorim, S., & Chamorro-Premuzic, T. (2009). Empathy deficits and trait emotional intelligence in psychopathy and Machiavellianism. *Personality and Individual Differences*, *47*, 758–762.

Ali, F., & Chamorro-Premuzic, T. (2010). Investigating theory of mind deficits in nonclinical psychopathy. *Personality and Individual Differences*, *49*, 169–174.

Andrew, J., Cooke, M., & Muncer, S. J. (2008). The relationship between empathy and Machiavellianism: An alternative to empathizing-systemizing theory. *Personality and Individual Differences*, *44*, 1203–1211.

Andrews, P. W. (2002). The influence of postreliance detection on the deceptive efficacy of dishonest signals of intent: Understanding facial clues to deceit as the outcome of signaling tradeoffs. *Evolution and Human Behavior*, *23*, 103–122.

Apperly, I. (2011). *Mindreaders: The Cognitive Basis of "Theory of Mind"*. New York: Psychology Press.

Austin, E. J., Farrelly, D., Black, C., & Moore, H. (2007). Emotional intelligence, Machiavellianism and emotional manipulation: Does EI have a dark side? *Personality and Individual Differences*, *43*, 179–189.

Austin, E. J., & O'Donell, M. M. (2013). Development and preliminary validation of a scale to assess managing the emotions of others. *Personality and Individual Differences*, *55*, 834–839.

Azizli, N., Atkinson, B. E., Baughman, H. M., Chin, K., Vernon, P. A., Harris, E., & Veselka, L. (2016). Lies and crimes: Dark Triad, misconduct, and high-stakes deception. *Personality and Individual Differences*, *89*, 34–39.

Batson, C. D. (2009). These things called empathy: Eight related but distinct phenomena. In: *The Social Neuroscience of Empathy* (Eds. J. Decety & W. Ickes). Cambridge: MIT Press, pp. 3–15.

Baughman, H. M., Jonason, P. K., Lyons, M., & Vernon, P. A. (2014). Liar liar pants on fire: Cheater strategies linked to the Dark Triad. *Personality and Individual Differences*, *71*, 35–38.

Baumgartner, T., Fischbacher, U., Feierabend, A., Lutz, K., & Fehr, E. (2009). The neural circuitry of a broken promise. *Neuron, 64*, 756–770.

Belsky, J., Steinberg, L., & Draper, P. (1991). Childhood experience, interpersonal development, and reproductive strategy: An evolutionary theory of socialization. *Child Development, 62*, 647–670.

Benjamin, J., Ebstein, R. P., & Belmaker, R. H. (2005). *Molecular Genetics and the Human Personality.* Washington: American Psychiatric Publishing.

Bereczkei, T. (2015). The manipulative skill: Cognitive devices and their neural correlates underlying Machiavellian's decision making. *Brain and Cognition, 99*, 24–31.

Bereczkei, T. (2017). Machiavellian intelligence hypothesis revisited: What evolved cognitive and social skills may underlie human manipulation. *Evolutionary Behavioral Sciences.* (In press).

Bereczkei, T., & Birkas, B. (2014). The insightful manipulator: Machiavellians' interpersonal tactics may be linked to their superior information processing skills. *International Journal of Psychological Studies.*

Bereczkei, T. Birkas, B., & Kerekes, Z. (2010). The presence of others, prosocial traits, Machiavellism: A personality X situation approach. *Social Psychology, 41*, 238–245.

Bereczkei, T., & Csanaky, A. (2001). Stressful family environment, mortality, and child socialization: Life-history strategies among adolescents and adults from unfavourable social circumstances. *International Journal of Behavioral Development, 25*, 501–508.

Bereczkei, T., & Czibor, A. (2014). Personality and situational factors differently influence high Mach and low Mach persons' decisions in a social dilemma game. *Personality and Individual Differences, 64*, 168–173.

Bereczkei, T., Szabo, Z. P., & Czibor, A. (2015). Abusing good intentions: Machiavellians strive for exploiting cooperators. *SAGE Open Publications*, April–June 1–5.

Bereczkei, T., Deak, A., Papp, P., Kincses, P., Perlaki, G., & Gergely, O. (2015). The neural bases of the Machiavellians' decision making in fair and unfair situations. *Brain and Cognition, 98*, 53–64.

Bereczkei, T., Deak, A., Papp, P., Perlaki, G., & Gergely, O. (2013). Neural correlates of Machiavellian strategies in a social dilemma task. *Brain and Cognition, 82*, 108–116.

Birkás, B. & Csathó, A. (2015) Size the day: The time perspectives of the Dark Triad. *Personality and Individual Differences*, 86, 318–320.

Birkás, B., Csathó, Á., Gács, B., & Bereczkei, T. (2015). Nothing ventured nothing gained: Strong associations between reward sensitivity and two measures of Machiavellianism. *Personality and Individual Differences, 74*, 112–115.

Birkás, B., Gács, B., & Csathó, Á. (2016). Keep calm and don't worry: Different Dark Triad traits predict distinct coping preferences. *Preferences and Individual Differences, 88*, 134–138.

Bogart, K., Geis, F., Levy, M., & Zimbardo, P. (1970). No dissonance for Machiavellians. In: *Studies in Machiavellianism* (Eds. R. Christie & F. Geis). New York: Academic Press, pp. 236–259.

Borgerhoff-Mulder, M. (1992). Reproductive decisions. In: *Evolutionary Ecology and Human Behavior* (Eds. E. A. Smith & B. Winterhalder). New York: Aldine de Gruyter, pp. 339–374.

Byrne, R. (1995). *Thinking Ape: Evolutionary Origins of Intelligence.* Oxford: Oxford University Press.

Byrne, R. (1997). The technical intelligence hypothesis: An additional evolutionary stimulus to intelligence? In: *Machiavellian Intelligence II* (Eds. A. Whiten & R. Byrne). Cambridge: Cambridge University Press, pp. 289–311.

Byrne, R. W., & Whiten, A. (Eds.) (1988). *Machiavellian Intelligence: Social Expertise and the Evolution of Intellect in Monkeys, Apes, and Humans.* Oxford: Clarendon Press.

Campbell, J. D., Schermer, J. A., Villani, V. C., Nguyen, B., Vickers, L., & Vernon, P. A. (2009). A behavioral genetic study of the Dark Triad of personality and moral development. *Twin Research and Human Genetics, 12,* 132–136.

Carver, C. S. and Scheier, M. (1998) *Perspectives on Personality.* New Jersey: Pearson Education, Inc.

Cherulnik, P. D., Way, J. H., Ames, S., & Hutto, D. B. (1981). Impressions of high and low Machiavellian men. *Journal of Personality, 49,* 388–400.

Christie, R., & Geis, F. (1970). *Studies in Machiavellianism.* New York: Academic Press.

Chung, K. L., & Charles, K. (2016). Giving the benefit of the doubt: The role of vulnerability in the perception of Dark Triad behaviors. *Personality and Individual Differences, 101,* 208–213.

Cooper, S., & Peterson, C. (1980). Machiavellianism and spontaneous cheating in competition. *Journal of Research in Personality, 14,* 70–75.

Cosmides, L., & Tooby, J. (1992). Cognitive adaptations for social exchange. In: *The Adapted Mind: Evolutionary Psychology and the Generation of Culture* (Eds. J. Barkow, L. Cosmides, & J. Tooby). New York: Oxford University Press, pp. 163–228.

Crawford, C. (1998). Environments and adaptations: Then and now. In: *Handbook of Evolutionary Psychology: Ideas, Issues, and Applications* (Eds. C. B. Crawford & D. L. Krebs). Mahwah, NJ: Lawrence Erlbaum, pp. 275–302.

Crook, J. H. (1988). The experimental context of intellect. In: *Machiavellian Intelligence: Social Expertise and the Evolution of Intellect in Monkeys, Apes, and Humans* (Eds. R. Byrne & A. Whiten). Oxford: Clarendon Press, pp. 347–362.

Crysel, L. C., Crosier, B. S., & Webster, G. D. (2013). The Dark Triad and risk behavior. *Personality and Individual Differences, 54,* 35–40.

Czibor, A., & Bereczkei, T. (2012). Machiavellian people's success results from monitoring their partners. *Personality and Individual Differences, 53,* 202–206.

Czibor, A., Vincze, O., & Bereczkei, T. (2014). Feelings and motives underlying Machiavellian behavioural strategies; narrative reports in a social dilemma situation. *International Journal of Psychology, 49,* 519–524.

Davies, M., & Stone, T. (2003). Synthesis: Psychological understanding and social skills. In: *Individual Differences in the Theory of Mind: Implications for Typical and Atypical Development* (Eds. B. Repacholi & V. Slaughter). Hove, UK: Psychology Press, pp. 305–352.

Dawkins, R., & Krebs, J. R. (1978). Animal signals: Information or manipulation? In: *Behavioral Ecology: An Evolutionary Approach* (Eds. J. R. Krebs & N. B. Davies). Oxford: Blackwell Scientific Publication, pp. 282–309.

Deluga, R. J. (2001). American presidential Machiavellianism: Implications for charismatic leadership and rated performance. *Leadership Quarterly, 12,* 339–363.

De Raad, B. (2005). The trait-coverage of emotional intelligence. *Personality and Individual Differences, 38,* 673–687.

Digman, J. M. (1990). Personality structure: Emergence of the five-factor model. *Annual Review of Psychology, 41,* 417–440.

Dreisbach, G., & Fischer, R. (2012). Conflicts as aversive signals. *Brain and Cognition, 78,* 94–98.

Dulebohn, J. H., Conlon, D. E., Sarinopulus, I., Davison, R. B., & McNamara, G. (2009). The biological bases of unfairness: Neuroimaging evidence for the distinctiveness of procedural and distributive justice. *Organizational Behavior and Human Decision Processes, 110,* 140–151.

Dunbar, R. I. M. (1992). Neocortex size as a constraint on group size in primates. *Journal of Human Evolution, 20,* 469–493.

Dunbar, R. I. M. (1998). The social brain hypothesis. *Evolutionary Anthropology, 6,* 178–190.

Dunbar, R. I. M. (2002). Why are apes so smart? In: *Primate Life Histories* (Eds. P. M. Kapeller & M. Perriera). Cambridge: MIT Press.

Durkin, J. E. (1970). Encountering: What low Machs do. In: *Studies in Machiavellianism* (Eds. R. Christie & F. Geis). New York: Academic Press, pp. 260–284.

Egan, V., Chan, S., & Shorter, G. W. (2014). The Dark Triad, happiness, and subjective well-being. *Personality and Individual Differences, 67*, 17–22.

Eibl-Eibesfeldt, I. (1989). *Human Ethology.* New York: Aldine de Gruyter.

Ekman, P. (1991). Who can catch a liar? *American Psychologist, 46*, 913–920.

Ellis, B. J., & Garber, J. (2000). Psychological antecedents of variation in girls' pubertal timing: Maternal depression, stepfather presence, and marital and family stress. *Child Development, 71*, 485–501.

Ellis, B. J., McFadyen-Ketchum, S., Dodge, K. A., Pettit, G. S., & Bates, J. E. (1999). Quality of early family relationships and individual differences in the timing of pubertal maturation in girls: A longitudinal test of an evolutionary model. *Journal of Personality and Social Psychology, 77*, 387–401.

Esperger, Zs. & Bereczkei, T. (2012) Machiavellianism and spontaneous mentalization: One step ahead of others. *European Journal of Personality, 26*, 580–587.

Etkin, A., Egner, T., & Kalisch, R. (2011). Emotional processing in anterior cingulated and medial prefrontal cortex. *Trends in Cognitive Sciences, 15*, 85–93.

Evans, J. St. B. T. (2010). *Thinking Twice: Two Minds in One Brain.* Oxford, England: Oxford University Press.

Exlinne, R. V., Thiabaut, J., Hickey, C., & Gumpart, P. (1970). Visual interaction in relation to Machiavellianism. In: *Studies in Machiavellianism* (Eds. R. Christie & F. Geis). New York: Academic Press, pp. 53–76.

Eysenck, H. J. (1970). *The Structure of Human Personality.* London: Methuen.

Fehr, B., Samsom, B., & Paulhus, D. L. (1992). The construct of Machiavellianism: Twenty years later. In: *Advances in Personality Assessment* (Eds. C. D. Spielberger & J. N. Butcher). Hillsdale, NJ: Erlbaum, pp. 77–116.

Figueredo, A. J., Vasquez, G., Brumbach, B. H., Sefcek, J. A., Kirsner, B. R., & Jacobs, W. J. (2005). The K-factor: Individual differences in life history strategy. *Personality and Individual Differences, 39*, 1349–1360.

Furnham, A., Richards, S. C., & Paulhus, D. L. (2013). The Dark Triad personality: A 10 year review. *Social and Personality Psychology Compass, 7*, 199–216.

Gable, M., Hollon, C., & Dangello, F. (1992). Managerial structuring of work as a moderator of the Machiavellianism and job performance relationship. *Journal of Psychology, 126*, 317–325.

Geis, F. (1970). The con game. In: *Studies in Machiavellianism* (Eds. R. Christie & F. Geis). New York: Academic Press, pp. 130–160.

Geis, F., & Christie, R. (1970). Overview of experimental Research. In: *Studies in Machiavellianism* (Eds. R. Christie & F. Geis). New York: Academic Press, pp. 285–313.

Geis, F., Christie, R., & Nelson, C. (1970). In search of the Machiavelianism. In *Studies in Machiavellianism* (Eds. R. Christie & F. L. Geis). New York: Academic Press, pp. 76–95.

Geis, F., & Levy, M. (1970). The eye of the beholder. In: *Studies in Machiavellianism* (Eds. R. Christie & F. Geis). New York: Academic Press, pp. 210–235.

Geis, F., Weinheimer, S., & Berger, D. (1970). Playing legislature: Cool heads and hot issues. In: *Studies in Machiavellianism* (Eds. R. Christie & F. Geis). New York: Academic Press, pp. 190–209.

Geis, F. L. (1978). Machiavellianism. In: *Dimensions of Personality* (Eds. H. London & J. E. Exner). New York: Wiley, pp. 305–363.

Geis, F. L., & Moon, H. (1981). Machiavellianism and deception. *Journal of Personality and Social Psychology, 41*, 766–775.

Giammarco, E. A., Atkinson, B., Baughman, H. M., Veselka, L., & Vernon, P. A. (2013). The relation between antisocial personality and the perceived ability to deceive. *Personality and Individual Differences, 54,* 246–250.

Gintis, H., Bowles, S., Boyd, R., & Fehr, E. (2003). Explaining altruistic behavior in humans. *Evolution and Human Behavior, 24,* 153–172.

Goody, E. N. (1997). Social intelligence and language: Another Rubicon. In: *Machiavellian Intelligence II: Extensions and Evaluations* (Eds. A. Whiten & R. W. Byrne). Cambridge: Cambridge University Press, pp. 365–396.

Graber, J. A., Brooks-Gunn, J., & Warren, M. P. (1995). The antecedents of menarcheal age: Heredity, family environment, and stressful life events. *Child Development, 66,* 346–359.

Grams, W. C., & Rogers, R. W. (1990). Power and personality: Effects of Machiavellianism, need for approval, and motivation on use of influence tactics. *The Journal of General Psychology, 117,* 71–82.

Grieve, R. (2011). Mirror mirror: The role of self-monitoring and sincerity in emotional manipulation. *Personality and Individual Differences, 51,* 981–985.

Gunnthorsdottir, A., McCabe, K., & Smith, V. (2002). Using the Machiavellianism instrument to predict trustworthiness in a bargaining game. *Journal of Economic Psychology, 23,* 49–66.

Harrell, W. A., & Hartnagel, T. (1976). The impact of Machiavellianism and the trustfulness of the victim on laboratory theft. *Sociometry, 39,* 157–165.

Hauser, M. D. (1997). Minding the behavior of deception. In: *Machiavellian Intelligence II: Extensions and Evaluations* (Eds. A. Whiten & R. W. Byrne). Cambridge: Cambridge University Press, pp. 112–143.

Hawley, P. H. (2006). Evolution and personality: A new look at Machiavellianism. In: *Handbook of Personality Development* (Eds. D. Mroczek & T. Little). Mahwah, NJ: Lawrence Erlbaum, pp. 147–161.

Heinrich, J., Boyd, R., Bowles, S., Camerer, C., Fehr, E., & Gintis, H. (2005). Economic man in cross-cultural perspective: Behavioral experiments in 15 small-scale societies. *Behavioral and Brain Sciences, 28,* 1–46.

Holtzman, N. S. (2011). Facing a psychopath: Detecting the Dark Triad from emotionally-neutral faces, using prototypes from the Personality Faceaurus. *Journal of Research in Personality, 45,* 648–654.

Humphrey, N. K. (1976). The social function of intellect. In: *Growing Points in Ethology* (Eds. P. P. G. Bateson & R. A. Hinde). Cambridge: Cambridge University Press, pp. 303–317.

Jacobwitz, S., & Egan, V. (2006). The Dark Triad and normal personality traits. *Personality and Individual Differences, 40,* 331–339.

Jonason, P. K., Koenig, B. L., & Tost, J. (2010). Living a fast life: The Dark Triad and life history theory. *Human Nature, 21,* 428–442.

Jonason, P. K., & Krause, L. (2013). The emotional deficits associated with the Dark Triad traits: Cognitive empathy, affective empathy, and alexithymia. *Personality and Individual Differences, 55,* 532–537.

Jonason, P. K., & Lavertu, A. N. (2017). The reproductive costs and benefits associated with the Dark Triad traits in women. *Personality and Individual Differences, 110,* 38–40.

Jonason, P. K., Li, N. P., Webster, G. D., & Scmitt, D. P. (2009). The Dark Triad: Facilitating a short-term mating strategy in men. *European Journal of Personality, 23,* 5–18.

Jonason, P. K., Luevano, V. X., & Adams, H. M. (2012). How the Dark Triad traits predict relationship choices. *Personality and Individual Differences, 53,* 180–184.

Jonason, P. K., Lyons, M., Baughman, H. M., & Vernon, P. A. (2014). What a tangled web we weave: The Dark Triad traits and deception. *Personality and Individual Differences, 70,* 117–119.

Jonason, P. K., Lyons, M., & Bethell, E. (2014). The making of Darth Vader: Parent-child care and the Dark Triad. *Personality and Individual Differences, 67,* 30–34.

Jonason, P. K., Strosser, G. L., Kroll, C. H., Duineveld, J. J., & Baruffi, S. A. (2015). Valuing myself over others: The Dark Triad traits and moral and social values. *Personality and Individual Differences, 81*, 102–106.

Jonason, P. K., & Webster, G. D. (2012). A protean approach to social influence: Dark Triad personalities and social influence tactics. *Personality and Individual Differences, 52*, 521–526.

Jones, D. N. (2014). Risk in the face of retribution: Psychopathic individuals persist in financial misbehavior among Dark Triad. *Personality and Individual Differences, 67*, 109–113.

Jones, D. N., & Figueredo, A. J. (2013). The core of darkness: Uncovering the heart of the Dark Triad. *European Journal of Personality, 27*, 521–531.

Jones, D. N., & Paulhus, D. L. (2009). Machiavellianism. In: *Individual Differences in Social Behavior* (Eds. M. R. Leary & R. H. Hoyle). New York: Guilford, pp. 93–108.

Jones, D. N., & Paulhus, D. L. (2010). Different provocations trigger aggression in narcissist and psychopaths. *Social Psychology and Personality Science, 1*, 12–18.

Jones, D. N., & Paulhus, D. L. (2011). The role of impulsivity in the Dark Triad of personality. *Personality and Individual Differences, 51*, 679–682.

Keating, C. F. (2003). Charismatic faces: Social status cues put face appeal in context. In: *Facial Attractiveness: Evolutionary, Cognitive, and Social Perspectives* (Eds. G. Rhodes & L. A. Zebrowitz). London: Ablex, pp. 153–192.

Keenan, T. (2003). Individual differences in theory of mind: The preschool years and beyond. In: *Individual Differences in the Theory of Mind: Implications for Typical and Atypical Development* (Eds. B. Repacholi & V. Slaughter). Hove, UK: Psychology Press, pp. 153–172.

Kim, K., & Smith, P. K. (1998). Retrospective survey of parental marital relations and child reproductive development. *International Journal of Behavioral Development, 22*, 729–751.

Knoch, D., Pascual-Leone, A., Meyer, K., Treyer, V., & Fehr, E. (2006). Diminishing reciprocal fairness by disrupting the right prefrontal cortex. *Science, 314*, 829–832.

Kolb, B., & Whishaw, I. Q. (1998). Brain plasticity and behaviour. *Annual Review of Psychology, 49*, 43–64.

Kowalski, C. M., Vernon, P. A., & Schermer, J. A. (2017). Vocational interests and Dark Triad personality: Are there dark career choices? *Personality and Individual Differences, 104*, 43–47.

Kraut, R. E., & Price, J. D. (1976). Machiavellianism in parents and their children. *Journal of Personality and Social Psychology, 33*, 782–786.

Krebs, J. R., & Davies, N. B. (1993). *An Introduction to Behavioral Ecology.* Oxford: Blackwell Scientific Publications.

Kringelbach, M. L. (2005). The human orbitofrontal cortex: Linking reward to hedonic experience. *Nature Reviews Neurosciences, 6*, 691–702.

Krystal, H. (1988). *Integration and Self-Healing.* Hillsdale, NJ: Analytic Press Inc.

Láng, A. (2015). Borderline personality organization predicts Machiavellian interpersonal tactics. *Personality and Individual Differences, 80*, 28–31.

Láng, A., & Birkás, B. (2014). Machiavellianism and perceived family functioning in adolescence. *Personality and Individual Differences, 63*, 69–74.

Liakakis, G., Nickel, J., & Seitz, R. J. (2011). Diversity of the inferior frontal gyrus: A meta-analysis of neuroimaging studies. *Behavioral Brain Research, 225*, 341–347.

Linton, D. K., & Power, J. L. (2013). The personality traits of workplace bullies are often shared by their victims: Is there a dark side to victims? *Personality and Individual Differences, 54*, 738–743.

Liu, J., Zhang, M., Jou, J., Wu, X., Li, W., & Qiu, J. (2012). Neural bases of falsification in conditional proposition testing: Evidence from an fMRI study. *International Journal of Psychophysiology, 85*, 249–256.

Liu, X., Hairston, J., Schrier, M., & Fan, J. (2011). Common and distinct networks underlying reward valence and processing stages: A meta-analysis of functional neuroimaging studies. *Neuroscience and Biobehavioral Reviews, 35*, 1219–1236.

Lyons, M., Caldwell, T., & Schultz, S. (2010). Mind-reading and manipulation: Is Machiavellianism related to theory of mind? *Journal of Evolutionary Psychology, 8*(3), 261–274.

Maguire, E. A., Woolett, K., & Spiers, H. J. (2006). London taxi drivers and bus drivers: A structural MRI and neuropsychological analysis. *Hippocampus, 16*, 1091–1101.

Malesza, M., & Ostaszewski, P. (2016). Dark side and impulsivity: Associations between the Dark Triad, self-report and behavioral measures of impulsivity. *Personality and Individual Differences, 88*, 197–201.

Martin, R. A., Lastuk, J. M., Jeffery, J., Vernon, P., & Veselka, L. (2012). Relationships between the Dark Triad and humor styles: A replication and extension. *Personality and Individual Differences, 52*, 178–182.

McDonald, M., Donellan, M. B., & Navarrete, C. D. (2012). A life history approach to understanding in the Dark Triad. *Personality and Individual Difference, 52*, 601–605.

McHoskey, J. W. (1995). Narcissism and Machiavellianism. *Psychological Reports, 77*, 755–759.

McHoskey, J. W. (1999). Machiavellianism, intrinsic versus extrinsic goals and social interest: A self-determination theory analysis. *Motivation and Emotion, 23*, 267–283.

McHoskey, J. W. (2001a). Machiavellianism and personality dysfunction. *Personality and Individual Differences, 31*, 791–798.

McHoskey, J. W. (2001b). Machiavellianism and sexuality: On the moderating role of biological sex. *Personality and Individual Differences, 31*, 779–789.

McIllwain, D. (2003). Bypassing empathy: A Machiavellian theory of mind and sneaky power. In: *Individual Differences in Theory of Mind* (Eds. B. Repacholi & V. Slaughter). Macquarie Monographs in Cognitive Science. Hove, E. Sussex: Psychology Press, pp. 39–66.

McLeod, B. A., & Genereux, R. L. (2008). Predicting the acceptability and likelihood of lying: The interaction of personality with type of lie. *Personality and Individual Differences, 45*, 591–596.

Meyer, H. (1992). Norms and self-interest in ultimatum bargaining: The prince's prudence. *Journal of Economic Psychology, 13*, 215–232.

Miller, G. F. (1997). Protean primates: The evolution of adaptive unpredictability in competition and courtship. In: *Machiavellian Intelligence II. Extensions and Evaluations* (Eds. A. Whiten & R. W. Byrne). Cambridge: Cambridge University Press, pp. 312–340.

Mithen, S. (2000). Paleoanthropological perspectives on the theory of mind. In: *Understanding Other Minds: Perspectives from Developmental Neuroscience* (Eds. S. Baron-Cohen, H. Tager-Flusberg, & D. J. Cohen). Oxford: Oxford University Press, pp. 488–502.

Montag, C., Hall, J., Plieger, T., Felten, A., Markett, S., Melchers, M., & Reuter, M. (2015). The DRD3 Ser9Gly polymorphism, Machiavellianism, and its link to schizotypal personality. *Journal of Neuroscience, Psychology, and Economics, 8*, 48–57.

Murphy, P. R. (2012). Attitude, Machiavellianism, and the rationalization of misreporting. *Accounting Organizations and Society, 37*, 242–259.

Nagler, U. K. J., Reiter, K. J., Furtner, M. R., & Rauthmann, J. F. (2014). Is there a "dark intelligence"? Emotional intelligence is used by dark personalities to emotionally manipulate others. *Personality and Individual Differences, 65*, 47–52.

Nettle, D. (2006). The evolution of personality variation in humans and other animals. *American Psychologist, 61*, 622–631.

Nettle, D. (2007). Individual differences. In: *Oxford Handbook of Evolutionary Psychology* (Eds. R. I. M. Dunbar & L. Barrett). Oxford: Oxford University Press, pp. 479–490.

O'Boyle, E. H., Forsyth, D., Banks, G. C., & McDaniel, A. (2013). A meta-analysis of the Dark Triad and work behavior: A social exchange perspective. *Journal of Applied Psychology, 97*, 557–559.

O'Boyle, E. H., Forsyth, D., Banks, G. C., & Story, P. A. (2013). A meta-analytical review of the Dark Triad–intelligence connection. *Journal of Research in Personality, 47*, 789–794.

O'Conner, P. J., & Athota, V. S. (2013). The intervening role of Agreeableness in the relationship between trait emotional intelligence and Machiavellianism: Reassessing the potential dark side of EI. *Personality and Individual Differences*, *55*, 750–754.

O'Doherty, J., Kringelbach, M. L., Rolls, E. T., Hornak, J., & Andrews, C. (2001). Abstract reward and punishment representations in the human orbitofrontal cortex. *Nature Neuroscience*, *4*, 95–102.

Ojha, H. (2007). Parent-child interaction and Machiavellian orientation. *Journal of the Indian Academy of Applied Psychology*, *33*, 285–289.

Orosz, A., & Bereczkei, T. (2015). Research of Machiavellianism by using a card game. *European Human Behavior and Evolution Society Conference*, Helsinki.

Paal, T., & Bereczkei, T. (2007). Adult theory of mind, cooperation, Machiavellianism: The effect of mindreading on social relations. *Personality and Individual Differences*, *43*, 541–551.

Pailing, A., Boon, J., & Egan, V. (2014). Personality, the Dark Triad, and violence. *Personality and Individual Differences*, *67*, 81–86.

Paulhus, D. L., & Williams, K. M. (2002). The Dark Triad of personality: Narcissism, Machiavellianism, and psychopathy. *Journal of Research in Personality*, *36*, 556–563.

Pawlowski, B., Dunbar, R., & Lowen, C. (1998). Neocortex size, social skills, and mating success in primates. *Behavior*, *135*, 357–368.

Penke, L., & Asendorf, J. B. (2008). Beyond global sociosexual orientation: A more differentiated look at sociosexuality and its effect on courtship and romantic relationships. *Journal of Social and Personality Psychology*, *95*, 1113–1135.

Perner, J. (1991). *Understanding the Representational Mind*. Brighton: Harvester.

Pilch, I., & Górnik-Durose, M. E. (2016). Do we need dark traits to explain materialism? The incremental validity of the Dark Triad over the HEXACO domains in predicting materialistic orientation. *Personality and Individual Differences*, *102*, 102–106.

Pilch, M. (2008). Machiavellianism, emotional intelligence, and social competence: Are Machiavellians interpersonally skilled? *Polish Psychological Bulletin*, *39*, 158–164.

Plattheicher, S. (2016). Testosterone, cortisol and the Dark Triad: Narcissism (but not Machiavellianism or psychopathy) is positively related to basal testosterone and cortisol. *Personality and Individual Differences*, *97*, 115–119.

Plomin, R., DeFries, J. C., McClearn, G. E., & McGuffin, P. (2005). *Behavioral Genetics*. New York: Worth Publishers.

Polosan, M., Baciu, M., Perrone, M., Pichat, T., & Bougerot, T. (2011). An fMRI study of the social competition in healthy subjects. *Brain and Cognition*, *77*, 401–411.

Qin, J., & Han, S. (2009). Neurocognitive mechanisms underlying identification of environmental risk. *Neuropsychologia*, *47*, 397–405.

Rada, F. M., Taracena, L., & Rodriguez, M. A. M. (2004). Assessment of Machiavellian intelligence in antisocial disorder with the Mach-IV scale. *Actas Española de Psiquiatría*, *32*, 65–70.

Rauthmann, J. F. (2011). The Dark Triad and interpersonal perception: Similarities and differences in the social consequences of Narcissism, Machiavellianism, and Psychopathy. *Social Psychological and Personality Science*, *3*, 1–10.

Rauthmann, J. F., & Kolar, G. P. (2013). The perceived attractiveness and traits of the Dark Triad: Narcissists are perceived as hot, Machiavellians and psychopaths not. *Personality and Individual Differences*, *54*, 582–586.

Richell, R. A., Mitchell, D. G. V., Newman, C., Leonard, A., Baron-Cohen, S., & Blair, R. J. R. (2003). Theory of mind and psychopathy: Can psychopathic individuals read the 'language of the eyes'? *Neuropsychologia*, *41*(5), 523–526.

Rilling, J. K., Goldsmith, D. R., Glenn, A. L., Jairam, M. R., Elfenbein, H. A., Dagenais, J. E., Murdock, C. D., & Pagnoni, G. (2008). The neural correlates of the affective response to unreciprocated cooperation. *Neuropsychologia*, *46*, 1256–1266.

Rilling, J. K., Gutman, D. A., Zeh, T. R., Pagnoni, G., Berns, G. S., & Kilts, C. D. (2002). A neural basis for social cooperation. *Neuron, 35*, 395–405.

Rilling, J. K., & Sanfey, A. G. (2009). Social interaction. In: *Encyclopedia of Neuroscience* (Ed. L. Squire). Vol. 9. London: Academic, pp. 41–48.

Sanfey, A. G., Rilling, J. K., Aronson, J. A., Nystrom, L. E., & Cohen, J. D. (2003). The neural basis of economic decision-making in the Ultimatum Game. *Science, 300*, 1755–1758.

Sárkány, A. & Bereczkei T. (2013) Machiavellianism in the Hungarian companies. University of Pécs, Institute of Psychology (in Hungarian).

Shultz, C. J. (1993). Situational and dispositional predictors of performance: A test of the hypothesized Machiavellianism X structure interaction among salespersons. *Journal of Applied Social Psychology, 23*, 478–498.

Sifenos, P. E. (1973). The prevalence of alexithimic characteristics in psychosomatic patients. *Psychotherapy and Psychosomatics, 22*, 255–262.

Slaughter, V. (2011). Early adoption of Machiavelliaan attitudes: Implications for children's interpersonal relationships. In: *Narcissism and Machiavellianism in Youth: Implications for the Development of Adaptive and Maladaptive Behavior* (Eds. T. Barry, C. P. Kerig, & K. Stellwagen). Washington, DC: APA Books, pp. 177–192.

Spitzer, M., Fischbacher, U., Herrnberger, B., Gron, G., & Fehr, E. (2007). The neural signature of social norm compliance. *Neuron, 56*, 185–196.

Steinmann, E., Schmalor, A., Prehn-Kristensen, A., Wolff, S., Galka, A., Möhring, J., Gerber, W., Petermann, F., Stephani, U., & Siniatchkin, M. (2014). Developmental changes of neuronal networks associated with strategic social decision-making. *Neurophychologia, 56*, 37–46.

Stellwagen, K. K., & Kerig, P. K. (2013). Dark Triad personality traits and theory of mind among school-age children. *Personality and Individual Differences, 54*, 123–127.

Strum, S. C., Forster, D., & Hutchins, E. (1997). In: *Machiavellian Intelligence II: Extensions and Evaluations* (Eds. A. Whiten & R. W. Byrne). Cambridge: Cambridge University Press, pp. 50–85.

Süß, H.-M., Oberauer, K., Wittmann, W. W., Wilhelm, O., & Schulze, R. (2002). Working-memory capacity explains reasoning ability – and a little bit more. *Intelligence, 30*, 261–288.

Sullivan, R. J., & Allen, J. S. (1999). Social deficits associated with schizophrenia defined in terms of interpersonal Machiavellianism. *Acta Psychiatria Scandinavia, 99*, 148–154.

Sutton, J., & Keogh, E. (2000). Social competition in school: Relationships with bullying, Machiavellianism, and personality. *The British Journal of Educational Psychology, 70*, 443–456.

Szabo, J., & Bereczkei, T. (under publication). Dark Triad and theory of mind: Mentalization as a device of manipulation for Machiavellians.

Szijjarto, L., & Bereczkei, T. (2015). The Machiavellians' "cool syndrome": They experience intensive feelings but have difficulties in expressing their emotions. *Current Psychology, 34*, 363–375.

Taborsky, B., & Oliveira, R. F. (2012). Social competence: An evolutionary approach. *Trends in Ecology and Evolution, 27*, 679–688.

Trivers, R. L. (1985). *Social Evolution*. Menlo Park, CA: Benjamin/Cummings.

Vangelisti, A. L., Daly, J. A., & Rudnick, J. R. (1991). Making people feel guilty in conversations: Techniques and correlates. *Human Communication Research, 18*, 3–39.

Verbeke, W. J. M. I., Bagozzi, R. P., Rietdijk, W. J. R., van den Berg, W. E., Dietworst, R. C., & Worm, L. (2011). The making of the Machiavellian brain: A structural MRI analysis. *Journal of Neuroscience, Psychology, and Economics, 4*, 205–216.

Vernon, P. A., Villani, J. C., Vickers, L. C., & Harris, J. A. (2008). A behavioural genetic investigation of the Dark Triad and the Big 5. *Personality and Individual Differences, 44*, 445–452.

Verplaetse, J., Vanneste, S., & Braeckman, J. (2007). You can judge a book by its cover: The sequel. A kernel of truth in predictive cheating detection. *Evolution and Human Behavior, 28*, 260–271.

Veselka, L., Schermer, J. A., Martin, R. A., & Vernon, P. A. (2010). Relations between humor styles and the Dark Triad traits of personality. *Personality and Individual Differences, 48*, 772–774.

Volmer, J., Koch, I. K., & Göritz, A. S. (2016). The bright and dark sides of leaders' Dark Triad traits: Effects on subordinates' career success and well-being. *Personality and Individual Differences, 101*, 413–418.

Vonk, J., Zeigler-Hill, V., Ewinga, D., Mercer, S., & Noser, A. E. (2015). Mindreading in the dark: Dark personality features and theory of mind. *Personality and Individual Differences, 87*, 50–54.

Wai, M., & Tiliopoulos, N. (2012). The affective and cognitive empathic nature of the Dark Triad personality. *Personality and Individual Differences, 52*, 794–799.

Wastell, C., & Booth, A. (2003a). Machiavellianism: An alexithymic perspective. *Journal of Social and Clinical Psychology, 22*, 63–68.

Wastell, C., & Booth, A. (2003b). Machiavellianism: An alexithymic perspective. *Journal of Social and Clinical Psychology, 22*, 730–744.

Weston, C. S. E. (2011). Another major function of the anterior cingulated cortex: The representation of requirements. *Neuroscience and Biobehavioral Reviews.*

Whiten, A., & Byrne, R. (Eds.) (1997). *Machiavellian Intelligence II: Extensions and Evaluations.* Cambridge: Cambridge University Press.

Wilson, D. S., Near, D., & Miller, R. R. (1996). Machiavellianism: A synthesis of the evolutionary and psychological literatures. *Psychological Bulletin, 119*(2), 285–299.

Wilson, D. S., Near, D., & Miller, R. R. (1998). Individual differences in Machiavellians as a mix of cooperative and exploitative strategies. *Evolution and Human Behavior, 19*, 203–212.

Wilson, E. O. (1975). *Sociobiology: The New Synthesis.* Cambridge: The Belknap Press of Harvard University.

Winkler, A. D., Hu, S., & Li, C. R. (2013). The influence of risky and conservative mental sets on cerebral activations of cognitive control. *International Journal of Psychophysiology, 87*, 254–261.

Woodley, H. J. R., & Allen, N. J. (2014). The dark side of equity sensitivity. *Personality and Individual Differences, 67*, 103–108.

Woolett, K., & Maguire, E. A. (2011). Acquiring "the knowledge" of London's layout drives structural brain changes. *Current Biology, 21*, 2109–2114.

Zajonc, R. B. (1965). Social facilitation. *Science, 149*, 269–274.

Zimbardo, P. G., & Boyd, J. N. (1999). Putting time in perspective: A valid, reliable individual-differences metric. *Journal of Personality and Social Psychology, 77*, 1271–1288.

Zuckerman, M. (1994). *Behavioral Expressions and Biosocial Bases of Sensation Seeking.* New York, NY: Cambridge University Press.

INDEX

Made in the USA
Las Vegas, NV
26 December 2021

39515704R00094